55th Annual Meeting of the Association for Computational Linguistics (ACL 2017)

System Demonstrations

Vancouver, Canada
30 July – 4 August 2017

ISBN: 978-1-5108-4570-1

ACL 2017

The 55th Annual Meeting of the Association for Computational Linguistics

Proceedings of System Demonstrations

July 30 - August 4, 2017
Vancouver, Canada

Introduction

Welcome to the proceedings of the system demonstrations session. This volume contains the papers of the system demonstrations presented at the 55th Annual Meeting of the Association for Computational Linguistics on July 30 - August 4, 2017 in Vancouver, Canada.

The system demonstrations program offers the presentation of early research prototypes as well as interesting mature systems. We received 68 submissions, of which 21 were selected for inclusion in the program (acceptance rate of 31%) after review by three members of the program committee.

We would like to sincerely thank the members of the program committee for their timely help in reviewing the submissions.

Organizers:

Heng Ji, Rensselaer Polytechnic Institute
Mohit Bansal, University of North Carolina, Chapel Hill

Program Committee:

Marianna Apidianaki
Simon Baker
Taylor Berg-Kirkpatrick
Laurent Besacier
Steven Bethard
Chris Biemann
Lidong Bing
Yonatan Bisk
Xavier Carreras
Asli Celikyilmaz
Arun Chaganty
Kai-Wei Chang
Chen Chen
Colin Cherry
Jackie Chi Kit Cheung
Christian Chiarcos
Hai Leong Chieu
Eunsol Choi
Christos Christodoulopoulos
Vincent Claveau
Anne Cocos
Bonaventura Coppola
Danilo Croce
Rajarshi Das
Leon Derczynski
Jesse Dodge
Doug Downey
Greg Durrett
James Fan
Benoit Favre
Yansong Feng
Radu Florian
Eric Fosler-Lussier
Annemarie Friedrich
Dimitris Galanis
Tao Ge
Kevin Gimpel
Filip Ginter
Dan Goldwasser
Pawan Goyal
Yvette Graham

Ben Hachey
Dilek Hakkani-Tur
Xianpei Han
Yifan He
Ales Horak
Hongzhao Huang
Lifu Huang
Shajith Ikbal
David Jurgens
Nobuhiro Kaji
Mamoru Komachi
Lingpeng Kong
Valia Kordoni
Jayant Krishnamurthy
Mathias Lambert
Carolin Lawrence
John Lee
Sujian Li
Xiao Ling
Pierre Lison
Kang Liu
Fei Liu
Wei Lu
Nitin Madnani
Wolfgang Maier
Suresh Manandhar
Benjamin Marie
Stella Markantonatou
Yuval Marton
Pascual Martínez-Gómez
Yelena Mejova
Margaret Mitchell
Makoto Miwa
Saif Mohammad
Taesun Moon
Roser Morante
Alessandro Moschitti
Philippe Muller
Preslav Nakov
Borja Navarro
Arvind Neelakantan

Vincent Ng
Hiroshi Noji
Pierre Nugues
Naoaki Okazaki
Constantin Orasan
Aasish Pappu
Yannick Parmentier
Siddharth Patwardhan
Stelios Piperidis
Maja Popović
Prokopis Prokopidis
Alessandro Raganato
Carlos Ramisch
Xiang Ren
German Rigau
Angus Roberts
Saurav Sahay
H. Andrew Schwartz
Djamé Seddah
Satoshi Sekine
Xing Shi
Michel Simard
Kiril Simov
Sameer Singh
Vivek Srikumar
Miloš Stanojević
Emma Strubell
Partha Talukdar
Xavier Tannier
Christoph Teichmann
Benjamin Van Durme
Andrea Varga
Andreas Vlachos
Ivan Vulić
V.G.Vinod Vydiswaran
Chi Wang
William Yang Wang
Ralph Weischedel
Marion Weller-Di Marco
Guillaume Wisniewski
Fabio Massimo Zanzotto

Ke Zhai
Jun Zhao
Hai Zhao

Shiqi Zhao
Guangyou Zhou
Imed Zitouni

Pierre Zweigenbaum

Table of Contents

Conference Program

Tuesday, August 1st

5:40pm–7:40pm ACL System Demonstrations Session

Annotating tense, mood and voice for English, French and German
Anita Ramm, Sharid Loáiciga, Annemarie Friedrich and Alexander Fraser

Automating Biomedical Evidence Synthesis: RobotReviewer
Iain Marshall, Joël Kuiper, Edward Banner and Byron C. Wallace

Benben: A Chinese Intelligent Conversational Robot
Wei-Nan Zhang, Ting Liu, Bing Qin, Yu Zhang, Wanxiang Che, Yanyan Zhao and
Xiao Ding

*End-to-End Non-Factoid Question Answering with an Interactive Visualization of
Neural Attention Weights*
Andreas Rücklé and Iryna Gurevych

ESTEEM: A Novel Framework for Qualitatively Evaluating and Visualizing Spatiotemporal Embeddings in Social Media
Dustin Arendt and Svitlana Volkova

Exploring Diachronic Lexical Semantics with JeSemE
Johannes Hellrich and Udo Hahn

Extended Named Entity Recognition API and Its Applications in Language Education
Tuan Duc Nguyen, Khai Mai, Thai-Hoang Pham, Minh Trung Nguyen, Truc-Vien
T. Nguyen, Takashi Eguchi, Ryohei Sasano and Satoshi Sekine

Hafez: an Interactive Poetry Generation System
Marjan Ghazvininejad, Xing Shi, Jay Priyadarshi and Kevin Knight

Interactive Visual Analysis of Transcribed Multi-Party Discourse
Mennatallah El-Assady, Annette Hautli-Janisz, Valentin Gold, Miriam Butt, Katharina Holzinger and Daniel Keim

Life-iNet: A Structured Network-Based Knowledge Exploration and Analytics System for Life Sciences
Xiang Ren, Jiaming Shen, Meng Qu, Xuan Wang, Zeqiu Wu, Qi Zhu, Meng Jiang,
Fangbo Tao, Saurabh Sinha, David Liem, Peipei Ping, Richard Weinshilboum and
Jiawei Han

Annotating tense, mood and voice for English, French and German

Anita Ramm[1,4]   **Sharid Loáiciga**[2,3]   **Annemarie Friedrich**[4]   **Alexander Fraser**[4]

[1]Institut für Maschinelle Sprachverarbeitung, Universität Stuttgart
[2]Département de Linguistique, Université de Genève
[3]Department of Linguistics and Philology, Uppsala University
[4]Centrum für Informations- und Sprachverarbeitung, Ludwig-Maximilians-Universität München

`ramm@ims.uni-stuttgart.de`   `sharid.loaiciga@unige.ch`
`{anne,fraser}@cis.uni-muenchen.de`

Abstract

We present the first open-source tool for annotating morphosyntactic tense, mood and voice for English, French and German verbal complexes. The annotation is based on a set of language-specific rules, which are applied on dependency trees and leverage information about lemmas, morphological properties and POS-tags of the verbs. Our tool has an average accuracy of about 76%. The tense, mood and voice features are useful both as features in computational modeling and for corpus-linguistic research.

1   Introduction

Natural language employs, among other devices such as temporal adverbials, *tense* and *aspect* to locate situations in time and to describe their temporal structure (Deo, 2012). The tool presented here addresses the automatic annotation of *morphosyntactic tense*, i.e., the tense-aspect combinations, expressed in the morphology and syntax of verbal complexes (VC). VCs are sequences of verbal tokens within a verbal phrase. We address German, French and English, in which the morphology and syntax also includes information on mood and voice. Morphosyntactic tenses do not always correspond to *semantic tense* (Deo, 2012). For example, the morphosyntactic tense of the English sentence "He is leaving at noon." is *present progressive*, while the semantic tense is *future*. In the remainder of this paper, we use the term *tense* to refer to the morphological tense and aspect information encoded in finite verbal complexes.

Corpus-linguistic research, as well as automatic modeling of mono- and cross-lingual use of tense, mood and voice will strongly profit from a reliable automatic method for identifying these clausal features. They may, for instance, be used to classify texts with respect to the epoch or region in which they have been produced, or for assigning texts to a specific author. Moreover, in cross-lingual research, tense, mood, and voice have been used to model the translation of tense between different language pairs (Santos, 2004; Loáiciga et al., 2014; Ramm and Fraser, 2016)). Identifying the morphosyntactic tense is also a necessary prerequisite for identifying the semantic tense in synthetic languages such as English, French or German (Reichart and Rappoport, 2010). The extracted tense-mood-voice (TMV) features may also be useful for training models in computational linguistics, e.g., for modeling of temporal relations (Costa and Branco, 2012; UzZaman et al., 2013).

As illustrated by the examples in Figure 1, relevant information for determining TMV is given by syntactic dependencies and partially by part-of-speech (POS) tags output by analyzers such as Mate (Bohnet and Nivre, 2012). However, the parser's output is not sufficient for determining TMV features; morphological features and lexical information needs to be taken into account as well. Learning TMV features from an annotated corpus would be an alternative; however, to the best of our knowledge, no such large-scale corpora exist.

A sentence may contain more than one VC, and the tokens belonging to a VC are not always contiguous in the sentence (see VCs A and B in the English sentence in Figure 1). In a first step, our tool identifies the tokens that belong to a VC by analysing their POS tags as well as the syntactic dependency parse of the sentence. Next, TMV values are assigned according to language specific hand-crafted sets of rules, which have been developed based on extensive data analysis. The system contains approximately 32 rules for English and 26 rules for German and for French. The TMV values are output along with some additional in-

Proceedings of the 55th Annual Meeting of the Association for Computational Linguistics-System Demonstrations, pages 1–6
Vancouver, Canada, July 30 - August 4, 2017. ©2017 Association for Computational Linguistics
https://doi.org/10.18653/v1/P17-4001

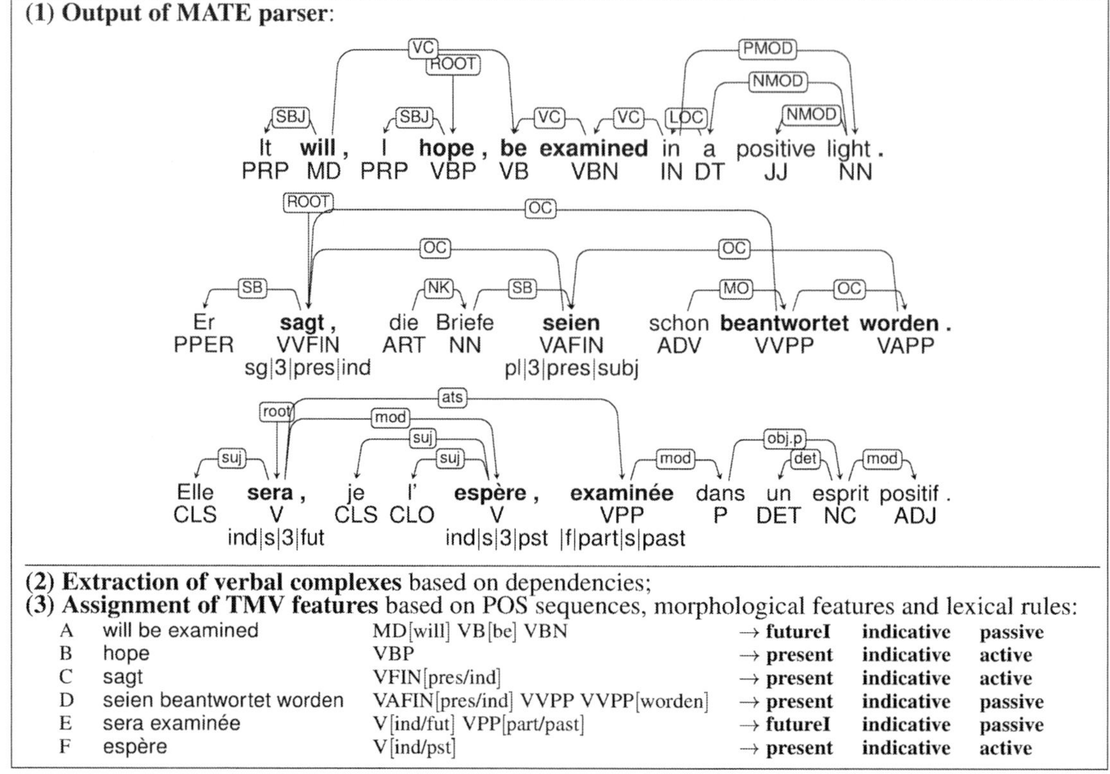

(2) **Extraction of verbal complexes** based on dependencies;
(3) **Assignment of TMV features** based on POS sequences, morphological features and lexical rules:

A	will be examined	MD[will] VB[be] VBN	→ **futureI**	**indicative**	**passive**
B	hope	VBP	→ **present**	**indicative**	**active**
C	sagt	VFIN[pres/ind]	→ **present**	**indicative**	**active**
D	seien beantwortet worden	VAFIN[pres/ind] VVPP VVPP[worden]	→ **present**	**indicative**	**passive**
E	sera examinée	V[ind/fut] VPP[part/past]	→ **futureI**	**indicative**	**passive**
F	espère	V[ind/pst]	→ **present**	**indicative**	**active**

Figure 1: **Example** for TMV extraction.

formation about the VCs into a TSV file which can easily be used for further processing.

Related work. Loáiciga et al. (2014) use rules to automatically annotate tense and voice information in English and French parallel texts. Ramm and Fraser (2016) use similar tense annotation rules for German. Friedrich and Pinkal (2015) provide a tool which, among other syntactic-semantic features, derives the tense of English verbal complexes. This tense annotation is based on the set of rules used by Loáiciga et al. (2014)

For English, PropBank (Palmer et al., 2005) contains annotations for tense, aspect and voice, but there are no annotations for subjunctive constructions including modals. The German TüBa-D/Z corpus only contains morphological features.[1]

Contributions. To the best of our knowledge, our system represents the first open-source[2] system which implements a reliable set of derivation

rules for annotating tense, mood and voice for English, French and German. Furthermore, the online demo[3] version of the tool allows for fast text processing without installing the tool.

2 Properties of the verbal complexes

In this section, we describe the morphosyntactic features that we extract for verbal complexes.

2.1 Finite and non-finite VCs

We define a verbal complex (VC) as a sequence of verbs within a verbal phrase, i.e. a sentence may include more than one VC. In addition to the verbs, a VC can also contain verbal particles and negation words but not arguments. We distinguish between finite VCs which need to have at least one finite verb (e.g. "sagt" in Figure 1), and non-finite VCs which do not; the latter consist of verb forms such as gerunds, participles or infinitives (e.g. "to support"). Infinitives in English and German have to occur with the particles *to* or *zu*, respectively,

---

[1] http://www.sfs.uni-tuebingen.de/ascl/ressourcen/corpora/tueba-dz.html
[2] https://github.com/aniramm/tmv-annotator

[3] https://clarin09.ims.uni-stuttgart.de/tmv/

while in French, infinitives may occur alone. We do not assign the TMV features to non-finite VCs. Our tool marks finiteness of a VC using a binary feature "yes" (finite) and "no" (non-finite).

2.2 Tense, mood, voice

The identification of TMV features for a VC requires the analysis of lexical and grammatical information, such as inflections, given by the combination of verbs. For example, the English *present continuous* requires the auxiliary *be* in present tense and the gerundive form of the main verb (e.g. "(I) am speaking").

Mood refers to the distinction between *indicative* and *subjunctive*. Both of these values are expressed in the inflection of finite verbs in all the considered languages. For example, the English verb "shall" is indicative, while its subjunctive form is "should." In English, tense forms used in subjunctive mood are often called *conditionals*; for German, they are referred to as *Konjunktiv*.

Voice differentiates between *active* and *passive* constructions. In all three languages, the passive voice can be recognized by searching for a specific verb. For example, the passive voice in English requires the auxiliary *be* in a tense-specific form, e.g., "(I) am **being** seen" for *present progressive* or "(he) has **been** seen" for *present perfect*.

Details on how our tool automatically identifies TMV features will be described in Section 3.

2.3 Negation

VCs may include negation. Our tool outputs a binary negation value to VCs depending on whether a negation word (identified by checking for a language-specific POS-tag) is part of the verbal dependency chain. If a negation exists, the feature value is "yes", and "no" otherwise.

2.4 Main verb

Within a VC, the main verb bears the semantic meaning. For example, in the English VC "would have read," the participle "read" is considered to be the main verb. The main verb feature may contain a single verb or a combination of a verb with the verb particle. In the following, we describe the detection of the main verbs for each of the three languages under consideration.

English and French. In English and French VCs, the very last verb in the VC is considered to be the main verb. For example, in the English VC "will be examined", "examined" is marked as the main verb. Verb particles are considered as a part of the main verb and are attached to the corresponding main verb, e.g., the main verb of the non-finite English VC "to move up" is "move-up."

German In general, the main verbs in German have specific POS-tags (*VV**) (see, for example, (Scheible et al., 2013)). In most German VCs, there is only one verb with such a POS-tag. However, there are a few exceptions. For example, the *recipient passive* is built with full verbs *bekommen, kriegen*, as well as *lernen, lassen, bleiben* and an additional meaning-bearing full verb. Thus, in such constructions, there are two verbs tagged as VV* (e.g. "Ich bekomme$_{VVFIN}$ das Buch geschenkt$_{VVPP}$." ("I receive the book donated")). Recipient verbs are not treated as main verbs if they occur with an additional full verb. In case there are no verbs tagged with *VV**, the last verb in the chain is considered to be the main verb.

3 Deriving tense, mood and voice

In this section, we give a short overview of the methods used to derive TMV information.

3.1 Extraction of VCs

The tokens of a VC are not necessarily contiguous. They may be separated by a coordination, adverbials, etc., or even include nested VCs as in Figure 1. This makes it necessary to take syntactic dependencies into account. The extraction of VCs in our tool is based on dependency parse trees in the CoNLL format.[4] The first step is the identification of all VC-beginning elements v_b within a sentence, which include finite verbs (English, French and German) and infinitival particles (English, German). They are identified by searching for specific POS-tags. For each v_b, the remaining elements of the VC are collected by following the dependency relations between verbs. Consider for example the finite verb "will" in Figure 1. It is identified as a v_b because of its POS tag *MD*. We now follow the dependency path from "will" to "be" and from "be" to "examined". The resulting VC is thus "will be examined."

---

[4] In this work, we use the Mate parser for all three languages. https://code.google.com/archive/p/mate-tools/wikis/ParserAndModels.wiki.

finite	mood	tense	voice	example (active voice)
yes	ind	present	act pass	(I) work
		presProg		(I) am working
		presPerf		(I) have worked
		presPerfProg		(I) have been working
		past		(I) worked
		pastProg		(I) was working
		pastPerf		(I) had worked
		pastPerfProg		(I) have been working
		futureI		(I) will work
		futureIProg		(I) will be working
		futureII		(I) will have worked
		futureIIProg		(I) will have been working
	subj	condI		(I) would work
		condIProg		(I) would be working
		condII		(I) would have worked
		condIIProg		(I) would have been working
no	-	-	-	to work

Table 1: TMV combinations for English.

finite	mood	tense	voice	example (active voice)
yes	ind	present	act pass	(je) travaille
		presPerf		(je) viens de travailler
		perfect		(j')ai travaillé
		imperfect		(je) travaillais
		pastSimp		(je) travaillai
		pastPerf		(j')eus travaillé
		pluperfect		(j')avais travaillé
		futureI		(je) travaillerai
		futureII		(j')aurai travaillé
		futureProc		(je) vais travailler
	subj	present		(je) travaille
		past		(j')aie travaillé
		imperfect		(je) travaillasse
no	-	-	-	travailler

Table 2: TMV Combinations for French.

3.2 TMV extraction rules

English. The rules for English make use of the combinations of the *functions* of the verbs within a given VC. Such functions are for instance *finite verb* or *passive auxiliary*. According to the POS combination of a VC and lexical information, first, the function of each verb within the VC is determined. Subsequently, the combination of the derived functions is mapped to TMV values. For example, the following functions will be assigned to the verbs of the VC "will be examined" in Figure 1: "will" → *finite-modal*, "be" → *passive-auxiliary*, "examined" → *past-participle*. This particular combination of verb functions leads to the TMV combination *futureI/indicative/passive*. Table 1 contains the set of possible TMV combinations that our tool extracts for English.

French. The rules for French are defined on the basis of the reduction of the verbs to their morphological features. The morphological features of the verbs are derived from the morphological analysis of the verbs, as well as their POS-tags. The rules specify TMV values for each of the possible sequences of the morphological features. For example, the VC "sera examinée" is mapped to the morphological feature combination *V-indfut-V-partpast* which, according to our rule set, leads to the TMV *futureI/indicative/passive*. In some cases, the lexical information is used to decide between ambiguous configurations. For example, some *perfect/active* forms are ambiguous with *present/passive* forms. For instance, "Jean est parti" and "Jean est menacé" are both composed of the verb "est" + past participle, but they have different meaning: "Jean has left" vs. "Jean is threatened." Information about the finite verb helps to

finite	mood	tense	voice	example (active voice)
yes	ind	present	act pass	(ich) arbeite
		perfect		(ich) habe gearbeitet
		imperfect		(ich) arbeitete
		pluperfect		(ich) hatte gearbeitet
		futureI		(ich) werde arbeiten
		futureII		(ich) werde gearbeitet haben
	konjI konjII	present		(er) arbeite/arbeitete
		past		(er) habe/hätte gearbeitet
		futureI+II		(er) würde arbeiten / gearbeitet haben
no	-	-	-	zu arbeiten

Table 3: TMV combinations for German.

distinguish between the two constructions. Table 2 shows the French TMV combinations.

German. The rules are based on POS tags, morphological analysis of the finite verbs and the lemmas of the verbs. We group the rules by the number of tokens contained in the VC, as we have observed that each combination of TMV features requires a particular number of tokens in the VC. For each length, we specify which tense and mood of the finite verb lead to a specific TMV. Similarly to French, in some contexts, we need to use lexical information to decide on TMV.

Take for example the VC "seien beantwortet worden" from Figure 1. Its POS sequence is *VAFIN-VVPP-VAPP*, so we use rules defined for the POS length of 3. We first check the mood of the finite verb "seien" which is *subj* (subjunctive). The combination of *subj* with the morphological tense of the finite verb *pres* leads to the mood value *konjunktivI* and the tense value *past*. As the verb *werden*, which is used for passive constructions in German, occurs in the VC, we derive the voice value *passive*. Thus, the resulting annotation is *past/konjunktivI/passive*. Table 3 shows TMV value combinations for German.

3.3 Extraction of voice

In all three languages, it is difficult to distinguish between stative passive and tenses in the active voice. For instance, the German VCs "ist geschrieben (is written)" and "ist gegangen (has gone)" are both built with the auxiliary *sein* and a past participle. The combination of POS tags is same for both cases, and the morphological features of the finite verb (*pres/ind*) correspond to the German perfect tense in active voice. This, however, holds only for verbs of movement and a few other verbs. Verbs such as "schreiben (to write)" are in this specific context *present/passive* (stative passive in present tense) and not *perfect/active* which is the case for the VC "ist gegangen".

To disambiguate between these constructions, we use a semi-automatically crafted list of the German and French verbs that form *perfect/active* with the auxiliary *sein/être (be)* instead of *haben/avoir (have)*, which is used for the majority of the verbs. We extract these lists from different corpora by counting how often verbs occur with *sein/haben* and *être/avoir*, respectively. We manually validate the resulting verb lists.

When a VC with a POS sequence that is ambiguous in the above explained way is detected, we check whether the main verb is in the list of "sein/être" verbs. If that is the case, the corresponding active tense is annotated. Otherwise, the VC is assigned the corresponding passive tense.

In the case of English, the disambiguation is somewhat easier. To differentiate between "is written" and "has written," we use information about the finite verb within the VC. In the case where we have *be*, we assume to have passive voice in combination with an appropriate tense. In case of *have*, the voice is active.

4 Annotation tool

The tool is implemented in Python. It takes as input the parsed text file in the CoNLL format. For the rule development, as well as evaluation, we used the Mate parser (Bohnet and Nivre, 2012), which can be applied on all of the three languages addressed here. For German and French, we use the joint model for parsing, tagging and morphological analysis including lemmatization. For English, only tagging and parsing is required. In general, the TMV annotation tool is applicable on the output of arbitrary parsers as long as their models use the same POS- and dependency tags as Mate.

The tool outputs a TSV file with TMV annotations. An example output is shown in Table 4. The columns are specified as follows: sentence number, indices of the elements of a VC separated by a comma, elements of a VC separated by a comma, finite, main verb (if more than one, separated by a comma), tense, mood, voice, progressive (only for English), coordination and negation. The German TSV output has an additional column with boundaries of a clause in which a VC is placed.[5] We additionally provide a script for the conversion of the annotations into HTML format which allows for quick and easy examination of the annotations.

5 Evaluation

We manually evaluate annotations for 157 German VCs, 151 English Vcs and 137 French VCs extracted from a set of randomly chosen sentences from Europarl (Koehn, 2005). The results are shown in Table 5.

Language	tense	mood	voice	all
EN	81.5	88.1	86.1	76.8
DE	80.8	84.0	81.5	76.4
FR	86.1	93.4	82.5	75.2

Table 5: Accuracy of TMV features according to manual evaluation.

For French, the overall acurracy is 75%, while the accuracy of German and English annotations is 76%. Based on the manually annotated sample, we estimate that 23/59/85% (for EN/DE/FR) of the erroneous annotations are due to parsing errors. For instance, in the case of English, the VC extraction process sometimes adds gerunds to the VC and interprets them as a present participle. Similarly, for French, a past participle is added, which erroneously causes the voice assignment to be passive. Contrary to German and English, French has higher mood accuracy, since mood is largely encoded unambiguously in the verb morphology. For German, false or missing morphological annotation of the finite verbs causes some errors, and there are cases not covered by our rules for identifying stative passive.

Our rule sets have been developed based on extensive data analysis. This evaluation presents a

---

[5]The clause boundary identification is based on the sentence punctuation (e.g. comma, colon, semicolon, hyphen, etc). For more sophisticated clause boundary identification for German, please refer to (Sidarenka et al., 2015).

sent num	verb id(s)	VC	main verb	fin	tense	mood	voice	neg	coord
1	6,7	has climbed	climbed	yes	presPerf	indicative	active	no	no
2	4,5	has crossed	crossed	yes	presPerf	indicative	active	no	no
2	13,14	can 't increase	increase	yes	present	indicative	active	yes	no

Table 4: TSV output of the annotation tool for two English sentences: "Since then, the index has climbed above 10,000. Now that gold has crossed the magic $1,000 barrier, why can't it increase ten-fold, too?"

snapshot of the tool's performance. The findings of this analysis will lead to improvement of the rules' precision in future development iterations.

6 Conclusion

We have presented an automatic tool which annotates English, French and German verbal complexes with tense, mood and voice. Our tool compensates for the lack of annotated data on this subject. It allows for large-scale studies of verbal tenses and their use within and across the three languages. This includes for instance typological studies of the temporal interpretation of tenses, or discourse studies interested in the referential properties of tense. Large-scale annotated data with reliable accuracy also creates the possibility to train classifiers, machine translation systems and other NLP tools. The same approach for extracting tense, aspect and mood could also be implemented for other languages.

Acknowledgment

This work has received funding from the DFG grant Models of Morphosyntax for Statistical Machine Translation (Phase 2), the European Union's Horizon 2020 research and innovation programme under grant agreement No. 644402 (*HimL*), and from the European Research Council (ERC) under grant agreement No. 640550.

We thank André Blessing for developing the demo version of the tool.

References

Bernd Bohnet and Joakim Nivre. 2012. A transition-based system for joint part-of-speech tagging and labeled non-projective dependency parsing. In *Proceedings of the 2012 Joint Conference on EMNLP*. Jeju Island, Korea.

Francisco Costa and António Branco. 2012. Aspectual type and temporal relation classification. In *Proceedings of the 13th Conference of the EACL*. Avignon, France.

Ashwini Deo. 2012. Morphology. In Robert I. Binnick, editor, *The Oxford Handbook of Tense and Aspect*, OUP.

Annemarie Friedrich and Manfred Pinkal. 2015. Automatic recognition of habituals: a three-way classification of clausal aspect. In *Proceedings of the 2015 Conference on EMNLP*. Lisbon, Portugal.

Philipp Koehn. 2005. Europarl: A parallel corpus for statistical machine translation. In *Conference Proceedings: the tenth Machine Translation Summit*. Phuket, Thailand.

Sharid Loáiciga, Thomas Meyer, and Andrei Popescu-Belis. 2014. English-French verb phrase alignment in Europarl for tense translation modeling. In *Proceedings of the 9th International Conference on LREC*. Reykjavik, Iceland.

Martha Palmer, Daniel Gildea, and Paul Kingsbury. 2005. The Proposition Bank: An Annotated Corpus of Semantic Roles. *Computational Linguistics* 31(1):71–106.

Anita Ramm and Alexander Fraser. 2016. Modeling verbal inflection for English to German SMT. In *Proceedings of the the First Conference on Machine Translation (WMT)*. Berlin, Germany.

Roi Reichart and Ari Rappoport. 2010. Tense sense disambiguation: a new syntactic polysemy task. In *Proceedings of the 2010 Conference on EMNLP*. Massachusetts, USA.

Diana Santos. 2004. *Translation-based corpus studies Contrasting English and Portuguese tense and aspect systems*. Rodopi.

Silke Scheible, Sabine Schulte im Walde, Marion Weller, and Max Kisselew. 2013. A compact but linguistically detailed database for german verb subcategorisation relying on dependency parses from a web corpus: Tool, guidelines and resource. In *In Proceedings of the WAC-8*. Lancaster, UK.

Uladzimir Sidarenka, Andreas Peldszus, and Manfred Stede. 2015. Discourse segmentation of German texts. *Journal for Language Technology and Computational Linguistics* 30(1):71–98.

Naushad UzZaman, Hector Llorens, Leon Derczynski, James Allen, Marc Verhagen, and James Pustejovsky. 2013. SemEval-2013 Task 1: TempEval-Events, and Temporal Relations. In *Proceedings of the SemEval 2013*. Atlanta, Georgia.

Automating Biomedical Evidence Synthesis: RobotReviewer

Iain J. Marshall,[1] **Joël Kuiper**,[2] **Edward Banner**[3] **and Byron C. Wallace**[3]

[1]Department of Primary Care and Public Health Sciences, Kings College London
[2]Doctor Evidence, [3]College of Computer and Information Science, Northeastern University
`iain.marshall@kcl.ac.uk`, `jkuiper@doctorevidence.com`
`banner.ed@husky.neu.edu`, `byron@ccs.neu.edu`

Abstract

We present *RobotReviewer*, an open-source web-based system that uses machine learning and NLP to semi-automate biomedical evidence synthesis, to aid the practice of Evidence-Based Medicine. RobotReviewer processes full-text journal articles (PDFs) describing randomized controlled trials (RCTs). It appraises the reliability of RCTs and extracts text describing key trial characteristics (e.g., descriptions of the population) using novel NLP methods. RobotReviewer then automatically generates a report synthesising this information. Our goal is for RobotReviewer to automatically extract and synthesise the full-range of structured data needed to inform evidence-based practice.

1 Introduction and Motivation

Decisions regarding patient healthcare should be informed by all available evidence; this is the philosophy underpinning *Evidence-based Medicine* (EBM) (Sackett, 1997). But realizing this aim is difficult, in part because clinical trial results are primarily disseminated as free-text journal articles. Moreover, the biomedical literature base is growing exponentially (Bastian et al., 2010). It is now impossible for a practicing clinician to keep up to date by reading primary research articles, even in a narrow specialty (Moss and Marcus, 2017). Thus healthcare decisions today are often made without full consideration of the existing evidence.

Systematic reviews (SRs) are an important tool for enabling the practice of EBM despite this data deluge. SRs are reports that exhaustively identify and synthesise all published evidence pertinent to a specific clinical question. SRs include an assessment of research biases, and often a statistical

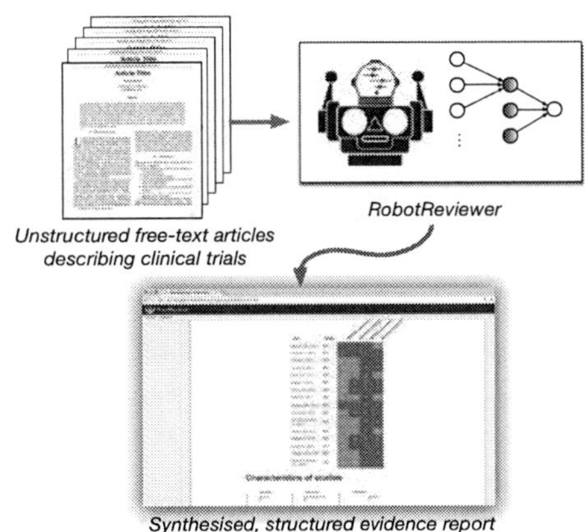

Figure 1: RobotReviewer is an open-source NLP system that extracts and synthesises evidence from unstructured articles describing clinical trials.

meta-analysis of trial results. SRs inform all levels of healthcare, from national policies and guidelines to bedside decisions. But the expanding primary research base has made producing and maintaining SRs increasingly onerous (Bastian et al., 2010; Wallace et al., 2013). Identifying, extracting, and combining evidence from free-text articles describing RCTs is difficult, time-consuming, and laborious. One estimate suggests that a single SR requires thousands of person hours (Allen and Olkin, 1999); and a recent analysis suggests it takes an average of nearly 70 weeks to publish a review (Borah et al., 2017). This incurs huge financial cost, particularly because reviews are performed by highly-trained persons.

To keep SRs current with the literature then we must develop new methods to expedite evidence synthesis. Specifically, we need tools that can help identify, extract, assess and summarize evidence relevant to specific clinical questions from free-text articles describing RCTs. Toward this end, this paper describes *RobotReviewer* (RR; Figure 1), an open-source system that automates aspects

Proceedings of the 55th Annual Meeting of the Association for Computational Linguistics-System Demonstrations, pages 7–12
Vancouver, Canada, July 30 - August 4, 2017. ©2017 Association for Computational Linguistics
https://doi.org/10.18653/v1/P17-4002

of the data-extraction and synthesis steps of a systematic review using novel NLP models.[1]

2   Overview of RobotReviewer (RR)

RR is a web-based tool which processes journal article PDFs (uploaded by end-users) describing the conduct and results of related RCTs to be synthesised. Using several machine learning (ML) data-extraction models, RR generates a report summarizing key information from the RCTs, including, e.g., details concerning trial participants, interventions, and reliability. Our ultimate goal is to automate the extraction of the full range of variables necessary to perform evidence synthesis. We list the current functionality of RR and future extraction targets in Table 1.

RR comprises several novel ML/NLP components that target different sub-tasks in the evidence synthesis process, which we describe briefly in the following section. RR provides access to these models both via a web-based prototype graphical interface and a REST API service. The latter provides a mechanism for integrating our models with existing software platforms that process biomedical texts generally and that facilitate reviews specifically (e.g., Covidence[2]). We provide a schematic of the system architecture in Figure 2. We have released the entire system as open source via the GPL v 3.0 license. A live demonstration version with examples, a video, and the source code is available at our project website.[3]

3   Tasks and Models

We now briefly describe the tasks RR currently automates and the ML/NLP models that we have developed and integrated into RR to achieve this.

3.1   Risks of Bias (RoB)

Critically appraising the conduct of RCTs (from the text of their reports) is a key step in evidence synthesis. If a trial does not rigorously adhere to a well-designed protocol, there is a risk that the results exhibit bias. Appraising such risks has been formalized into the Cochrane[4] Risk of Bias (RoB) tool (Higgins et al., 2011). This defines several 'domains' with respect to which the risk of bias is

___
[1]We described an early version of what would become RR in (Kuiper et al., 2014); we have made substantial progress since then, however.

[2]http://covidence.com

[3]http://www.robotreviewer.net/acl2017

[4]Cochrane is a non-profit organization dedicated to conducting SRs of clinical research: http://www.cochrane.org/.

to be assessed, e.g., whether trial participants were adequately blinded.

EBM aims to make evidence synthesis transparent. Therefore, it is imperative to provide support for one's otherwise somewhat subjective appraisals of risks of bias. In practice, this entails extracting quotes from articles supporting judgements, i.e. *rationales* (Zaidan et al., 2007). An automated system needs to do the same. We have therefore developed models that jointly (1) categorize articles as describing RCTs at 'low' or 'high/unknown' risk of bias across domains, and, (2) extract rationales supporting these categorizations (Marshall et al., 2014; Marshall et al., 2016; Zhang et al., 2016).

We have developed two model variants for automatic RoB assessment. The first is a multi-task (across domains) linear model (Marshall et al., 2014). The model induces sentence rankings (w.r.t. to how likely they are to support assessment for a given domain) which directly inform the overall RoB prediction through 'interaction' features (interaction of n-gram features with whether identified as rationale [yes/no]).

To assess the quality of extracted sentences, we conducted a blinded evaluation by expert systematic reviewers, in which they assessed the quality of manually and automatically extracted sentences. Sentences extracted using our model were scored comparably to those extracted by human reviewers (Marshall et al., 2016). However, the accuracy of the overall classification of articles as describing *high/unclear* or *low* risk RCTs achieved by our model remained 5-10 points lower than that achieved in published (human authored) SRs (estimated using articles that had been independently assessed in multiple SRs).

We have recently improved overall document classification performance using a novel variant of Convolutional Neural Networks (CNNs) adapted for text classification (Kim, 2014; Zhang and Wallace, 2015). Our model, the 'rationale-augmented CNN' (RA-CNN), explicitly identifies and up-weights sentences likely to be rationales. RA-CNN induces a document vector by taking a weighted sum over sentence vectors (output from a sentence-level CNN), where weights are set to reflect the predicted probability of sentences being rationales. The composite document vector is fed through a softmax layer for overall article classification. This model achieved gains of 1-2% abso-

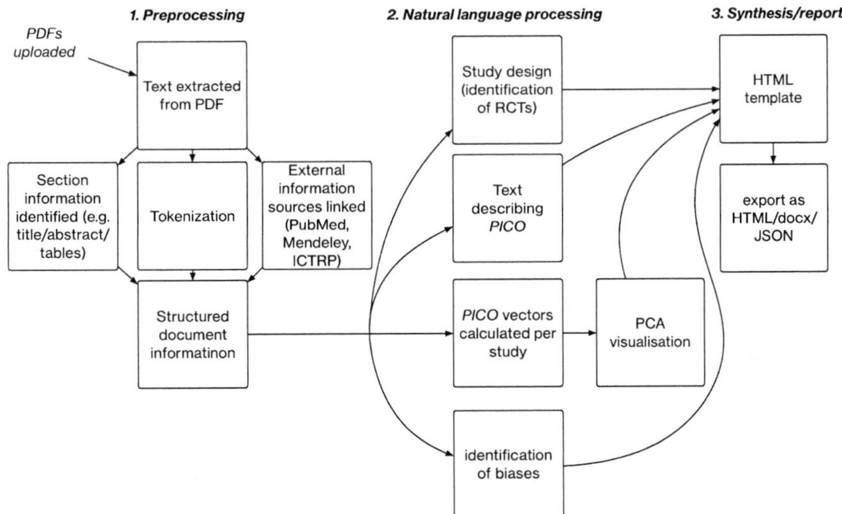

Figure 2: Schematic of RR document processing. A set of PDFs are uploaded, processed and run through models; the output from these are used to construct a summary report.

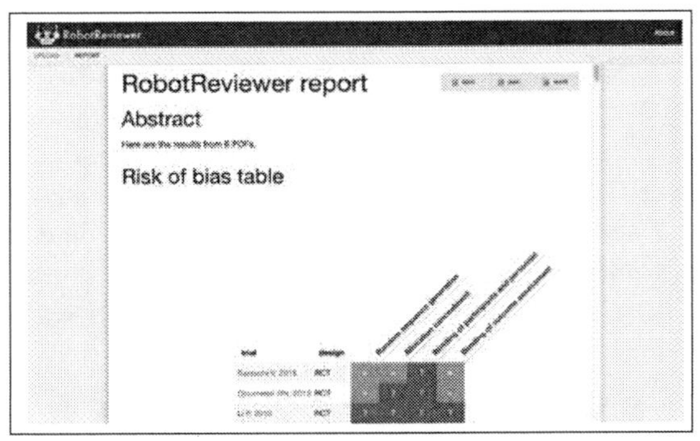

Figure 3: Report view. Here one can see the automatically generated risk of bias matrix; scrolling down reveals PICO and RoB textual tables

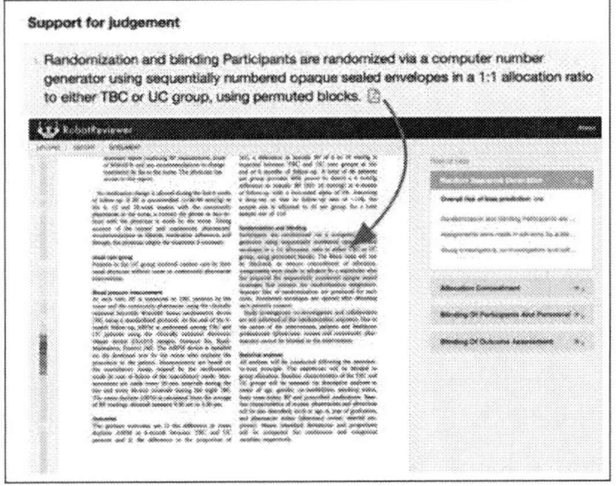

Figure 4: Links are maintained to the source document. We show predicted annotations for the risk of bias w.r.t. *random sequence generation*. Clicking on the PDF icon in the report view (top) brings the user to the annotation in-place in the source document (bottom).

lute accuracy across domains (Zhang et al., 2016).

RR incorporates these linear and neural strategies using a simple ensembling strategy. For bias classification, we average the predicted probabilities of RCTs being at *low* risk of bias from the linear and neural models. To extract corresponding rationales, we induce rankings over all sentences in a given document using both models, and then aggregate these via Borda count (de Borda, 1784).

3.2 PICO

The Population, Interventions/Comparators and Outcomes (PICO) together define the clinical question addressed by a trial. Characterising and representing these is therefore an important aim for automating evidence synthesis.

3.2.1 Extracting PICO sentences

Past work has investigated identifying PICO elements in biomedical texts (Demner-Fushman and Lin, 2007; Boudin et al., 2010). But these efforts have largely considered only article abstracts, limiting their utility: not all clinically salient data is always available in abstracts. One exception to this is a system called ExaCT (Kiritchenko et al., 2010), which does operate on full-texts, although

Extraction type	Text	Structured	Extraction type	Text	Structured
General			**Intervention and setting**		
Record number	✓	✓	Setting	✓	
Author	✓	✓	Interventions and controls	✓	
Article title	✓	✓	co-interventions	✓	
Citation	✓	✓	**Outcome data/results**		
Type of Publication	✓		Unit of analysis		
Country of origin			Statistical techniques		
Source of funding			Outcomes reported?	✓	
Study characteristics			Outcome definitions	✓	
Aims/objectives			Measures used	✓	
Study design	✓	✓	Length of follow up		
Inclusion criteria	✓		N participants enrolled	✓	
Randomization/blinding	✓	✓	N participants analyzed	✓	
Unit of allocation			Withdrawals/exclusions	✓	
Participants			Summary outcome data		
Age	✓		Adverse events		
Gender	✓				
Ethnicity	✓				
Socio-economic status	✓				
Disease characteristics	✓	✓			
Co-morbidities	✓	✓			

Table 1: Typical variables required for an evidence synthesis (Centre for Reviews and Dissemination, 2009), and current RR functionality. *Text*: extracted text snippets describing the variable (e.g. 'The randomization schedule was produced using a statistical computer package'). *Structured*: translation to e.g., standard bias scores or medical ontology concepts.

assumes HTML/XML inputs, rather than PDFs. ExaCT was hindered by the modest amount of available training data ($\sim$160 annotated articles).

Scarcity of training data is an important problem in this domain. We have thus taken a *distant supervision* (DS) approach to train PICO sentence extraction models, deriving a corpus of tens of thousands of 'pseudo-annotated' full-text PDFs. DS is a training regime in which noisy labels are induced from existing structured resources via rules (Mintz et al., 2009). Here, we exploited a training corpus derived from an existing database of SRs using a novel training paradigm: *supervised distant supervision* (Wallace et al., 2016).

Briefly, the idea is to replace the heuristics usually used in DS to derive labels from the available structured resource with a function $\tilde{f}_{\tilde{\theta}}$ that maps from instances $\tilde{\mathcal{X}}$ and DS derived labels $\tilde{\mathcal{Y}}$ to higher precision labels $\mathcal{Y}$; $\tilde{f}_{\tilde{\theta}}(\tilde{\mathcal{X}}, \tilde{\mathcal{Y}}) \rightarrow \mathcal{Y}$. Crucially, the $\tilde{\mathcal{X}}$ representations include features derived from the available DS; such features will thus not be available for test instances. Parameters $\tilde{\theta}$ are to be estimated using a small amount of direct supervision. Once a higher precision label set $\mathcal{Y}$ is induced via $\tilde{f}_{\tilde{\theta}}$, we can train a model as usual, training the final classifier f_{θ} using $(\mathcal{X}, \mathcal{Y})$. Further, we can incorporate the predicted probability distribution over true labels $\mathcal{Y}$ estimated by $\tilde{f}_{\tilde{\theta}}$ directly in the loss function used to train f_{θ}. This approach results in improved model performance,

at least for our case of PICO sentence extraction from full-text articles (Wallace et al., 2016).

Text describing PICO elements is identified in RR using this strategy; the results are displayed both as tables and as annotations on individual articles (see Figures 3 and 4, respectively).

3.2.2 PICO embeddings

We have begun to explore learning dense, low-dimensional embeddings of biomedical abstracts specific to each PICO dimension. In contrast to monolithic document embedding approaches, such as doc2vec (Le and Mikolov, 2014), PICO embeddings are an example of *disentangled* representations.

Briefly, we have developed a neural approach which assumes access to manually generated free-text aspect summaries (here, one per PICO element) with corresponding documents (abstracts). The objective is to induce vector representations (via an encoder model) of abstracts and aspect summaries that satisfy two desiderata. (1) The embedding for a given abstract/aspect should be close to its matched aspect summary; (2) but far from the embeddings of aspect summaries for *other* abstracts, specifically those which differ with respect to the aspect in question.

To train this model, we used data recorded for previously conducted SRs to train our embedding model. Specifically we collected

30,000+ abstract/aspect summary pairs stored in the Cochrane Database of Systematic Reviews (CDSR). We have demonstrated that the induced aspect representations improve performance an information retrieval task for EBM: ranking RCTs relevant to a given systematic review.[5]

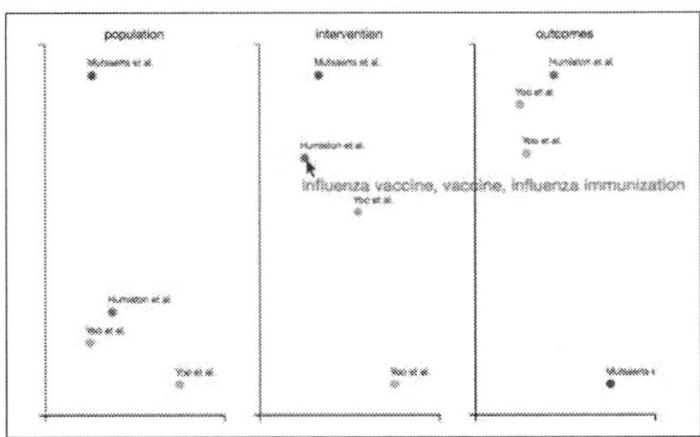

Figure 5: PICO embeddings. Here, a mouse-over event has occurred on the point corresponding to *Humiston et al.* in the *intervention* embedding space, triggering the display of the three uni-/bigrams that most excited the encoder model.

For RR, we incorporate these models to induce abstract representations and then project these down to two dimensions using a PCA model pretrained on the CDSR. We then present a visualisation of study positions in this reduced space, thus revealing relative similarities and allowing one, e.g., to spot apparently outlying RCTs. To facilitate interpretation, we display the uni and bigrams most activated for each study by filters in the learned encoder model on mouse-over. Figure 5 shows such an example. We are actively working to refine our approach to further improve the interpretability of these embeddings.

3.3 Study design

RCTs are regarded as the gold standard for providing evidence on of the effectiveness of health interventions (Chalmers et al., 1993) Yet these articles form a small minority of the available medical literature. We employ an ensemble classifier, combining multiple CNN models, Support Vector Machines (SVMs), and which takes account of meta-data obtained from PubMed. Our evaluation on an independent dataset has found this approach achieves very high accuracy (area under the Recevier Operating Characteristics curve = 0.987), outperforming previous ML approaches and manually created boolean filters.[6]

4 Discussion

We have presented RobotReviewer, an open-source tool that uses state-of-the-art ML and NLP to semi-automate biomedical evidence synthesis. RR incorporates the underlying trained models with a prototype web-based user interface, and a REST API that may be used to access the models. We aim to continue adding functionality to RR, automating the extraction and synthesis of additional fields: particularly structured *PICO* data, outcome statistics, and trial participant flow. These additional data points would (if extracted with sufficient accuracy) provide the information required for statistical synthesis.

For example, for assessing bias, RR is competitive with, but modestly inferior to the accuracy of a conventional manually produced systematic review (Marshall et al., 2016) We therefore recommended that RR be used as a time-saving tool for manual data extraction, or that one of two humans in the conventional data-extraction process be replaced by the automated process.

However, there is an increasing need for methods that trade a small amount of accuracy for increased speed (Tricco et al., 2015). The opportunity cost of maintaining current rigor in SRs is vast: reviews do not exist for most clinical questions (Smith, 2013), and most reviews are out of date soon after publication (Shojania et al., 2007).

RR used in a fully automatic workflow (without manual checks) might improve upon relying on the source articles alone, particularly given those in clinical practice are unlikely to have time to read the full texts. To explore how automation should be used in practice, we plan to experimentally evaluate RR in real-world use: in terms of time saved, user experience, and the resultant review quality.

Acknowledgments

RobotReviewer is supported by the National Library of Medicine (NLM) of the National Institutes of Health (NIH) under award R01LM012086. The content is solely the

---

[5]Under review: preprint available at `http://www.byronwallace.com/static/articles/PICO-vectors-preprint.pdf`.

[6]Under review; pre-print available at `https://kclpure.kcl.ac.uk/portal/iain.marshall.html`

responsibility of the authors and does not necessarily represent the official views of the National Institutes of Health. IJM is supported of the Medical Research Council (UK), through its Skills Development Fellowship program (MR/N015185/1).

References

IE Allen and I Olkin. 1999. Estimating time to conduct a meta-analysis from number of citations retrieved. *The Journal of the American Medical Association (JAMA)*, 282(7):634–635.

H Bastian, P Glasziou, and I Chalmers. 2010. Seventy-five trials and eleven systematic reviews a day: how will we ever keep up? *PLoS medicine*, 7(9).

R Borah, AW Brown, PL Capers, and Kathryn A Kaiser. 2017. Analysis of the time and workers needed to conduct systematic reviews of medical interventions using data from the prospero registry. *BMJ open*, 7(2):e012545.

F Boudin, J-Y Nie, and M Dawes. 2010. Positional language models for clinical information retrieval. In *EMNLP*, pages 108–115.

Centre for Reviews and Dissemination. 2009. *Systematic reviews: CRD's guidance for undertaking reviews in health care*. University of York, York.

I Chalmers, M Enkin, and MJNC Keirse. 1993. Preparing and updating systematic reviews of randomized controlled trials of health care. *Milbank Q.*, 71(3):411.

J de Borda. 1784. A paper on elections by ballot. *Sommerlad F, McLean I (1989, eds) The political theory of Condorcet*, pages 122–129.

D Demner-Fushman and J Lin. 2007. Answering clinical questions with knowledge-based and statistical techniques. *Computational Linguistics*, 33(1):63–103.

JPT Higgins, DG Altman, PC Gøtzsche, P Jüni, D Moher, AD Oxman, J Savović, KF Schulz, L Weeks, and JAC Sterne. 2011. The Cochrane Collaborations tool for assessing risk of bias in randomised trials. *BMJ*, 343:d5928.

Y Kim. 2014. Convolutional neural networks for sentence classification. *arXiv preprint arXiv:1408.5882*.

S Kiritchenko, B de Bruijn, S Carini, J Martin, and I Sim. 2010. ExaCT: automatic extraction of clinical trial characteristics from journal publications. *BMC medical informatics and decision making*, 10(1):56.

J Kuiper, IJ Marshall, BC Wallace, and MA Swertz. 2014. Spá: A web-based viewer for text mining in evidence based medicine. In *ECML-PKDD*, pages 452–455. Springer.

QV Le and T Mikolov. 2014. Distributed representations of sentences and documents. In *ICML*, volume 14, pages 1188–1196.

IJ Marshall, J Kuiper, and BC Wallace. 2014. Automating risk of bias assessment for clinical trials. In *ACM-BCB*, pages 88–95.

IJ Marshall, J Kuiper, and BC Wallace. 2016. RobotReviewer: Evaluation of a System for Automatically Assessing Bias in Clinical Trials. *Journal of the American Medical Informatics Association (JAMIA)*, 23(1):193–201.

M Mintz, S Bills, R Snow, and D Jurafsky. 2009. Distant supervision for relation extraction without labeled data. In *IJCNLP*, pages 1003–1011.

AJ Moss and FI Marcus. 2017. Changing times in cardiovascular publications: A commentary. *Am. J. Med.*, 130(1):11–13, January.

DL Sackett. 1997. *Evidence-based medicine: how to practice and teach EBM*. WB Saunders Company.

K G Shojania, M Sampson, M T Ansari, J Ji, C Garritty, T Rader, and D Moher. 2007. *Updating Systematic Reviews. Technical Review No. 16*. Agency for Healthcare Research and Quality (US), 1 September.

Richard Smith. 2013. The Cochrane collaboration at 20. *BMJ*, 347:f7383, 18 December.

Andrea C Tricco, Jesmin Antony, Wasifa Zarin, Lisa Strifler, Marco Ghassemi, John Ivory, Laure Perrier, Brian Hutton, David Moher, and Sharon E Straus. 2015. A scoping review of rapid review methods. *BMC Med.*, 13:224, 16 September.

BC Wallace, IJ Dahabreh, CH Schmid, J Lau, and TA Trikalinos. 2013. Modernizing the systematic review process to inform comparative effectiveness: tools and methods. *Journal of Comparative Effectiveness Research (JCER)*, 2(3):273–282.

BC Wallace, J Kuiper, A Sharma, M Zhu, and IJ Marshall. 2016. Extracting PICO Sentences from Clinical Trial Reports using Supervised Distant Supervision. *Journal of Machine Learning Research*, 17(132):1–25.

O Zaidan, J Eisner, and CD Piatko. 2007. Using "annotator rationales" to improve machine learning for text categorization. In *NAACL*, pages 260–267.

Y Zhang and B Wallace. 2015. A sensitivity analysis of (and practitioners' guide to) convolutional neural networks for sentence classification. *arXiv preprint arXiv:1510.03820*.

Y Zhang, IJ Marshall, and BC Wallace. 2016. Rationale-Augmented Convolutional Neural Networks for Text Classification. In *EMNLP*, pages 795–804.

Benben: A Chinese Intelligent Conversational Robot

Wei-Nan Zhang, Ting Liu, Bing Qin, Yu Zhang, Wanxiang Che,
Yanyan Zhao, Xiao Ding
Research Center for Social Computing and Information Retrieval
Harbin Institute of Technology
{wnzhang,tliu,qinb,zhangyu,wxche,yyzhao,xding}@ir.hit.edu.cn

Abstract

Recently, conversational robots are widely used in mobile terminals as the virtual assistant or companion. The goals of prevalent conversational robots mainly focus on four categories, namely chit-chat, task completion, question answering and recommendation. In this paper, we present a Chinese intelligent conversational robot, Benben, which is designed to achieve these goals in a unified architecture. Moreover, it also has some featured functions such as diet map, implicit feedback based conversation, interactive machine reading, news recommendation, etc. Since the release of Benben at June 6, 2016, there are 2,505 users (till Feb 22, 2017) and 11,107 complete human-robot conversations, which totally contain 198,998 single turn conversation pairs.

1 Introduction

The research of conversational robot can be traced back to 1950s, when Alan M. Turing presented the Turing test to answer the proposed question *"Can machine think?"* (Turing, 1950). It then becomes an interesting and challenging research in artificial intelligence. Conversational robot can be applied to many scenarios of human-computer interaction, such as question answering (Crutzen et al., 2011), negotiation (Rosenfeld et al., 2014), e-commence (Goes et al., 2011), tutoring (Pilato et al., 2005), etc. Recently, with the widespread of mobile terminals, it is also applied as the virtual assistant, such as Apple Siri[1], Microsoft Cortana[2], Facebook Messenger[3], Google Assistant[4], etc., to

---

[1] https://en.wikipedia.org/wiki/Siri
[2] https://en.wikipedia.org/wiki/Cortana_(software)
[3] https://www.messenger.com/
[4] https://assistant.google.com/

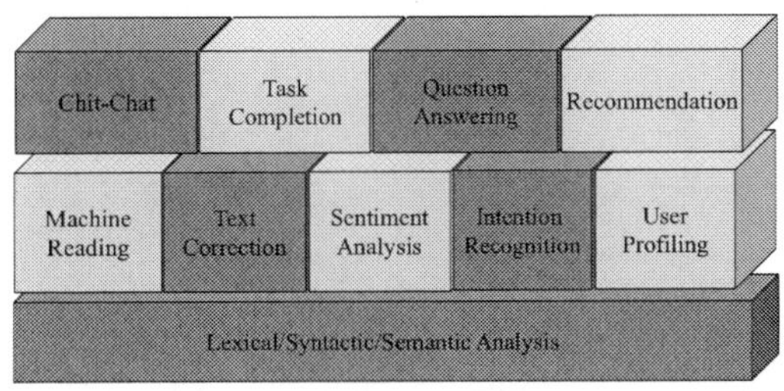

Figure 1: The technical structure of Benben.

make users acquire information and services with the terminals more conveniently.

The goals of the prevalent conversational robots can be grouped into four categories. First is chit-chat which is usually designed for responding greeting, emotional and entertainment messages. Second is task completion aiming to assist users to complete some specific tasks, such as restaurant and hotel reservation, flight inquiry, tourist guide, web search, etc. Third is question answering that is to satisfy the need of information and knowledge acquisition. Fourth is recommendation that can actively recommend personalized content through the user interest profiling and conversation history. Despite the success of the existing conversational robots, they tend to only focus on one or several goals and hardly achieve all of them in a unified framework.

In this paper, we present a Chinese intelligent conversational robot, Benben, which is based on massive Natural Language Processing (NLP) techniques and takes all of the goals in design.

Figure 1 shows the technical structure of Benben. The bottom layer contains the basic techniques of NLP, such as Chinese word segmentation, part-of-speech tagging, word sense disambiguation, named entity recognition, dependency parsing, semantic role labelling and semantic de-

Proceedings of the 55th Annual Meeting of the Association for Computational Linguistics-System Demonstrations, pages 13–18
Vancouver, Canada, July 30 - August 4, 2017. ©2017 Association for Computational Linguistics
https://doi.org/10.18653/v1/P17-4003

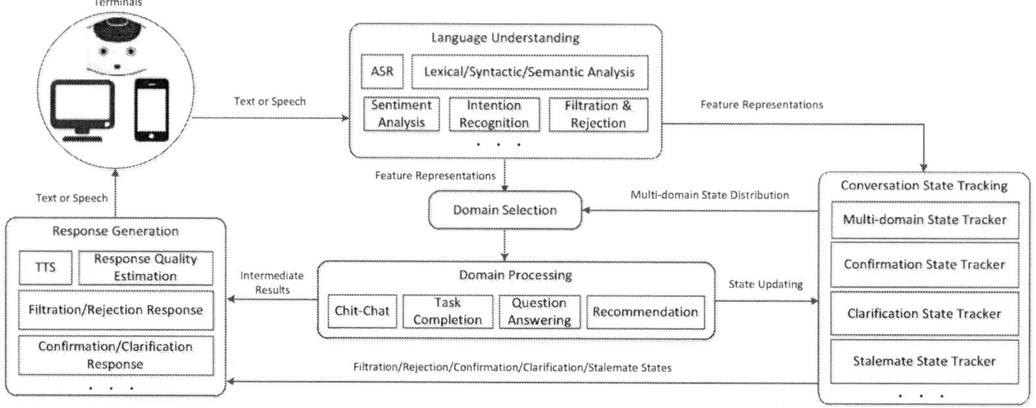

Figure 2: The simplified architecture of Benben.

pendency parsing, etc. These techniques are from the language technique platform (LTP)[5]. The middle layer includes the core techniques that are supported by the basic NLP techniques. The top layer is the four functionalities of Benben.

2 Architecture

In this section, we will introduce the architecture of Benben. Figure 2 shows the simplified architecture of Benben. It mainly consists of four components: 1) language understanding, 2) conversation state tracking, 3) domain selection and processing and 4) response generation. As can be seen, the architecture of Benben can be corresponded to the classic architecture of spoken dialogue systems (Young et al., 2013). Concretely, the natural language understanding, dialogue management and natural language generation in spoken dialogue systems are corresponding to the 1), 2) and 3), 4) components of the Benben architecture, respectively. We will next detail each component in the following sections.

2.1 Language Understanding

The user input can be either text or speech. Therefore, the first step is to understand both the speech transcription and text. In Benben, the LTP toolkit (Che et al., 2010) is utilized to the basic language processing, including Chinese word segmentation, part-of-speech tagging, word sense disambiguation, named entity recognition, dependency parsing, semantic role labelling and semantic

dependency parsing. The results of these processing are finally taken as the lexical, syntactic and semantic features and transferred to different representations to the following processing steps.

We obtain the results of sentence-level sentiment analysis by using our proposed approach (Tang et al., 2015). The results are then used in two aspects. One is to directly generate consoling responses and the other is to take the sentiment as an implicit feedback of users to optimize the long-term goal of conversations.

We utilize the proposed weakly-supervised approach (Fu and Liu, 2013) to recognize the intention of users. User intention can be either used as clues for response generation or features for domain selection. For example, if a user says:"*I want to go to Beijing.*", he/she may want to book an airplane or train ticket or further reserve a hotel room in Beijing.

We also design a scheme to filter out the sentences that contain vulgar, obscene or sensitive words. A classifier is trained to automatically identify these sentences with manually collated lexicons. Meanwhile, the rejection scheme is also needed as Benben should cope with the inputs that are out of its responding scope.

2.2 Conversation State Tracking

After the language understanding step, an input sentence is transferred to several feature representations. These feature representations are then taken as the inputs of the conversation state tracking and domain selection. The conversation state

[5]http://www.ltp-cloud.com

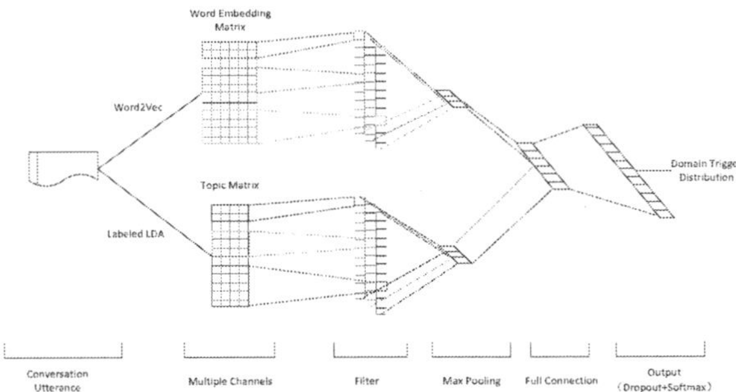

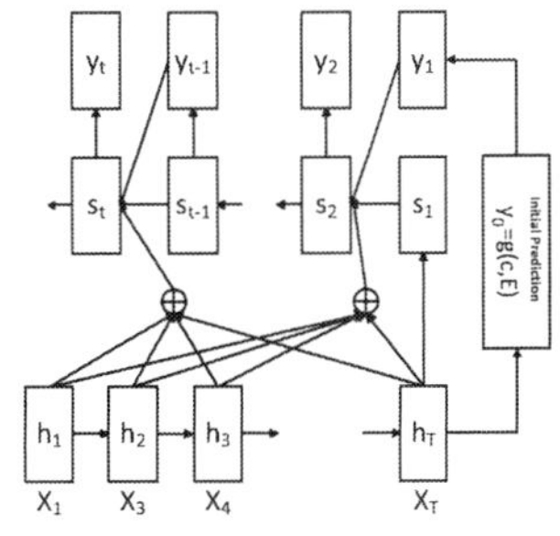

Figure 3: The framework of the proposed topic augmented convolutional neural network for domain selection.

Figure 4: The framework of the proposed LTS model for response generation.

tracker records the historical content, the current domain and the historically triggered domains, the sequences of the states of confirmation, clarification, filtration, rejection, etc., and their combinations. Given the feature representations of an input, the multi-domain state tracker will produce a probability distribution of the states over multiple domains, which is then used to domain selection. The trackers of confirmation, clarification, filtration, rejection, etc., estimate their triggered probabilities, respectively. These probabilities are directly sent to the response generation as their current states or triggered confidences. It is worth noting that the conversations may come to a stalemate state, which indicates that the users are not interesting to the current conversation topic or they are unsatisfied to the responses generated by Benben. Once the stalemate state is detected, Benben will transfer the current conversation topic to another topic to sustain the conversation.

Meanwhile, as can be seen from Figure 2, there is an iterative interaction among conversation state tracking, domain selection and domain processing. The interactive loop denotes that the state tracking module provides the current state distribution of multiple domains for the domain selection. The triggered domains are then processing to update the conversation state as well as generate the intermediate results for response generation.

2.3 Domain Selection

The domain selection module is to trigger one or more domains to produce the intermediate results for response generation. It takes the feature representations from language understanding and the current multi-domain state distribution from con-versation state tracking as inputs and estimates the triggered domain distribution using a convolutional neural network.

In Benben, we proposed a topic augmented convolutional neural network to integrate the continuous word representations and the discrete topic information into a unified framework for domain selection. Figure 3 shows the framework of the proposed topic augmented convolutional neural network for domain selection. The word embedding matrix and the topic matrix are obtained using the word2vec[6] and Labeled LDA (Ramage et al., 2009), respectively. The two representations of the input conversation utterance are combined in the full connection layer and output the domain triggered distribution. At last, the domains whose triggered probabilities are larger than a threshold are selected to execute the following domain processing step. Note that after the domain selection step, there may be one or more triggered domains. If there is no domain to be triggered, the conversation state is updated and then sent to the response generation module.

2.4 Domain Processing

Once a domain is selected, the corresponding processing step is triggered. We will next details the processing manners of the four domains.

Chit-Chat

The chit-chat processing consists of two components. First is the retrieval based model for generating chit-chat conversations. Here, we have indexed 3 million single turn post-response pairs collected from the online forum and microblog

---

[6]https://code.google.com/archive/p/word2vec/

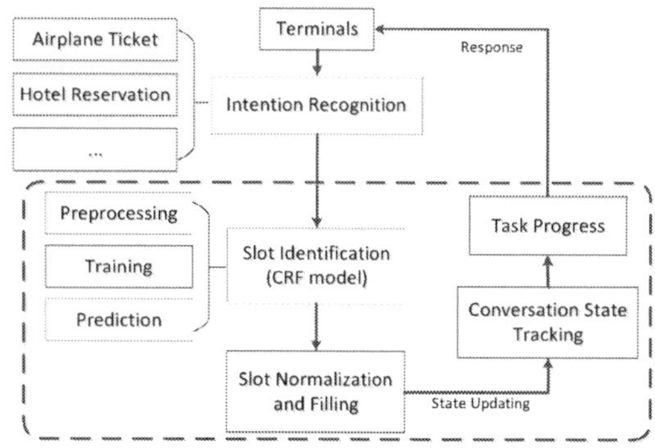

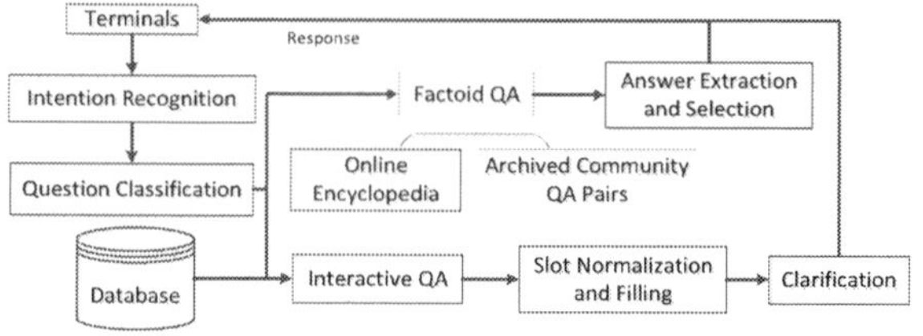

Figure 5: The process of task completion for each sub-domain.

conversations, using Lucene toolkit[7]. Second, the use of "<EOS>" to initialize the sequence to sequence (Seq2Seq) learning based response generation models usually leads to vague or non-committal responses, such as *"I don't know."*, *"Me too."*, etc. To address the problem, we used an optimized approach (Zhu et al., 2016), namely learning to start (LTS) model, to utilize a specific neural network to learn how to generate the first word of a response. Figure 4 is the framework of the proposed LTS model. 5 million post and comment pairs that are released by the short text conversation in NTCIR-12[8] are used to train the LTS model.

Task Completion

The domain of task completion also has sub-domains, such as restaurant and hotel reservation, airplane and train ticket booking, bus and metro line guidance, etc. For each sub-domain, the task completion process is shown in Figure 5. As can be seen, after recognizing the user intention, a conditional random field (CRF) model is utilized to identify the values, in the user input, to fill the semantic slots according to the characteristics of the sub-domain. For the same semantic slot, there may be different forms of values can be filled in. Therefore, we also proposed a value normalization scheme for the semantic slots. The conversation state is then updated after a slot has been filled. In a task progress, the task completion is an interactive process between terminals and users so that it needs a multi-turn conversation controller. In Benben, the multi-turn conversation is jointly

Figure 6: The process of the question answering in Benben.

controlled by the conversation state tracking and domain selection. The domain alternation is implemented by the confirmation and clarification state trackers as well as the response generation.

Question Answering

The question answering (QA) domain has two modes, namely factoid QA and interactive QA. After the intention recognition of user input, the question classification module routes the user questions into the factoid QA or interactive QA. For the factoid QA, we retrieve the candidate paragraphs, sentences, infobox messages from the online encyclopedia, and QA pairs from a large scale archived community QA repository, which are collected from a community QA website. As Benben currently processes the Chinese conversations, the Baidu Encyclopedia[9] and Baidu Zhidao[10] are selected as the online encyclopedia and the community QA website, respectively. The answer extraction module then extract the candidate answers from the retrieved paragraphs, sentences, infobox messages and QA pairs. The answer selection is to rank the candidate answers and the top 1 answer is sent to the user as a response. The interactive QA is similar to the task completion and they share the common processes of slot normalization, slot filling and clarification. An example interactive QA is the weather forecast and inquiry as the weather is related to the date and location. Figure 6 shows the process of the question answering in Benben.

Recommendation

The recommendation in Benben has two functions. The first is to satisfy the users' information need on specific content, such as news. The second is to break the stalemate in conversation.

[7]http://lucene.apache.org/core/
[8]http://ntcir12.noahlab.com.hk/stc.htm
[9]https://baike.baidu.com/
[10]https://zhidao.baidu.com/

Taking the news recommendation as an example, Benben can respond to the requirement of news reading in some specific topics, such as sports, fashion, movie, finance, etc. For example, users say: *"Show me the most recent news about movies."* as well as they can also say *"Once more"* to see another movie news. Besides the querying mode, when a stalemate is detected during a conversation, Benben will recommend a recent news, according to the user profiling information, by a random alternation to the conversation topic transferring to break the stalemate. Note that the news recommendation is also in an interactive way, which means that Benben will ask the user whether he/she wants to read a news of a specific topic in an euphemism way.

2.5 Response Generation

As shown in Figure 2, the response generation takes the conversation states and the intermediate results as input to generate text or speech responses to users. The filtration, rejection, confirmation and clarification responses are generated by considering the corresponding states that obtained from the conversation state tracking. The transferred topic and recommendation responses are generated to break the stalemate in conversations. It is worth noting that there may be more than one triggered domains in domain selection and processing steps. Therefore, the intermediate results may contain multiple outputs from different domains. These outputs are actually the generated responses from the corresponding domains. However, in each turn of a conversation, there is only one response that should be responded to users. Hence, the response quality estimation module is proposed to generate a unique response to users. The quality estimation process considers the states, the output confidences and the response qualities of the domains. For example, if the triggered probability of QA is higher than other domains and the confidence of the generated answer is larger than a threshold, the answer is more likely to be a response to users. The module will also identify an answer type to check whether the generated answer is matched to the predicted type or not. For example, the expected answer type of the question *"When was the Titanic first on?"* is *"Date"*. If the QA domain outputs a location or a human name, the answer type is mismatched so that the answer should not be a response to users.

3 Featured Functions of Benben

Diet Map based Conversation: The diet map is a database that contains the geographical distribution of diet in China. It is constructed by mining the location and diet pairs from a microblog service in China, named Sina Weibo. The diet map not only includes the related diet and location information, but also distinguishes the breakfast, lunch, dinner as well as the gender of users. These aspects can be seen as the slots in conversations. Based on the diet map, we develop a function for querying the location specific diet through chatting with Benben.

Implicit Feedback based Conversation: We find that users may express their emotion, opinion, sentiment, etc., on the inputs during the conversation process. These can be seen as the implicit feedback from users. We thus explore the implicit feedback in the conversation to optimize the long-term goal of conversation generation and model the implicit feedback as a reward shaping scheme towards a basic reward function in a reinforcement learning framework.

Interactive Machine Reading: Given a document or a paragraph about a specific topic or event, Benben can continuously talk to users about the given content which is our proposed interactive machine reading function. Benben will first reads and understands the given material using the proposed approach (Cui et al., 2016) and users can ask several factoid questions according to the material content. Note that as these questions are context related, there are many anaphora and ellipsis phenomenons. We thus utilize the proposed approaches (Liu et al., 2016; Zhang et al., 2016) for anaphora and zero-anaphora resolution.

4 Implementation

There are three implementations of Benben. 1) First is the webpage version for PC or mobile phone(The link is http://iqa.8wss.com/dialogue-test). Users can open the link and type to chat with Benben in Chinese. 2) Second is the Nao robot version. We carry the Benben service in a cloud server and link a Nao robot to the service. Users thus can chat with Benben in speech. The ASR and TTS are implemented by calling the services from the voice cloud[11] of iFLYTEK[12]. Besides the conversation, the Nao robot version can

---

[11]http://www.voicecloud.cn/
[12]http://www.iflytek.com/en/index.html

Figure 7: The QR code of Benben in WeChat.

be also controlled by speech instructions of spoken language to execute some actions. Please see the video in Youtube[13] 3) Third, Benben is also carried in WeChat[14] App, which is the most convenient platform as it allows to chat with Benben in text and speech as well as images and emoticons. The quick response (QR) code is shown in Figure 7. Please scan the QR code using the WeChat App and chat with Benben.

5 Conclusion

In this paper, we present a Chinese conversational robot, Benben, which is designed to achieve the goals of chit-chat, task completion, question answering and recommendation in human-robot conversations. In the current version, Benben is implemented in three platforms, namely PC, mobile phone and Nao robot. In the future, we plan to apply it to other scenarios such as vehicle, home furnishing, toys, etc. Meanwhile, we plan to transfer Benben from Chinese version to English version.

Acknowledgments

The authors would like to thank all the anonymous reviewers for their insight reviews and the members of the conversational robot group of the research center for social computing and information retrieval, Harbin Institute of Technology. This paper is funded by 973 Program (No. 2014CB340503) and NSFC (No. 61502120, 61472105).

References

Wanxiang Che, Zhenghua Li, and Ting Liu. 2010. Ltp: A chinese language technology platform. In *COLING*. pages 13–16.

Rik Crutzen, Gjaltjorn Y Peters, Sarah Dias Portugal, Erwin M Fisser, and J J J Grolleman. 2011. An artificially intelligent chat agent that answers adolescents' questions related to sex, drugs, and alcohol: An exploratory study. *Journal of Adolescent Health* 48(5):514–519.

Yiming Cui, Zhipeng Chen, Si Wei, Shijin Wang, Ting Liu, and Guoping Hu. 2016. Attention-over-attention neural networks for reading comprehension .

B. Fu and T. Liu. 2013. Weakly-supervised consumption intent detection in microblogs. *Journal of Computational Information Systems* 9(6):2423–2431.

Paulo Goes, Noyan Ilk, Wei T. Yue, and J. Leon Zhao. 2011. Live-chat agent assignments to heterogeneous e-customers under imperfect classification. *ACM TMIS* 2(4):1–15.

Ting Liu, Yiming Cui, Qingyu Yin, Shijin Wang, Weinan Zhang, and Guoping Hu. 2016. Generating and exploiting large-scale pseudo training data for zero pronoun resolution. *CoRR* abs/1606.01603.

Giovanni Pilato, Giorgio Vassallo, Manuel Gentile, Agnese Augello, and Salvatore Gaglio. 2005. Lsa for intuitive chat agents tutoring system. pages 461–465.

Daniel Ramage, David Hall, Ramesh Nallapati, and Christopher D. Manning. 2009. Labeled LDA: A supervised topic model for credit attribution in multi-labeled corpora. In *EMNLP*. pages 248–256.

Avi Rosenfeld, Inon Zuckerman, Erel Segalhalevi, Osnat Drein, and Sarit Kraus. 2014. Negochat: A chat-based negotiation agent. *Autonomous Agents and Multi-Agent Systems* .

Duyu Tang, Bing Qin, Furu Wei, Li Dong, Liu Ting, and Zhou Ming. 2015. A joint segmentation and classification framework for sentence level sentiment classification. *IEEE/ACM TASLP* 23(11):1750–1761.

Alan M Turing. 1950. Computing machinery and intelligence. *Mind* 59(236):433–460.

S Young, M Gasic, B Thomson, and J. D Williams. 2013. Pomdp-based statistical spoken dialog systems: A review. *Proceedings of the IEEE* 101(5):1160–1179.

Weinan Zhang, Ting Liu, Qingyu Yin, and Yu Zhang. 2016. Neural recovery machine for chinese dropped pronoun. *CoRR* abs/1605.02134.

Qingfu Zhu, Weinan Zhang, Lianqiang Zhou, and Ting Liu. 2016. Learning to start for sequence to sequence architecture. http://arxiv.org/abs/1608.05554.

---

[13] https://youtu.be/wfPv9-I4q7s.

[14] https://en.wikipedia.org/wiki/WeChat

End-to-End Non-Factoid Question Answering with an Interactive Visualization of Neural Attention Weights

Andreas Rücklé[†] and **Iryna Gurevych**[††]
[†]Ubiquitous Knowledge Processing Lab (UKP)
Department of Computer Science, Technische Universität Darmstadt
[‡]Ubiquitous Knowledge Processing Lab (UKP-DIPF)
German Institute for Educational Research
`www.ukp.tu-darmstadt.de`

Abstract

Advanced attention mechanisms are an important part of successful neural network approaches for non-factoid answer selection because they allow the models to focus on few important segments within rather long answer texts. Analyzing attention mechanisms is thus crucial for understanding strengths and weaknesses of particular models. We present an extensible, highly modular service architecture that enables the transformation of neural network models for non-factoid answer selection into fully featured end-to-end question answering systems. The primary objective of our system is to enable researchers a way to interactively explore and compare attention-based neural networks for answer selection. Our interactive user interface helps researchers to better understand the capabilities of the different approaches and can aid qualitative analyses. The source-code of our system is publicly available.[1]

1 Introduction

Attention-based neural networks are increasingly popular because of their ability to focus on the most important segments of a given input. These models have proven to be extremely effective in many different tasks, for example neural machine translation (Luong et al., 2015; Tu et al., 2016), neural image caption generation (Xu et al., 2015), and multiple sub-tasks in question answering (Hermann et al., 2015; Tan et al., 2016; Yin et al., 2016; Andreas et al., 2016).

Attention-based neural networks are especially successful in answer selection for non-factoid ques-

tions, where approaches have to deal with complex multi-sentence texts. The objective of this task is to re-rank a list of candidate answers according to a non-factoid question, where the best-ranked candidate is selected as an answer. Models usually learn to generate dense vector representations for questions and candidates, where representations of a question and an associated correct answer should lie closely together within the vector space (Feng et al., 2015). Accordingly, the ranking score can be determined with a simple similarity metric. Attention in this scenario works by calculating weights for each individual segment in the input (attention vector), where segments with a higher weight should have a stronger impact on the resulting representation. Several approaches have been recently proposed, achieving state-of-the-art results on different datasets (Dos Santos et al., 2016; Tan et al., 2016; Wang et al., 2016).

The success of these approaches clearly shows the importance of sophisticated attention mechanisms for effective answer selection models. However, it has also been shown that attention mechanisms can introduce certain biases that negatively influence the results (Wang et al., 2016). As a consequence, the creation of better attention mechanisms can improve the overall answer selection performance. To achieve this goal, researchers are required to perform in-depth analyses and comparisons of different approaches to understand what the individual models learn and how they can be improved. Due to the lack of existing tool-support to aid this process, such analyses are complex and require substantial development effort. This important issue led us to creating an integrated solution that helps researchers to better understand the capabilities of different attention-based models and can aid qualitative analyses.

In this work, we present an extensible service architecture that can transform models for non-

---

[1] `https://github.com/UKPLab/`
`acl2017-non-factoid-qa`

Proceedings of the 55th Annual Meeting of the Association for Computational Linguistics-System Demonstrations, pages 19–24
Vancouver, Canada, July 30 - August 4, 2017. ©2017 Association for Computational Linguistics
https://doi.org/10.18653/v1/P17-4004

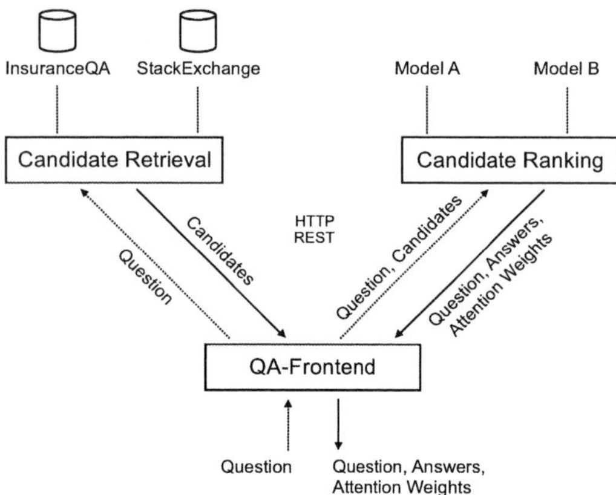

Figure 1: A high-level view on our service architecture.

factoid answer selection into fully featured end-to-end question answering systems. Our sophisticated user interface allows researchers to ask arbitrary questions while visualizing the associated attention vectors with support for both, one-way and two-way attention mechanisms. Users can explore different attention-based models at the same time and compare two attention mechanisms side-by-side within the same view. Due to the loose coupling and the strictly separated responsibilities of the components in our service architecture, our system is highly modular and can be easily extended with new datasets and new models.

2 System Overview

To transform attention-based answer selection models into end-to-end question answering systems, we rely on a service orchestration that integrates multiple independent webservices with separate responsibilities. Since all services communicate using a well-defined HTTP REST API, our system achieves strong extensibility properties. This makes it simple to replace individual services with own implementations. A high-level view on our system architecture is shown in Figure 1. For each question, we retrieve a list of candidate answers from a given dataset (candidate retrieval). We then rank these candidates with the answer selection component (candidate ranking), which integrates the attention-based neural network model that should be explored. The result contains the top-ranked answers and all associated attention weights,

which enables us to interactively visualize the attention vectors in the user interface.

Our architecture is similar to the pipelined structures of earlier work in question answering that rely on a retrieval step followed by a more expensive supervised ranking approach (Surdeanu et al., 2011; Higashinaka and Isozaki, 2008). We primarily chose this architecture because it allows the user to directly relate the results of the system to the answer selection model. The use of more advanced components (e.g. query expansion or answer merging) would negate this possibility due to the added complexity.

Because all components in our extensible service architecture are loosely coupled, it is possible to use multiple candidate ranking services with different attention mechanisms at the same time. The user interface exploits this ability and allows researchers to interactively compare two models side-by-side within the same view. A screenshot of our UI is shown in Figure 2, and an example of a side-by-side comparison is available in Figure 4.

In the following sections, we describe the individual services in more detail and discuss their technical properties.

3 Candidate Retrieval

The efficient retrieval of answer candidates is a key component in our question answering approach. It allows us to narrow down the search space for more sophisticated, computationally expensive attention-based answer selection approaches in the subsequent step, and enables us to retrieve answers within seconds. We index all existing candidates of the target dataset with ElasticSearch, an open-source high-performance search engine. Our service provides a unified interface for the retrieval of answer candidates, where we query the index with the question text using BM25 as a similarity measure.

The service implementation is based on *Scala* and the *Play Framework*. Our implementation contains data readers that allow to index InsuranceQA (Feng et al., 2015) and all publicly available dumps of the StackExchange platform.[2] Researchers can easily add new datasets by implementing a single data reader class.

Analysis Enabling researchers to directly relate the results of our question answering system to

---

[2]`https://archive.org/details/stackexchange`

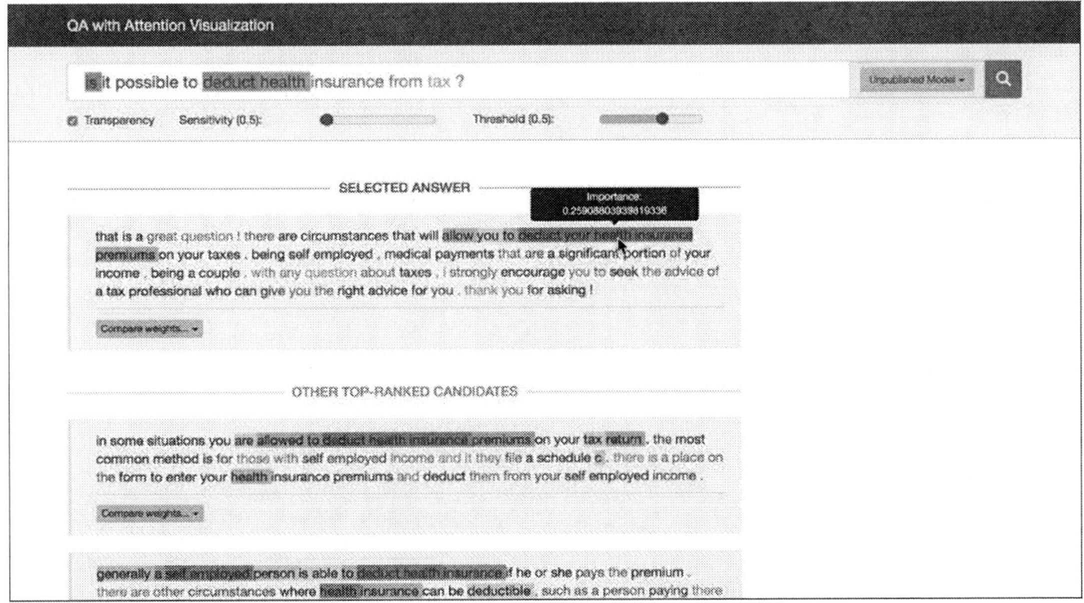

Figure 2: The user interface of our question answering system with the interactive visualization of neural attention weights. The UI includes several options to adapt the attention visualization.

the answer selection component requires the absence of major negative influences from the answer retrieval component. To analyze the potential influence, we evaluated the list of retrieved candidates (size 500) for existing questions of InsuranceQA and of different StackExchange dumps. Questions in these datasets have associated correct answers,[3] which we treat as the ground-truth that should be included in the retrieved list of candidates. Otherwise it would be impossible for the answer selection model to find the correct answer, and the results would be negatively affected. Table 1 shows the number of questions with candidate lists that include at least one ground-truth answer. Since the ratio is sufficiently high for all analyzed datasets (83% to 88%), we conclude that the chosen retrieval approach is a valid choice for our end-to-end question answering system.

4   Candidate Ranking

The candidate ranking service provides an interface to the attention-based neural network, which the researcher chose to analyze. It provides a method to rank a list of candidate answers according to a given question text. An important property is the

Dataset	Candidate Lists with Ground-Truth
InsuranceQA (v1)	84.1% (13,200/15,687)
InsuranceQA (v2)	83.3% (14,072/16,889)
StackExchange/Travel	85.8% (13,978/16,294)
StackExchange/Cooking	88.0% (12,025/13,668)
StackExchange/Photo	83.0% (10,856/13,079)

Table 1: Performance of the retrieval service for different datasets.

retrieval of attention vectors from the model. These values are bundled with the top-ranked answers and are returned as a result of the service call.

Since our primary objective was to enable researchers to explore different attention-based approaches, we created a fully configurable and modular framework that includes different modules to train and evaluate answer selection models. The key properties of this framework are:

- Fully configurable with external *YAML* files.
- Dynamic instantiation and combination of configured module implementations (e.g. for the data reader and the model).
- Highly extensible: researchers can integrate new (TensorFlow) models by implementing a single class.
- Seamless integration with a webapplication that implements the service interface.

---

[3] For StackExchange, we consider all answers as correct that have a positive user voting. We only include questions with a positive user voting and at least one correct answer.

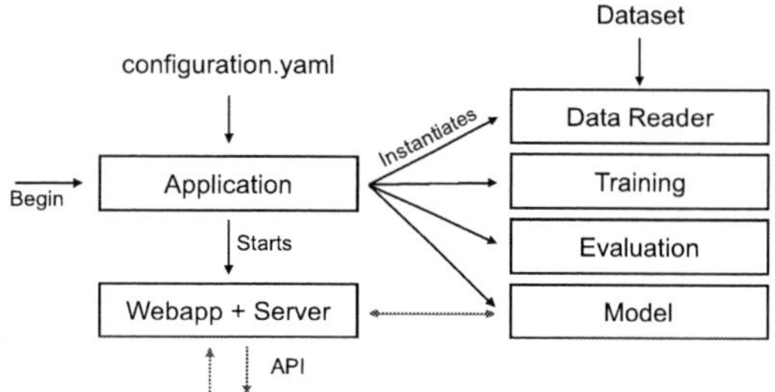

Figure 3: Our answer selection framework and candidate ranking service.

Our framework implementation is based on *Python* and relies on *TensorFlow* for the neural network components. It uses *Flask* for the service implementation.

A high-level view on the framework structure is shown in Figure 3. A particularly important property is the dynamic instantiation and combination of module implementations. A central configuration file is used to define all necessary options that enable to train and evaluate neural networks within our framework. An excerpt of such configuration is shown in Listing 1. The first four lines describe the module import paths of the desired implementations. Our framework dynamically loads and instantiates the configured modules and uses them to perform the training procedure. The remaining lines define specific configuration options to reference resource paths or to set specific neural network settings. This modular structure enables a high flexibility and provides a way to freely combine different models, training procedures, and data readers.

Additionally, our framework is capable of starting a seamlessly integrated webserver that uses a configured model to rank candidate answers. Since model states can be saved, it is possible to load pretrained models to avoid a lengthy training process.

5 QA-Frontend and User Interface

The central part of our proposed system is the QA-Frontend. This component coordinates the other services and combines them into a fully functional question answering system. Since our primary goal was to provide a way to explore and compare attention-based models, we especially focused on the user interface. Our UI fulfills the following requirements:

```
1   data-module: data.insuranceqa.v2
2   model-module: model.ap_lstm
3   training-module: training.dynamic
4   evaluation-module: evaluation.default
5
6   data:
7       map_oov: true
8       embeddings: data/glove.6B.100d.txt
9       insuranceqa: data/insuranceQA
10      ...
11
12  model:
13      lstm_cell_size: 141
14      margin: 0.2
15      trainable_embeddings: true
16      ...
17
18  training:
19      negative_answers: 50
20      batchsize: 20
21      epochs: 100
22      save_folder: checkpoints/ap_lstm
23      dropout: 0.3
24      optimizer: adam
25      scorer: accuracy
26      ...
```

Listing 1: An excerpt of a *YAML* configuration file for the candidate ranking framework.

- Use a visualization for the attention vectors similar to Hermann et al. (2015) and Dos Santos et al. (2016).
- Support for both, one-way attention mechanisms (Tan et al., 2016) and two-way attention mechanisms (Dos Santos et al., 2016).
- Enable to query multiple models within the same view.
- Provide a side-by-side comparison of different attention-based models.

We implemented the user interface with modern web technologies, such as *Angular*, *TypeScript*, and *SASS*. The QA-Frontend service was implemented in *Python* with *Flask*. It is fully configurable and allows multiple candidate ranking services to be used at the same time.

A screenshot of our user interface is shown in Figure 2. In the top row, we include an input field that allows users to enter the question text. This input field also contains a dropdown menu to select the target model that should be used for the candidate ranking. This makes it possible to ask the same question for multiple models and compare the outputs to gain a better understanding of the key differences. Below this input field we offer multiple ways to interactively change the attention visualization. In particular, we allow to change the sensitivity s and the threshold t of the visualization component. We calculate the opacity of an attention highlight o_i that corresponds to the weight w_i in position i as follows:

$$a = min\left(w_{std},\ w_{max} - w_{avg}\right) \qquad (1)$$

$$o_i = \begin{cases} s \cdot \frac{w_i - w_{avg}}{a}, & if\ \ w_i \geq w_{avg} + a \cdot t \\ 0, & otherwise \end{cases} \qquad (2)$$

Where w_{avg}, w_{std} and w_{max} are the average, standard deviation and maximum of all weights in the text. We use a instead of w_{std} because in rare cases it can occur that $w_{std} > w_{max} - w_{avg}$, which would lead to visualizations without fully opaque positions. These two options make it possible to adapt the attention visualization to fit the need of the analysis. For example, it is possible to only highlight the most important sections by increasing the threshold. On the other hand, it is also possible to highlight all segments that are slightly relevant by increasing the sensitivity and at the same time reducing the threshold.

When the user hovers over an answer and the target model employs a two-way attention mechanism, the question input visualizes the associated attention weights. To get a more in-depth view on the attention vectors, the user can hover over any specific word in a text to view the exact value of the associated weight. This enables numerical comparisons and helps to get an advanced understanding of the employed answer selection model.

Finally, each answer offers the option to compare the attention weights to the output of another configured model. This action enables a side-by-side comparison of different attention mechanisms and gives researchers a powerful tool to explore the advantages and disadvantages of the different approaches. A screenshot of a side-by-side visualization is shown in Figure 4. It displays two attention mechanisms that result in very different behavior. Whereas the model to the left strongly focuses on few individual words (especially in the question), the model to the right is less selective and focuses on more segments that are similar. Our user interface makes it simple to analyze such attributes in detail.

6 Conclusion

In this work, we presented a highly extensible service architecture that can transform non-factoid answer selection models into fully featured end-to-end question answering systems. Our key contribution is the simplification of in-depth analyses of attention-based models to non-factoid answer selection. We enable researchers to interactively explore and understand their models qualitatively. This can help to create more advanced attention mechanisms that achieve better answer selection results. Besides enabling the exploration of individual models, our user interface also allows researchers to compare different attention mechanisms side-by-side within the same view.

All components of our system are highly modular which allows it to be easily extended with additional functionality. For example, our modular answer retrieval component makes it simple to integrate new datasets, and our answer ranking framework allows researchers to add new models without requiring to change any other part of the application.

The source-code of all presented components as well as the user interface is publicly available. We provide a documentation for all discussed APIs.

Acknowledgements

This work has been supported by the German Research Foundation as part of the QA-EduInf project (grant GU 798/18-1 and grant RI 803/12-1). We gratefully acknowledge the support of NVIDIA Corporation with the donation of the Tesla K40 GPU used for this research.

References

Jacob Andreas, Marcus Rohrbach, Trevor Darrell, and Dan Klein. 2016. Learning to Compose Neural Networks for Question Answering. In *Proceedings of the 2016 Conference of the North American Chapter of the Association for Computational Linguistics.* pages 1545–1554. https://doi.org/10.18653/v1/N16-1181.

Cicero Dos Santos, Ming Tan, Bing Xiang, and Bowen Zhou. 2016. Attentive Pooling Networks. *arXiv preprint* https://arxiv.org/abs/1602.03609.

Minwei Feng, Bing Xiang, Michael R. Glass, Lidan Wang, and Bowen Zhou. 2015. Applying deep learning to answer selection: A study and an open task. In *2015 IEEE Workshop on Automatic Speech Recognition and Understanding.* pages 813–820. https://doi.org/10.1109/ASRU.2015.7404872.

Karl Moritz Hermann, Tomáš Kočiský, Edward Grefenstette, Lasse Espeholt, Will Kay, Mustafa Suleyman, and Phil Blunsom. 2015. Teaching machines to read

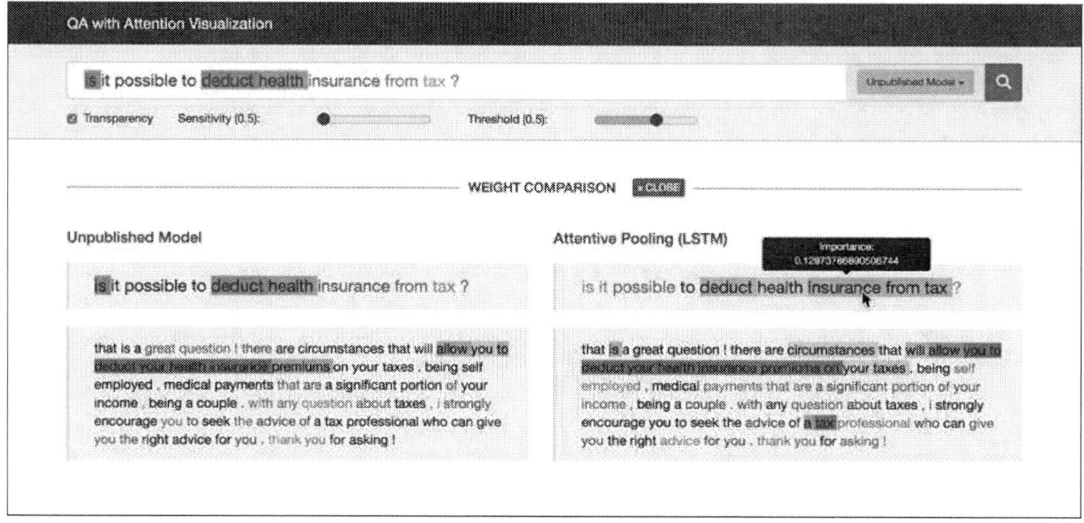

Figure 4: A side-by-side comparison of two different attention-based models. It allows the user to quickly spot the differences of the used models and can be used to better analyze their benefits and drawbacks.

and comprehend. In *Advances in Neural Information Processing Systems*. pages 1693–1701.

Ryuichiro Higashinaka and Hideki Isozaki. 2008. Corpus-based question answering for why-questions. In *Proceedings of the Third International Joint Conference on Natural Language Processing*. pages 418–425. http://aclweb.org/anthology/I08-1055.

Thang Luong, Hieu Pham, and Christopher D. Manning. 2015. Effective approaches to attention-based neural machine translation. In *Proceedings of the 2015 Conference on Empirical Methods in Natural Language Processing*. pages 1412–1421. https://doi.org/10.18653/v1/D15-1166.

Mihai Surdeanu, Massimiliano Ciaramita, and Hugo Zaragoza. 2011. Learning to rank answers to non-factoid questions from web collections. *Computational Linguistics* 37(2). http://aclweb.org/anthology/J11-2003.

Ming Tan, Cicero dos Santos, Bing Xiang, and Bowen Zhou. 2016. Improved representation learning for question answer matching. In *Proceedings of the 54th Annual Meeting of the Association for Computational Linguistics*. pages 464–473. https://doi.org/10.18653/v1/P16-1044.

Zhaopeng Tu, Zhengdong Lu, Yang Liu, Xiaohua Liu, and Hang Li. 2016. Modeling Coverage for Neural Machine Translation. *Proceedings of the 54th Annual Meeting of the Association for Computational Linguistics* pages 76–85. https://doi.org/10.1145/2856767.2856776.

Bingning Wang, Kang Liu, and Jun Zhao. 2016. Inner attention based recurrent neural networks for answer selection. In *Proceedings of the 54th Annual Meeting of the Association for Computational Linguistics*. pages 1288–1297. https://doi.org/10.18653/v1/P16-1122.

Kelvin Xu, Jimmy Ba, Ryan Kiros, Kyunghyun Cho, Aaron C Courville, Ruslan Salakhutdinov, Richard S Zemel, and Yoshua Bengio. 2015. Show, Attend and Tell: Neural Image Caption Generation with Visual Attention. *Proceedings of The 32nd International Conference on Machine Learning* pages 2048–2057. https://doi.org/10.1109/72.279181.

Wenpeng Yin, Hinrich Schütze, Bing Xiang, and Bowen Zhou. 2016. Abcnn: Attention-based convolutional neural network for modeling sentence pairs. *Transactions of the Association of Computational Linguistics* 4:259–272. http://aclweb.org/anthology/Q16-1019.

ESTEEM: A Novel Framework for Qualitatively Evaluating and Visualizing Spatiotemporal Embeddings in Social Media

Dustin Arendt[1] and Svitlana Volkova[2]
[1]Visual Analytics, [2]Data Sciences and Analytics
National Security Directorate
Pacific Northwest National Laboratory
Richland, WA 99354
`firstname.lastname@pnnl.gov`

Abstract

Analyzing and visualizing large amounts of social media communications and contrasting short-term conversation changes over time and geolocations is extremely important for commercial and government applications. Earlier approaches for large-scale text stream summarization used dynamic topic models and trending words. Instead, we rely on text embeddings – low-dimensional word representations in a continuous vector space where similar words are embedded nearby each other.

This paper presents ESTEEM,[1] a novel tool for visualizing and evaluating spatiotemporal embeddings learned from streaming social media texts. Our tool allows users to monitor and analyze query words and their closest neighbors with an interactive interface. We used state-of-the-art techniques to learn embeddings and developed a visualization to represent dynamically changing relations between words in social media over time and other dimensions. This is the first interactive visualization of streaming text representations learned from social media texts that also allows users to contrast differences across multiple dimensions of the data.

1 Motivation

Social media is an example of high volume dynamic communications. Understanding and summarizing large amounts of streaming text data is extremely challenging. Traditional techniques that rely on experts, keywords and ontologies do not scale in this scenario. Dynamic topic models, trending topics are widely used as text stream summarization techniques but they are biased and do not allow exploring dynamically changing relationship between concepts in social media or contrasting them across multiple dimensions.

Text embeddings represent words as numeric vectors in a continuous space, where words within similar contexts appear close to one another (Harris, 1954). Mapping words into a lower-dimensional vector space not only solves the dimensionality problem for predictive tasks (Mikolov et al., 2013a), but also goes beyond topics and word clouds by capturing word similarities on syntactic, semantic and morphological levels (Gladkova and Drozd, 2016).

Most past work has learned text representations from static corpora and visualized[2] the relationships between embedding vectors, measured using cosine or Euclidian distance similarity, using Principal Component Analysis (PCA) projection in 2D (Hamilton et al., 2016b; Smilkov et al., 2016) or t-Distributed Stochastic Neighbor Embedding (t-SNE) technique (Van Der Maaten, 2014). Unlike static text corpora, in dynamically changing text streams the associations between words are changing over time e.g., days (Hamilton et al., 2016b,a), years (Kim et al., 2014) or centuries (Gulordava and Baroni, 2011). These changes are compelling to evaluate quantitatively, but, given the scale and complexity of the data, interesting findings are very difficult to capture without qualitative evaluation through visualization.

Moreover, the majority of NLP applications are using word embeddings as features for downstream prediction tasks e.g., part-of-speech tagging (Santos and Zadrozny, 2014), named entity recognition (Passos et al., 2014) and dependency

---

[1]Demo video: `http://goo.gl/3N9Ozj`

[2]TensorBoard Embedding Visualization:
`https://www.tensorflow.org/get_started/embedding_viz`

Proceedings of the 55th Annual Meeting of the Association for Computational Linguistics-System Demonstrations, pages 25–30
Vancouver, Canada, July 30 - August 4, 2017. ©2017 Association for Computational Linguistics
https://doi.org/10.18653/v1/P17-4005

parsing (Lei et al., 2014). However, in the computational social sciences domain, embeddings are used to explore and characterize specific aspects of a text corpus by measuring, tracking and visualizing relationships between words. For example, Bolukbasi et al. (2016) evaluate cultural stereotypes between occupation and gender, Stewart et al. (2017) predicted short-term changes in word meaning and usage in social media.

In this paper we present and publicly release a novel tool ESTEEM[3] for visualizing text representations learned from dynamic text streams across multiple dimensions e.g., time and space.[4] We present several practical use cases that focus on visualizing text representation changes in streaming social media data. These include visualizing word embeddings learned from tweets over time and across (A) geo-locations during crisis (Brussels Bombing Dataset), (B) verified and suspicious news posts (Suspicious News Dataset).

2 Background

2.1 Embedding Types

Most existing algorithms for learning text representations model the context of words using a continuous bag-of-words approach (Mikolov et al., 2013a), skip-grams with negative sampling (Mikolov et al., 2013b) – Word2Vec,[5] modified skip-grams with respect to the dependency tree of the sentence (Levy and Goldberg, 2014), or optimized ratio of word co-occurrence probabilities (Pennington et al., 2014) – GloVe.[6]

2.2 Embedding Evaluation

There are two principle ways one can evaluate embeddings: (a) intrinsically and (b) extrinsically.

(a) *Intrinsic evaluations* directly test syntactic or semantic relationships between the words, and rely on existing NLP resources e.g., WordNet and subjective human judgements e.g., crowdsourcing.

(b) *Extrinsic methods* evaluate word vectors by measuring their performance when used for downstream NLP tasks e.g., dependency parsing, named entity recognition (Passos et al., 2014; Godin et al., 2015).

Recent work suggests that intrinsic and extrinsic measures correlate poorly with one another (Schnabel et al., 2015; Gladkova and Drozd, 2016; Zhang et al., 2016). In many cases we want an embedding not just to capture relationships within the data, but also to do so in a way which can be usefully applied. In these cases, both intrinsic and extrinsic evaluation must be taken into account.

3 Use Cases

For demonstration purposes we rely on the Word2Vec implementation in gensim, but our tool can take any type of pre-trained embedding vectors. To ensure the quality of embeddings learned from social media streams, we lowercased, tokenized and stemmed raw posts,[7] and also applied standard NLP preprocessing to clean noisy social media texts e.g., remove punctuation, mentions, digits, emojis etc. Below we discuss two Twitter datasets we collected to demonstrate our tool for visualizing spatiotemporal text representations.

3.1 Brussels Bombing Dataset

We collected a large sample of tweets (with geo-locations and language IDs assigned to each tweet) from 240 countries in 66 languages from Twitter. Data collection lasted two weeks, beginning on March 15th, 2016 and ending March 29th, 2016. We chose this 15 day period because it includes the attacks on Brussels on March 22 (a widely-discussed event) as well as one whole week before and after the attacks. We used 140 million tweets in English to learn daily spatiotemporal embeddings over time and across 10 European countries.

Dimensions	Tweets
Belgium	1,795,906
France	7,627,599
Germany	5,186,523
Ireland	4,866,775
Spain	5,743,715
United Kingdom	81,733,747
Verified News	9,618,825
Suspicious News	8,492,905

Table 1: Brussels and news dataset statistics: the number of tweets we used to learn embeddings.

3.2 Suspicious News Dataset

We manually constructed a list of trusted news accounts that tweet in English and checked

---

[3]Live demo: http://esteem.labworks.org

[4]Code: https://github.com/pnnl/esteem/

[5]Word2Vec in gensim: https://radimrehurek.com/gensim/models/word2vec.html

[6]GloVe: https://cran.r-project.org/web/packages/text2vec/vignettes/glove.html

[7]Stemming is rarely done when learning embeddings. We stemmed our data because we are not interested in recovering syntactic relationships between the words.

whether they are verified on Twitter. The example verified accounts include @cnn, @bbcnews, @foxnews. We found the list of accounts that spread suspicious news – propaganda, clickbait, hoaxes and satire,[8] e.g., @TheOnion, @ActivistPost, @DRUDGE_REPORT. We collected retweets generated in 2016 by any user that mentions one of these accounts and assigned the corresponding label propagated from suspicious or trusted news sources. In total, we collected 9.6 million verified news posts and 8.4 million suspicious news tweets. We used 18 million tweets to learn monthly embeddings over time and across suspicious and verified news account types.

4 Visualization

Our objective was to provide users with a way to to visually understand how embeddings are changing across multiple dimensions. Lets consider the Brussels Twitter dataset as an example where text representations vary over time and space. We accomplish this by allowing the user to query our tool with a given keyword across set of locations, which produces corresponding visual representations of the embeddings across time and space. The user can then inspect these visual embedding representations side by side, or combine them into a single representation for a more explicit comparison across regions.

4.1 Design

The main challenge we faced in designing dynamic embedding representations was with the scale and complexity of the embeddings, which have tens of thousands of words and hundreds of dimensions. Existing embedding visualization techniques have primarily relied on scatter plot representations of projected data (Hamilton et al., 2016b), using principal components analysis or other dimension reduction techniques e.g., t-Distributed Stochastic Neighbor Embedding.

However, these techniques are problematic because they can create visual clutter if too many entities are projected, and they can be difficult to interpret. Embeddings, having high dimension, can not necessarily be projected into a 2- or 3- dimensional space without incurring significant visual distortion, which can degrade users' trust in the visualization (Chuang et al., 2012). Furthermore,

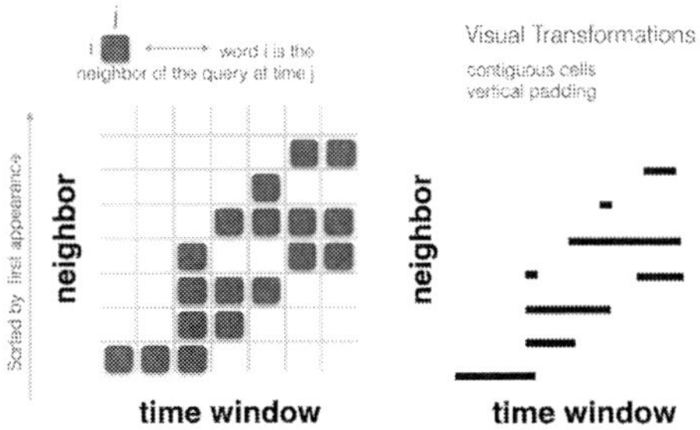

Figure 1: Our visual metaphor stems from an adjacency representation A of the nearest neighbors of the query term. The rows of the matrix correspond to nearest neighbors, and the columns correspond to time windows. The cell a_{ij} is filled if word i is a neighbor of the query term at time j. To this matrix to make the matrix more readable by the user, we apply a visual transformation.

in our experience, many non-expert users are confused by the meaninglessness of the x- and y- coordinate space of the projected data, and have to be trained how to interpret such visualizations.

These problems are amplified when we consider dynamic data, where entities move throughout an embedding space over time. In our case, because embeddings are trained online, the meanings of the dimensions in the embeddings are changing, in addition to the words embedded therein. So, it is not correct to use traditional approaches to project an entities at different time points into the same space using the features directly.

Our solution was to rely on a user driven querying and nearest neighbor technique to address these challenges. We allow users to query the embedding using a single keyword, as we assume the user has a few items of interest they wish to explore, and is not concerned with understanding the entire embedding. This allows us to frame our dynamic embedding visualization problem as a dynamic graph visualization problem (Beck et al., 2014), specifically visualizing dynamic ego-networks.

Our visual representation shows how the nearest neighbors of a user-provided query term change over time. The user can choose the k nearest neighbor words shown in the visualization. We encode time on the x-axis, whereas the y-axis is used to represent each nearest neighbor word returned by the query. This is a matrix representation of the nearest neighbors of the query term over time, as illustrated in Figure 1.

We apply a visual transformation to this matrix to make it easier to understand by replacing adjacent matrix cells with contiguous lines, and

---

[8]http://www.fakenewswatch.com/
http://www.propornot.com/p/the-list.html

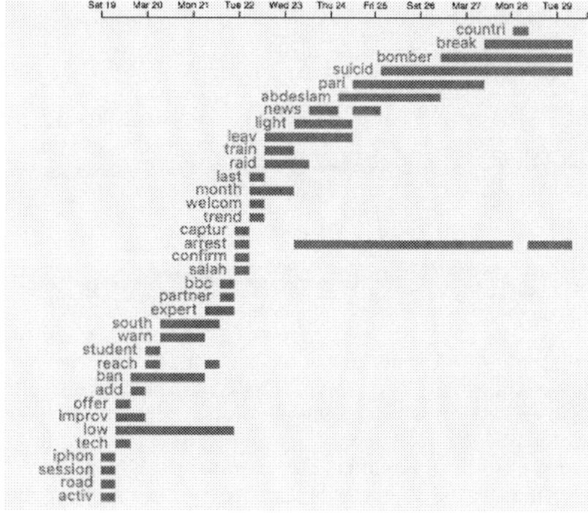

(a) Belgium

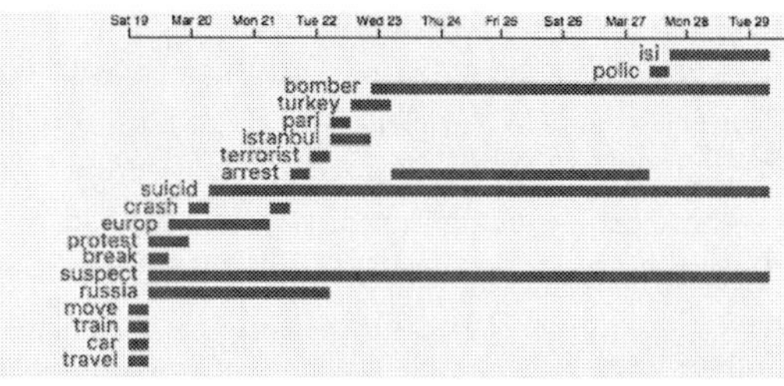

(b) Germany

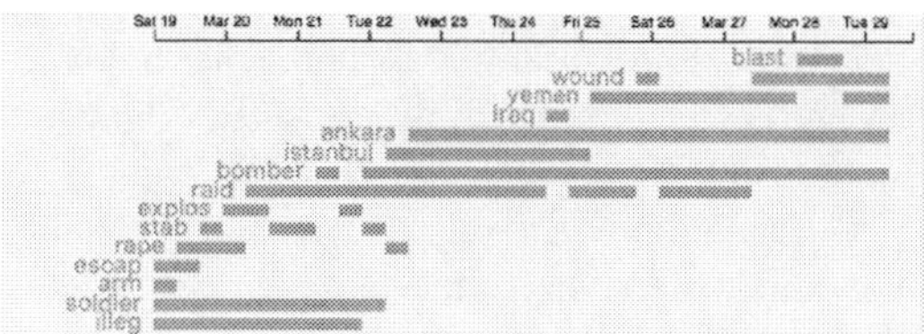

(c) United Kingdom

Figure 2: Visualization of dynamic embedding queries for the word "bomb" across the regions "Belgium," "Germany," and "United Kingdom" are shown. Time is encoded on the horizontal axis, and words are sorted by first occurrence (as a nearest neighbor) for the query term.

adding spacing between rows to help distinguish the query results. The words on the y-axis are sorted in the order they first become a neighbor of the query term. This helps the user see more recent terms, as they will float to the top, versus more persistent terms, which sink to the bottom, and have longer lines. Figure 2 shows a screenshot of our interface containing three of regional dynamic embeddings available for the term "bomb."

Users can compare visualizations of query results side by side in the interface, but we also designed a more explicit comparison of embeddings using a modified version of our visualization technique. Our goal for this comparison was to high-light similarities across two or more dynamic embedding queries over time. We accomplish this by first finding the shared neighbors of these queries within each time step, which is illustrated in Figure 3. We show the results of these queries using the same visual metaphor as described above with an additional embellishment. The thickness of the line at a given time now encodes the number of shared neighbors across the query results at that time. Also, when a query result is shared by more than one query in the combined chart, its corresponding line is filled black, otherwise it retains its original color corresponding to its region. Figure 4 shows an example of combining the query results for "bomb" across regions "Belgium," "Germany," and "United Kingdom."

4.2 Implementation

Our tool is a web application (i.e., client-server model) implemented using Python and Flask[9] for the server and React[10] and D3[11] for the client. The server is responsible for executing the query on the embeddings, whereas the client is responsible managing the users queries and visualizing the results. This separation of concerns means that the server assumes a large memory footprint[12] and processing burden, allowing the clients (i.e., web browsers) to be lightweight. This enables the interface to be used on a typical desktop or even a mobile device by multiple users simultaneously.

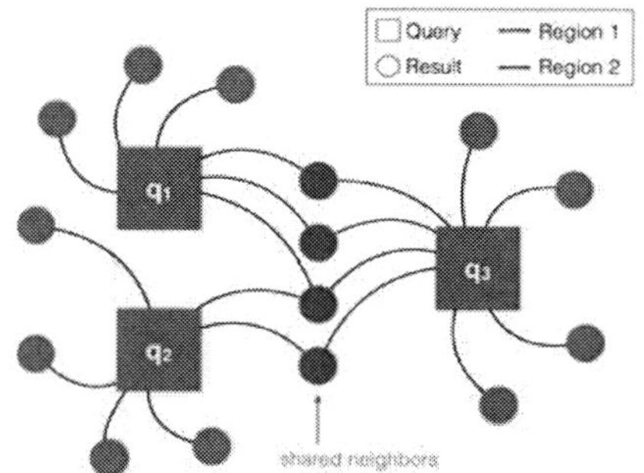

Figure 3: Dynamic embedding queries are combined by finding the shared neighbors across their query results at each time step. This example shows how three separate queries $\{q_1, q_2, q_3\}$ across two regions could have overlap in the result words within a single timestamp.

---

[9] http://flask.pocoo.org
[10] https://facebook.github.io/react/
[11] http://d3js.org
[12] For our Brussels data set, each dynamic embedding requires approximately 500MB of disk space and 2GB in memory after the data structures are created.

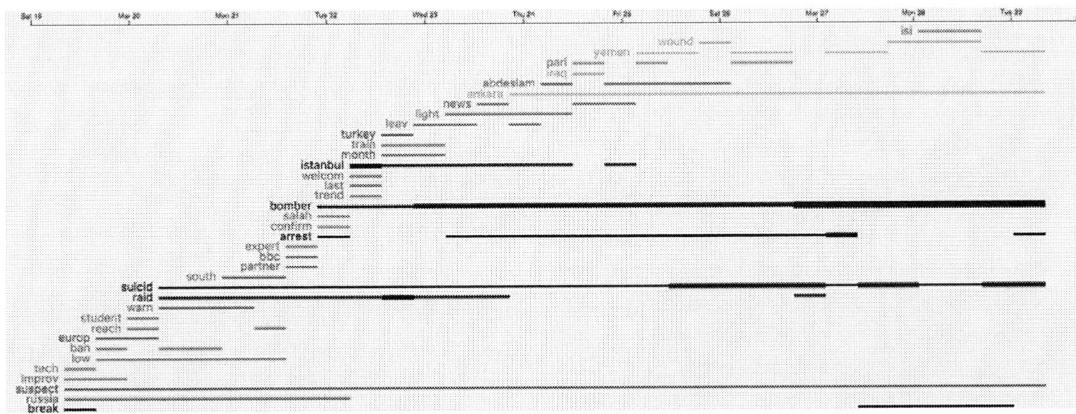

Figure 4: The dynamic embedding queries from Figure 2 are combined into a single chart to support a more explicit comparison of the dynamic embeddings across countries – Belgium (green), German (purple), UK (orange). Where the results overlap from the individual queries, a thicker black line is drawn.

Finding the k-nearest neighbors of a query term in the embedding could take a long time to query for dynamic embeddings with many dimensions and entities. We relied on the "ball tree" data structure available in scikit-learn[13] to help speed up the query. This data structure relies on the Euclidean distance metric, instead of cosine distance, which is considered a best practice. However, after spot checking a few relevant queries using cosine distance, we did not see a qualitative difference between the two metrics, and continued using the ball tree because of the performance advantage. One ball tree is computed for each region and time window, which has a large up front cost, but afterwards our tool provides embedding queries responsively (within 1 second per region). This approach is scalable because each query can divided independently into (region × time window) sub-tasks, allowing the overall calculation to be distributed easily in a map-reduce architecture.

Analyzing Brussels Embeddings Figure 4 shows an example of combining the query results for "bomb" across regions "Belgium," "Germany," and "United Kingdom." We observe that the shared neighbors of the query word "bomb" are *Istanbul* (March 22 - 25), *suicide* (March 20 - 29), *arrest* (March 23 - 27), and *bomber* (March 22 - 29). The words *Paris* and *Abdeslam* are the neighbors only in Belgium, *wound*, *Yemen* and *Iraq* – in the UK, and *Europe, suspect* and *Russia* – in Germany.

---

[13]http://scikit-learn.org/stable/
modules/generated/sklearn.neighbors.
BallTree.html

Analyzing Suspicious News Embeddings Figure 5 shows the results for an example query word pairs: (a) "zika" and "risk" and (b) "Europe" and "refugee" learned from content extracted from suspicious and verified news in 2016. We found that *potential, mosquito, increase, virus* and *concern* are shared neighbors of two query words "zika" and "risk". We observed that *European, Greece, Germany* and *migrant* are shared neighbors of two query words "Europe" and "refugee".

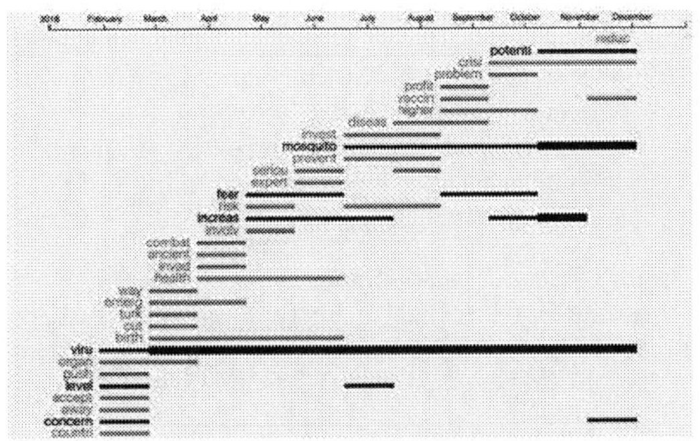

(a) Zika and Risk

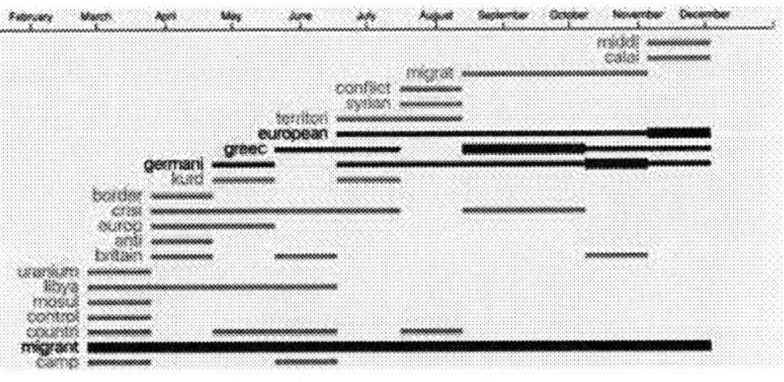

(b) Europe and Refugee

Figure 5: Visualization of dynamic embeddings for the words "zika" and "risk" with 2 neighbors learned from verified (green) and unverified (orange) news on Twitter.

5 Conclusion

We have presented ESTEEM, a novel framework for visualizing and qualitatively evaluating spatiotemporal embeddings learned from large amounts of dynamic text data. Our system allows users to explore specific aspects of text streaming corpus using continuous word representations. Unlike any other embedding visualization, our tool allows contrasting word representation differences over time across other dimensions e.g., geolocation, news types etc. For future work we plan to improve the tool by allowing the user to query using phrases and hashtags.

6 Acknowledgments

This research was conducted under the High-Performance Analytics Program at Pacific Northwest National Laboratory, a multiprogram national laboratory operated by Battelle for the U.S. Department of Energy. The authors would like to thank L. Phillips, J. Mendoza, K. Shaffer, J. Yea Jang and N. Hodas for their help with this work.

References

Fabian Beck, Michael Burch, Stephan Diehl, and Daniel Weiskopf. 2014. The state of the art in visualizing dynamic graphs. *EuroVis STAR* 2.

Tolga Bolukbasi, Kai-Wei Chang, James Y Zou, Venkatesh Saligrama, and Adam T Kalai. 2016. Man is to computer programmer as woman is to homemaker? debiasing word embeddings. In *Proceedings of NIPS*. pages 4349–4357.

Jason Chuang, Daniel Ramage, Christopher Manning, and Jeffrey Heer. 2012. Interpretation and trust: Designing model-driven visualizations for text analysis. In *Proceedings of SIGCHI*. pages 443–452.

Anna Gladkova and Aleksandr Drozd. 2016. Intrinsic evaluations of word embeddings: What can we do better? *Proceedings of ACL* .

Fréderic Godin, Baptist Vandersmissen, Wesley De Neve, and Rik Van de Walle. 2015. Named entity recognition for twitter microposts using distributed word representations. In *Proceedings of ACL-IJCNLP*.

Kristina Gulordava and Marco Baroni. 2011. A distributional similarity approach to the detection of semantic change in the Google Books Ngram corpus. In *Proceedings of GEMS*. pages 67–71.

William Hamilton, Jure Leskovec, and Dan Jurafsky. 2016a. Diachronic word embeddings reveal statistical laws of semantic change. In *Proceedings of ACL.*

William L Hamilton, Jure Leskovec, and Dan Jurafsky. 2016b. Cultural shift or linguistic drift? comparing two computational measures of semantic change. In *Proceedings of EMNLP*.

Zellig S Harris. 1954. Distributional structure. *Word* 10(2-3):146–162.

Yoon Kim, Yi-I Chiu, Kentaro Hanaki, Darshan Hegde, and Slav Petrov. 2014. Temporal analysis of language through neural language models. *Proceedings of ACL* .

Tao Lei, Yuan Zhang, Regina Barzilay, and Tommi Jaakkola. 2014. Low-rank tensors for scoring dependency structures. In *Proceedings of ACL.*

Omer Levy and Yoav Goldberg. 2014. Dependency-based word embeddings. In *Proceedings of ACL.*

Tomas Mikolov, Kai Chen, Greg Corrado, and Jeffrey Dean. 2013a. Efficient estimation of word representations in vector space. In *Proceedings of ICLR.*

Tomas Mikolov, Ilya Sutskever, Kai Chen, Greg S Corrado, and Jeff Dean. 2013b. Distributed representations of words and phrases and their compositionally. In *Proceedings of NIPS.*

Alexandre Passos, Vineet Kumar, and Andrew McCallum. 2014. Lexicon infused phrase embeddings for named entity resolution. In *Proceedings of CoNLL.*

Jeffrey Pennington, Richard Socher, and Christopher D Manning. 2014. Glove: Global vectors for word representation. In *Proceedings of EMNLP.*

Cícero Nogueira Santos and Bianca Zadrozny. 2014. Learning character-level representations for part-of-speech tagging. In *Proceedings ICML.*

Tobias Schnabel, Igor Labutov, David Mimno, and Thorsten Joachims. 2015. Evaluation methods for unsupervised word embeddings. In *Proceedings of EMNLP*.

Daniel Smilkov, Nikhil Thorat, Charles Nicholson, Emily Reif, Fernanda B Viégas, and Martin Wattenberg. 2016. Embedding projector: Interactive visualization and interpretation of embeddings. *arXiv preprint arXiv:1611.05469* .

Ian Stewart, Dustin Arendt, Eric Bell, and Svitlana Volkova. 2017. Measuring, predicting and visualizing short-term change in word representation and usage in vkontakte social network. In *Proceedings of ICWSM.*

Laurens Van Der Maaten. 2014. Accelerating t-sne using tree-based algorithms. *Journal of machine learning research* 15(1):3221–3245.

Yating Zhang, Adam Jatowt, and Katsumi Tanaka. 2016. Towards understanding word embeddings: Automatically explaining similarity of terms. In *Proceedings of Big Data*. IEEE, pages 823–832.

Exploring Diachronic Lexical Semantics with JeSemE

Johannes Hellrich
Graduate School "The Romantic Model.
Variation – Scope – Relevance"
Friedrich-Schiller-Universität Jena
Jena, Germany
johannes.hellrich@uni-jena.de

Udo Hahn
Jena University Language & Information
Engineering (JULIE) Lab
Friedrich-Schiller-Universität Jena
Jena, Germany
udo.hahn@uni-jena.de

Abstract

Recent advances in distributional semantics combined with the availability of large-scale diachronic corpora offer new research avenues for the Digital Humanities. JeSemE, the Jena Semantic Explorer, renders assistance to a non-technical audience to investigate diachronic semantic topics. JeSemE runs as a website with query options and interactive visualizations of results, as well as a REST API for access to the underlying diachronic data sets.

1 Introduction

Scholars in the humanities frequently deal with texts whose lexical items have become antiquated or have undergone semantic changes. Thus their proper understanding is dependent on translational knowledge from manually compiled dictionaries. To complement this workflow with modern NLP tooling, we developed JeSemE,[1] the Jena Semantic Explorer. It supports both lexicologists and scholars with easy-to-use state-of-the-art distributional semantics machinery via an interactive public website and a REST API. JeSemE can be queried for change patterns of lexical items over decades and centuries (resources permitting). The website and the underlying NLP pipelines are open source and available via GitHub.[2]

JeSemE currently covers five diachronic corpora, two for German and three for English. To the best of our knowledge, it is the first tool ever with such capabilities. Its development owes credits to the interdisciplinary Graduate School "The Romantic Model" at Friedrich-Schiller-Universität Jena (Germany).

[1] http://jeseme.org
[2] https://github.com/hellrich/JeSemE

2 Related Work

2.1 Distributional Semantics

Distributional semantics can be broadly conceived as a staged approach to capture the semantics of a lexical item in focus via contextual patterns. *Concordances* are probably the most simple scheme to examine contextual semantic effects, but leave semantic inferences entirely to the human observer. A more complex layer is reached with *collocations* which can be identified automatically via statistical word co-occurrence metrics (Manning and Schütze, 1999; Wermter and Hahn, 2006), two of which are incorporated in JeSemE as well: Positive pointwise mutual information (PPMI), developed by Bullinaria and Levy (2007) as an improvement over the probability ratio of normal pointwise mutual information (PMI; Church and Hanks (1990)) and Pearson's χ^2 , commonly used for testing the association between categorical variables (e.g., POS tags) and considered to be more robust than PMI when facing sparse information (Manning and Schütze, 1999).

The currently most sophisticated and most influential approach to distributional semantics employs *word embeddings*, i.e., low (usually 300–500) dimensional vector word representations of both semantic and syntactic information. Alternative approaches are e.g., graph-based algorithms (Biemann and Riedl, 2013) or ranking functions from information retrieval (Claveau et al., 2014).

The premier example for word embeddings is skip-gram negative sampling, which is part of the word2vec family of algorithms (Mikolov et al., 2013). The random processes involved in training these embeddings lead to a lack of reliability which is dangerous during interpretation—experiments cannot be repeated without predicting severely different relationships between words (Hellrich and Hahn, 2016a, 2017).

Proceedings of the 55th Annual Meeting of the Association for Computational Linguistics-System Demonstrations, pages 31–36
Vancouver, Canada, July 30 - August 4, 2017. ©2017 Association for Computational Linguistics
https://doi.org/10.18653/v1/P17-4006

Word embeddings based on singular value decomposition (SVD; historically popular in the form of Latent Semantic Analysis (Deerwester et al., 1990)) are not affected by this problem. Levy et al. (2015) created SVD$_{PPMI}$ after investigating the implicit operations performed while training neural word embeddings (Levy and Goldberg, 2014). As SVD$_{PPMI}$ performs very similar to word2vec on evaluation tasks while avoiding reliability problems we deem it the best currently available word embedding method for applying distributional semantics in the Digital Humanities (Hamilton et al., 2016; Hellrich and Hahn, 2016a).

2.2 Automatic Diachronic Semantics

The use of statistical methods is getting more and more the status of a commonly shared methodology in diachronic linguistics (see e.g., Curzan (2009)). There exist already several tools for performing statistical analysis on user provided corpora, e.g., WORDSMITH[3] or the UCS TOOLKIT,[4] as well as interactive websites for exploring precompiled corpora, e.g., the "advanced" interface for Google Books (Davies, 2014) or DIACOLLO (Jurish, 2015).

Meanwhile, word embeddings and their application to diachronic semantics have become a novel state-of-the-art methodology lacking, however, off-the-shelves analysis tools easy to use for a typically non-technical audience. Most work is centered around word2vec (e.g., Kim et al. (2014); Kulkarni et al. (2015); Hellrich and Hahn (2016b)), whereas alternative approaches are rare, e.g., Jo (2016) using GloVe (Pennington et al., 2014) and Hamilton et al. (2016) using SVD$_{PPMI}$. Embeddings trained on corpora specific for multiple time spans can be used for two research purposes, namely, screening the semantic evolution of lexical items over time (Kim et al., 2014; Kulkarni et al., 2015; Hamilton et al., 2016) and exploring the meaning of lexical items during a specific time span by finding their closest neighbors in embedding space. This information can then be exploited for automatic (Buechel et al., 2016) or manual (Jo, 2016) interpretation.

3 Corpora

Sufficiently large corpora are an obvious, yet often hard to acquire resource, especially for diachronic research. We employ five corpora, including the four largest diachronic corpora of acceptable quality for English and German.

The *Google Books Ngram Corpus* (GB; Michel et al. (2011), Lin et al. (2012)) contains about 6% of all books published between 1500 and 2009 in the form of n-grams (up to pentagrams). GB is multilingual; its English subcorpus is further divided into regional segments (British, US) and genres (general language and fiction texts). It can be argued to be not so useful for Digital Humanities research due to digitalization artifacts and its opaque and unbalanced nature, yet the English Fiction part is least effected by these problems (Pechenick et al., 2015; Koplenig, 2017). We use its German (GB German) and English Fiction (GB fiction) subcorpora.

The *Corpus of Historical American English*[5] (COHA; Davies (2012)) covers texts from 1800 to 2009 from multiple genres balanced for each decade, and contains annotations for lemmata.

The *Deutsches Textarchiv*[6] (DTA, 'German Text Archive'; Geyken (2013); Jurish (2013)) is a German diachronic corpus and consists of manually transcribed books selected for their representativeness and balance between genres. A major benefit of DTA are its annotation layers which offer both orthographic normalization (mapping archaic forms to contemporary ones) and lemmatization via the CAB tool (Jurish, 2013).

Finally, the *Royal Society Corpus* (RSC) contains the first two centuries of the *Philosophical Transactions of the Royal Society of London* (Kermes et al., 2016), thus forming the most specialized corpus in our collection. Orthographic normalization as well as lemmatization information are provided, just as in DTA. RSC is far smaller than the other corpora, yet was included due to its relevance for research projects in our graduate school.

4 Semantic Processing

The five corpora described in Section 3 were divided into multiple non-overlapping temporal slices, covering 10 years each for COHA and the two GB subcorpora, 30 years each for the smaller DTA and finally two 50 year slices and one 19 year slice for the even smaller RSC (as

---

[3]http://lexically.net/wordsmith
[4]http://www.collocations.de/software.html

[5]http://corpus.byu.edu/coha/
[6]TCF version from May 11th 2016, available via www.deutschestextarchiv.de/download

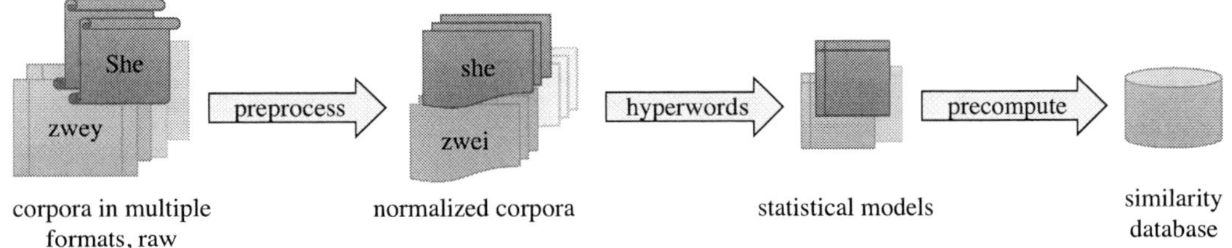

Figure 1: Diagram of JESEME's processing pipeline.

provided in the corpus, roughly similar in size). We removed non-alphanumeric characters during pre-processing and transformed all English text to lowercase. Lemmata were used for the stronger inflected German (provided in DTA, respectively a mapping table created with the CAB webservice (Jurish, 2013) for the German GB subcorpus) and the rather antiquated RSC (provided in the corpus).

We calculated PPMI and χ^2 for each slice, with a context window of 4 words, no random sampling, context distribution smoothing of 0.75 for PPMI, and corpus dependent minimum word frequency thresholds of 50 (COHA, DTA and RSC) respectively 100 (GB subcorpora).[7] The PPMI matrices were then used to create SVD_{PPMI} embeddings with 500 dimensions. These calculations were performed with a modified version of HYPERWORDS[8] (Levy et al., 2015), using custom extensions for faster pre-processing and χ^2. The resulting models have a size of 32 GB and are available for download on JESEME's Help page.[9]

To ensure JESEME's responsiveness, we finally pre-computed similarity (by cosine between word embeddings), as well as context specificity based on PPMI and χ^2. These values are stored in a POSTGRESQL[10] database, occupying about 60GB of space. Due to both space constraints (scaling with $\mathcal{O}(n^2)$ for vocabulary size n) and the lower quality of representations for infrequent words, we limited this step to words which were among the 10k most frequent words for all slices of a corpus, resulting in 3,1k – 6,5k words per corpus. In accordance with this limit, we also discarded slices with less than 10k (5k for RSC)

Corpus	Years	Words
COHA	1830–2009	5,101
DTA	1751–1900	5,338
GB Fiction	1820–2009	6,492
GB German	1830–2009	4,449
RSC	1750-1869	3,080

Table 1: Years and number of words modelled for each corpus in JESEME.

words above the minimum frequency threshold used during PPMI and χ^2 calculation, e.g., the 1810s and 1820s COHA slices. Figure 1 illustrates this sequence of processing steps, while Table 1 summarizes the resulting models for each corpus.

5 Website and API

JESEME provides both an interactive website and an API for querying the underlying database. Both are implemented with the SPARK[11] framework running inside a JETTY[12] Web server.

On JESEME's initial landing page, users can enter a word into a search field and select a corpus. They are then redirected to the result page, as depicted in Figure 2. Query words are automatically lowercased or lemmatized, depending on the respective corpus (see Section 4). The result page provides three kinds of graphs, i.e., Similar Words, Typical Context and Relative Frequency.

Similar Words depicts the words with the highest similarity relative to the query term for the first and last time slice and how their similarity values changed over time. We follow Kim et al. (2014) in choosing such a visualization, while we refrain from using the two-dimensional projection used in other studies (Kulkarni et al., 2015; Hamilton et al., 2016). We stipulate that the latter could

---

[7] Parameters were chosen in accordance with Levy et al. (2015) and Hamilton et al. (2016).

[8] https://bitbucket.org/omerlevy/hyperwords

[9] http://jeseme.org/help.html#download

[10] https://www.postgresql.org

[11] http://sparkjava.com

[12] http://www.eclipse.org/jetty

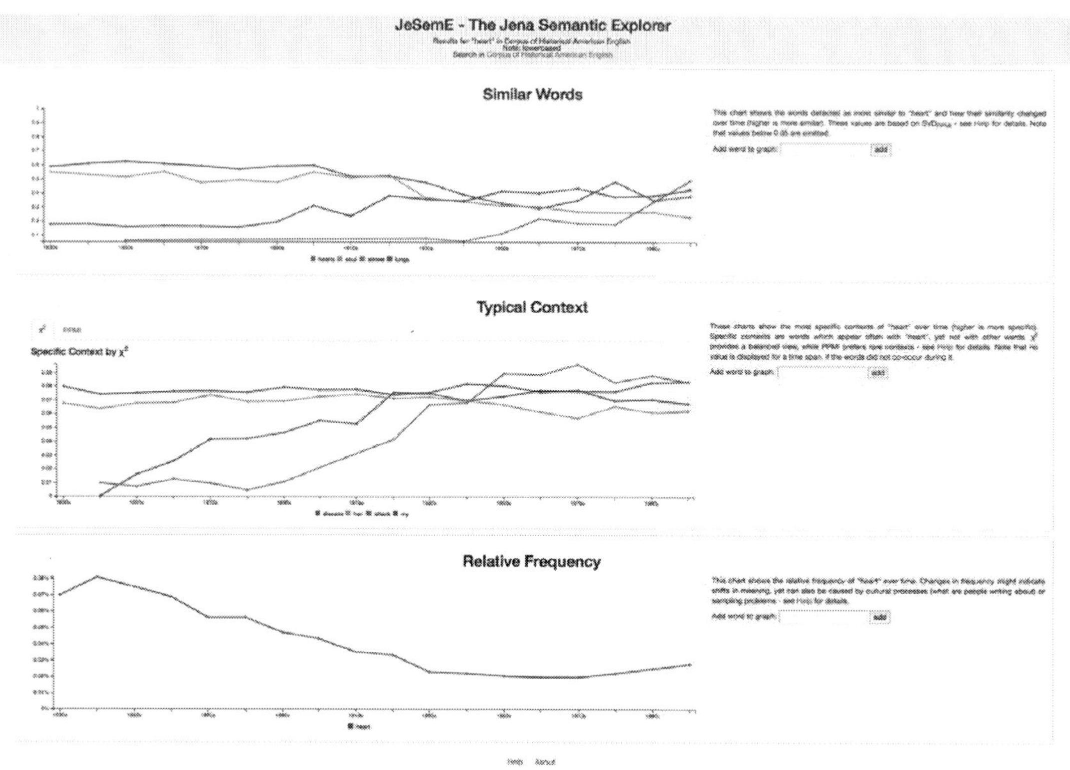

Figure 2: Screenshot of JeSemE's result page when searching for the lexical item *"heart"* in COHA.

be potentially misleading by implying a constant meaning of those words used as the background (which are actually positioned by their meaning at a single point in time).

Typical Context offers two graphs, one for χ^2 and one for PPMI, arranged in tabs. Values in typical context graphs are normalized to make them comparable across different metrics.

Finally, Relative Frequency plots the relative frequency measure against all words above the minimum frequency threshold (see Section 4). All graphs are accompanied by a short explanation and a form for adding further words to the graph under scrutiny. The result page also provides a link to the corresponding corpus, to help users trace JeSemE's computational results.

As an example, consider JeSemE's search for *"heart"* in COHA as depicted in Figure 2. The Similar Words graph depicts a lowered similarity to *"soul"* and increased similarity to *"lungs"*, and more recently also *"stroke"*, which we interpret as a gradual decrease in metaphorical usage. Since COHA is balanced, we assume this pattern to indicate a true semantic change;

a similar change is also observable in the GB Fiction dataset, yet not in the highly domain-specific RSC. Note that this change is unlikely to be linked with the decreased frequency of *"soul"*, as PMI-derived metrics are known to be biased towards infrequent words (Levy et al., 2015). This shift in meaning is also visible in the Typical Context graphs, with *"attack"* and *"disease"* being increasingly specific by both χ^2 and PPMI. Note that metaphorical or metonymical usage of *"heart"* is historically quite common (Niemeier, 2003), despite its long-known anatomical function (Aird, 2011).

The database underlying JeSemE's graphs can also be queried via a REST API which provides JSON encoded results. API calls need to specify the corpus to be searched and one (frequency) or two (similarity, context) words as GET parameters.[13] Calling conventions are further detailed on JeSemE's Help page.[14]

---

[13]For example `http://jeseme.org/api/similarity?word1=Tag&word2=Nacht&corpus=dta`

[14]`http://jeseme.org/help.html#api`

6 Conclusion

We presented JeSemE, the Jena Semantic Explorer, an interactive website and REST API for exploring changes in lexical semantics over long periods of time. In contrast to other corpus exploration tools, JeSemE is based on cutting-edge word embedding technology (Levy et al., 2015; Hamilton et al., 2016; Hellrich and Hahn, 2016a, 2017) and provides access to five popular corpora for the English and German language. JeSemE is also the first tool of its kind and under continuous development.

Future technical work will add functionality to compare words **across** corpora which might require a mapping between embeddings (Kulkarni et al., 2015; Hamilton et al., 2016) and provide optional stemming routines. Both goals come with an increase in precomputed similarity values and will thus necessitate storage optimizations to ensure long-term availability. Finally, we will conduct a user study to investigate JeSemE's potential for the Digital Humanities community.

Acknowledgments

This research was conducted within the Graduate School *"The Romantic Model.   Variation – Scope – Relevance"* supported by grant GRK 2041/1 from *Deutsche Forschungsgemeinschaft (DFG)* (http://www.modellromantik. uni-jena.de/).

References

William C. Aird. 2011. Discovery of the cardiovascular system: from Galen to William Harvey. *Journal of Thrombosis and Haemostasis* 9(s1):118–129.

Chris Biemann and Martin Riedl. 2013. Text: now in 2D! A framework for lexical expansion with contextual similarity. *Journal of Language Modelling* 1(1):55–95.

Sven Buechel, Johannes Hellrich, and Udo Hahn. 2016. Feelings from the past: adapting affective lexicons for historical emotion analysis. In *LT4DH — Proceedings of the Workshop on Language Technology Resources and Tools for Digital Humanities @ COLING 2016. December 11, 2016, Osaka, Japan.* pages 54–61.

John A. Bullinaria and Joseph P. Levy. 2007. Extracting semantic representations from word co-occurrence statistics: a computational study. *Behavior Research Methods* 39(3):510–526.

Kenneth Ward Church and Patrick Hanks. 1990. Word association norms, mutual information, and lexicography. *Computational Linguistics* 16(1):22–29.

Vincent Claveau, Ewa Kijak, and Olivier Ferret. 2014. Improving distributional thesauri by exploring the graph of neighbors. In *COLING 2014 – Proceedings of the 25th International Conference on Computational Linguistics: Technical Papers. Dublin, Ireland, August 23-29, 2014.* pages 709–720.

Anne Curzan. 2009. Historical corpus linguistics and evidence of language change. In Anke Lüdeling and Merja Kytö, editors, *Corpus Linguistics. An International Handbook.* Mouton de Gruyter, Berlin; New York/NY, volume 2 of *Handbooks of Linguistics and Communication Science, 29,* pages 1091–1109.

Mark Davies. 2012. Expanding horizons in historical linguistics with the 400-million word Corpus of Historical American English. *Corpora* 7(2):121–157.

Mark Davies. 2014. Making Google Books n-grams useful for a wide range of research on language change. *International Journal of Corpus Linguistics* 19(3):401–416.

Scott C. Deerwester, Susan T. Dumais, George W. Furnas, Thomas K. Landauer, and Richard A. Harshman. 1990. Indexing by latent semantic analysis. *Journal of the American Society for Information Science* 41(6):391–407.

Alexander Geyken. 2013. Wege zu einem historischen Referenzkorpus des Deutschen: das Projekt Deutsches Textarchiv. In Ingelore Hafemann, editor, *Perspektiven einer corpusbasierten historischen Linguistik und Philologie,* Berlin-Brandenburgische Akademie der Wissenschaften, number 4 in Thesaurus Linguae Aegyptiae, pages 221–234.

William L. Hamilton, Jure Leskovec, and Dan Jurafsky. 2016. Diachronic word embeddings reveal statistical laws of semantic change. In *ACL 2016 — Proceedings of the 54th Annual Meeting of the Association for Computational Linguistics: Long Papers. Berlin, Germany, August 7-12, 2016.* pages 1489–1501.

Johannes Hellrich and Udo Hahn. 2016a. Bad company: Neighborhoods in neural embedding spaces considered harmful. In *COLING 2016 — Proceedings of the 26th International Conference on Computational Linguistics: Technical Papers. Osaka, Japan, December 11-16, 2016.* pages 2785–2796.

Johannes Hellrich and Udo Hahn. 2016b. Measuring the dynamics of lexico-semantic change since the German Romantic period. In *Digital Humanities 2016 — Conference Abstracts of the 2016 Conference of the Alliance of Digital Humanities Organizations (ADHO). 'Digital Identities: The Past and the Future'. Kraków, Poland, 11-16 July 2016.* pages 545–547.

Johannes Hellrich and Udo Hahn. 2017. Don't get fooled by word embeddings: better watch their neighborhood. In *Digital Humanities 2017 — Conference Abstracts of the 2017 Conference of the Alliance of Digital Humanities Organizations (ADHO). Montréal, Quebec, Canada, August 8-11, 2017*.

Eun Seo Jo. 2016. Diplomatic history by data. Understanding Cold War foreign policy ideology using networks and NLP. In *Digital Humanities 2016 — Conference Abstracts of the 2016 Conference of the Alliance of Digital Humanities Organizations (ADHO). 'Digital Identities: The Past and the Future'. Kraków, Poland, 11-16 July 2016*. pages 582–585.

Bryan Jurish. 2013. Canonicalizing the Deutsches Textarchiv. In Ingelore Hafemann, editor, *Perspektiven einer corpusbasierten historischen Linguistik und Philologie*. Berlin-Brandenburgische Akademie der Wissenschaften, number 4 in Thesaurus Linguae Aegyptiae, pages 235–244.

Bryan Jurish. 2015. DiaCollo: on the trail of diachronic collocations. In *Proceedings of the CLARIN Annual Conference 2015. Book of Abstracts. Wroław,, Poland, 14-16 October, 2015*. pages 28–31.

Hannah Kermes, Stefania Degaetano-Ortlieb, Ashraf Khamis, Jörg Knappen, and Elke Teich. 2016. The Royal Society Corpus: from uncharted data to corpus. In *LREC 2016 — Proceedings of the 10th International Conference on Language Resources and Evaluation. Portorož, Slovenia, 23-28 May 2016*. pages 1928–1931.

Yoon Kim, Yi-I Chiu, Kentaro Hanaki, Darshan Hegde, and Slav Petrov. 2014. Temporal analysis of language through neural language models. In *Proceedings of the Workshop on Language Technologies and Computational Social Science @ ACL 2014. Baltimore, Maryland, USA, June 26, 2014*. pages 61–65.

Alexander Koplenig. 2017. The impact of lacking metadata for the measurement of cultural and linguistic change using the Google Ngram data sets: reconstructing the composition of the German corpus in times of WWII. *Digital Scholarship in the Humanities* 32(1):169–188.

Vivek Kulkarni, Rami Al-Rfou, Bryan Perozzi, and Steven Skiena. 2015. Statistically significant detection of linguistic change. In *WWW '15 — Proceedings of the 24th International Conference on World Wide Web: Technical Papers. Florence, Italy, May 18-22, 2015*. pages 625–635.

Omer Levy and Yoav Goldberg. 2014. Neural word embedding as implicit matrix factorization. In *Advances in Neural Information Processing Systems 27 — Proceedings of the Annual Conference on Neural Information Processing Systems 2014. Montréal, Quebec, Canada, December 8-13, 2014*. pages 2177–2185.

Omer Levy, Yoav Goldberg, and Ido Dagan. 2015. Improving distributional similarity with lessons learned from word embeddings. *Transactions of the Association for Computational Linguistics* 3:211–225.

Yuri Lin, Jean-Baptiste Michel, Erez Lieberman Aiden, Jon Orwant, William Brockman, and Slav Petrov. 2012. Syntactic annotations for the Google Books Ngram Corpus. In *ACL 2012 — Proceedings of the 50th Annual Meeting of the Association for Computational Linguistics: System Demonstrations. Jeju Island, Korea, July 10, 2012*. pages 169–174.

Chris Manning and Hinrich Schütze. 1999. *Foundations of Statistical Natural Language Processing*, MIT Press, Cambridge, MA, chapter 5: Collocations.

Jean-Baptiste Michel, Yuan Kui Shen, Aviva Presser Aiden, Adrian Veres, Matthew K. Gray, The Google Books Team, Joseph P. Pickett, Dale Hoiberg, Dan Clancy, Peter Norvig, Jon Orwant, Steven Pinker, Martin A. Nowak, and Erez Lieberman Aiden. 2011. Quantitative analysis of culture using millions of digitized books. *Science* 331(6014):176–182.

Tomas Mikolov, Kai Chen, Gregory S. Corrado, and Jeffrey Dean. 2013. Efficient estimation of word representations in vector space. In *ICLR 2013 — Workshop Proceedings of the International Conference on Learning Representations. Scottsdale, Arizona, USA, May 2-4, 2013*.

Susanne Niemeier. 2003. Straight from the heart: metonymic and metaphorical explorations. In Antonio Barcelona, editor, *Metaphor and Metonymy at the Crossroads: A Cognitive Perspective*, Mouton de Gruyter, Berlin; New York/NY, number 30 in Topics in English Linguistics, pages 195–211.

Eitan Adam Pechenick, Christopher M. Danforth, and Peter Sheridan Dodds. 2015. Characterizing the Google Books Corpus: strong limits to inferences of socio-cultural and linguistic evolution. *PLoS One* 10(10):e0137041.

Jeffrey Pennington, Richard Socher, and Christopher D. Manning. 2014. Glove: global vectors for word representation. In *EMNLP 2014 — Proceedings of the 2014 Conference on Empirical Methods in Natural Language Processing. Doha, Qatar, October 25-29, 2014*. pages 1532–1543.

Joachim Wermter and Udo Hahn. 2006. You can't beat frequency (unless you use linguistic knowledge): a qualitative evaluation of association measures for collocation and term extraction. In *COLING-ACL 2006 — Proceedings of the 21st International Conference on Computational Linguistics & 44th Annual Meeting of the Association for Computational Linguistics. Sydney, Australia, 17-21 July 2006*. volume 2, pages 785–792.

Extended Named Entity Recognition API and
Its Applications in Language Education

**Nguyen Tuan Duc[1], Khai Mai[1], Thai-Hoang Pham[1], Nguyen Minh Trung[1],
Truc-Vien T. Nguyen[1], Takashi Eguchi[1], Ryohei Sasano[2], Satoshi Sekine[3]**

[1]Alt Inc   [2]Nagoya University   [3]New York University

`nguyen.tuan.duc@alt.ai,  sekine@cs.nyu.edu`

Abstract

We present an Extended Named Entity Recognition API to recognize various types of entities and classify the entities into 200 different categories. Each entity is classified into a hierarchy of entity categories, in which the categories near the root are more general than the categories near the leaves of the hierarchy. This category information can be used in various applications such as language educational applications, online news services and recommendation engines. We show an application of the API in a Japanese online news service for Japanese language learners.

1   Introduction

Named entity recognition (NER) is one of the most fundamental tasks in Information Retrieval, Information Extraction and Question Answering (Bellot et al., 2002; Nadeau and Sekine, 2007). A high quality named entity recognition API (Application Programming Interface) is therefore important for higher level tasks such as entity retrieval, recommendation and automatic dialogue generation. To extend the ability of named entity recognition, Sekine et al. (Sekine et al., 2002; Sekine and Nobata, 2004) have proposed an Extended Named Entity (ENE) hierarchy, which refines the definition of named entity. The ENE hierarchy is a three-level hierarchy, which contains more than ten coarse-grained categories at the top level and 200 fine-grained categories at the leaf level.

The top level of the hierarchy includes traditional named entity categories, such as Person, Location or Organization. The middle level and leaf level refine the top level categories to more fine-

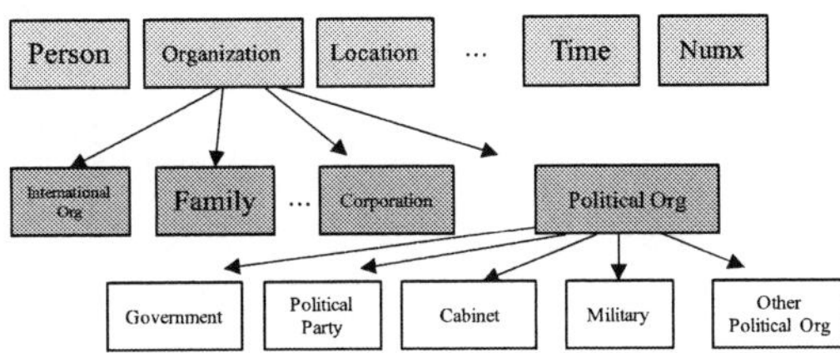

Figure 1: Extended Named Entity hierarchy

grained categories. Figure 1 shows a partial hierarchy for the top level category *Organization*. In Extended Named Entity recognition (ENER) problem, given an input sentence, such as "Donald Trump was officially nominated by the Republican Party", the system must recognize and classify the ENEs in the sentence, such as "Donald Trump" as *Person* and "Republican Party" as *Political Party*.

In this paper, we present the architecture design and implementation of an ENER API for Japanese. We named this API as "AL+ ENER API". The proposed architecture works well with a large number of training data samples and responses fast enough to use in practical applications. To illustrate the effectiveness of the AL+ ENER API, we describe an application of the API for automatic extraction of glossaries in a Japanese online news service for Japanese language learners. Feedbacks from the users show that the presented ENER API gives high precision on the glossary creation task.

The rest of this paper is organized as follows. Section 2 describes the design and implementation of the ENER API. Experiment results are presented in Section 3 to evaluate the performance of the API. Section 4 describes an application of the ENER API into an online news service for Japanese learners, the method to get user feedbacks from this service to improve the ENER system, and the statistics obtained from the user feed-

Proceedings of the 55th Annual Meeting of the Association for Computational Linguistics-System Demonstrations, pages 37–42
Vancouver, Canada, July 30 - August 4, 2017. ©2017 Association for Computational Linguistics
https://doi.org/10.18653/v1/P17-4007

backs. Section 5 reviews related systems and compares with the presented system. Finally, Section 6 concludes the paper.

2 Extended Named Entity Recognition API

2.1 Overview of the AL+ ENER API

The AL+ ENER API is an API for Extended Named Entity recognition, which takes an input sentence and outputs a JSON containing a list of ENEs in the sentence, as shown in Figure 2.

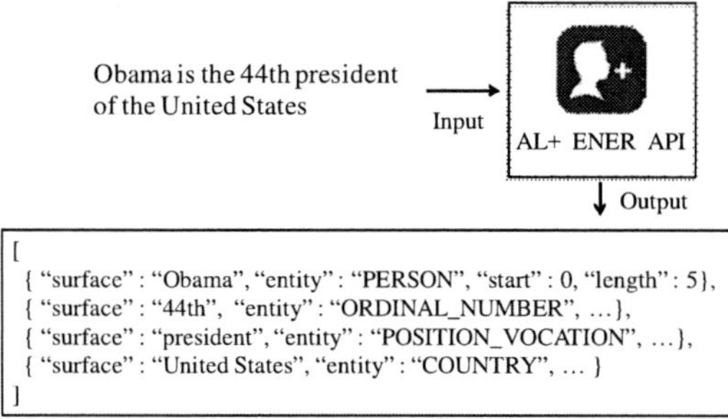

Figure 2: AL+ ENE Recognition API

Different from traditional NER APIs, this ENER API is capable of tagging 200 categories[1], including some entities that are actually not named entities (therefore, they are called "extended" named entities, as described in (Sekine and Nobata, 2004)). In Figure 2, "president" is not a traditional named entity, but it is tagged as POSITION_VOCATION, which is a category in the ENE hierarchy. For each entity, we output its surface (e.g., "president"), its ENE tag ("POSITION_VOCATION"), its index in the input sentence (the "start" field in the JSON) and its length. A developer who uses the ENER API can utilize the start and length information to calculate the exact position of the entity in the input sentence. The ENE tag can then be used in various subsequent tasks such as Relation Extraction (RE), Question Answering (QA) or automatic dialogue generation. The AL+ ENER API is freely accessible online.[2] Currently, the API supports Japanese only, but we are also developing an API for English ENER. Figure 3 shows an example input sentence and output ENE tags.

Figure 3: An example input sentence and output ENE tags. Translated sentence with tags: "I caught 3/N_Animal cicadas/Insect at Meiji Shrine/Worship_Place".

2.2 Extended Named Entity recognition algorithms

Existing NER systems often use Conditinal Random Fields (CRFs) (McCallum and Li, 2003; Finkel et al., 2005), HMM (Zhou and Su, 2002) or SVM (Yamada et al., 2002; Takeuchi and Collier, 2002; Sasano and Kurohashi, 2008) to assign tags to the tokens in an input sentence. However, these methods are supposed to work with only small number of categories (e.g., 10 categories). In the ENER problem, the number of categories is 200, which is very large, compared with the number in traditional NER. Consequently, traditional approaches might not achieve good performance and even be infeasible. Actually, we have tried to use CRF for 200 classes, but the training process took too long time and did not finish.

In this system, we use a combination approach to recognize ENEs. We first implement four base algorithms, namely, CRF-SVM hierarchical ENER, RNN-based ENER, Wikification-based ENER and Rule-based ENER. We then combine these algorithms by a selection method, as shown in Figure 4.

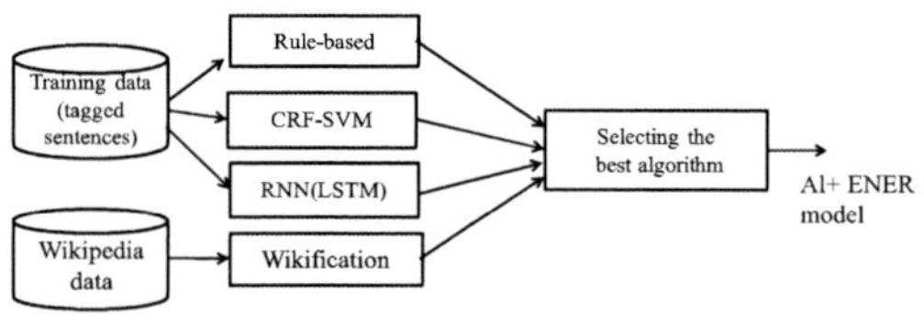

Figure 4: Overview of the proposed ENER algorithm

In the Rule-based method, we extend the rule-based method in (Sekine and Nobata, 2004) (by adding new rules for the new categories that are not recognized in their work) and we also use a dictionary containing 1.6 million Wikipedia entities. In the 1.6 million entities in the dictionary, only 70 thousands entities are assigned ENE tags by human, the rest are assigned by an existing Wikipedia ENE labeling algorithm (Suzuki et al.,

---

[1]The list of categories is here: http://nlp.cs.nyu.edu/ene/
[2]http://enerdev.alt.ai:8030/#!/Chatbot/

2016), which gives a score for each (entity, ENE category) pair. For the entities that are assigned automatically, we only take the entities with high scores to ensure that the algorithm assigns correct labels. If the rules fail to extract some entities, we extract all noun-phrases and lookup in the dictionary to check if they can be ENEs or not.

We use a training dataset which contains ENE-tagged sentences to train a CRF model to tag input sentences with the top-level ENE categories (in the training dataset, we get the correct labels for these ENEs from the parent or grandparent category in the ENE hierarchy). As illustrated in Figure 1, at the top level, we only have 11 ENE categories that we need to recognize by CRF-SVM (other categories such as Date, Time, Number can be recognized by rules), thus using a CRF model here would achieve comparable performance with existing NER systems. After tagging the sentences with the top-level ENE categories, we can convert the ENER problem into a simple classification problem (not a sequence labeling problem anymore), thus we can use SVM to classify the extracted ENEs at the top level into leaf-level categories. Therefore, we have a CRF model to tag the input sentences with top-level categories, and several SVM models (each for a top-level category) to classify the ENEs into the leaf-level ENE categories. The features that we use in CRF and SVM are bag-of-words, POS-tag, the number of digits in the word, the Brown cluster of the current word, the appearance of the word as a substring of a word in the Wikipedia ENE dictionary, the orthography features (the word is written in Kanji, Hiragana, Katakana or Romaji), whether the word is capitalized, and the last 2-3 characters. Because the number of leaf-level categories in each top-level category is also not too large (e.g., less than 15), SVM can achieve a reasonable performance at this step.

We also train an LSTM (Long-Short Term Memory network), a kind of RNN (Recurrent Neural Network) to recognize ENEs. We use LSTM because it is appropriate for sequence labeling problems. The inputs of the LSTM are the word embedding of the current word and the POS-tag of the current word. The POS-tags are automatically generated using JUMAN[3], a Japanese morphological analyzer. The word embedding is obtained by training a word2vec model with Japanese Wikipedia text. We hope that LSTM can memorize the patterns in the training data and interpolate to the CRF-SVM method in many cases.

To cope with free-text ENEs, we use Wikification approach. Free-text ENEs refer to the entities that can be of any text, such as a movie name or a song name (e.g., "What is your name" is a famous movie name in Japanese). If these names are famous, they often become the titles of some Wikipedia articles. Consequently, using Wikification-based approach could work well with these types of entities.

We also create an algorithm selection model by evaluating the F-scores of the four base algorithms (Rule, CRF-SVM, RNN and Wikification) with a development dataset (which is different from the test set). In the final phase, after having all labels from the four base algorithms for each entity, we select the label of the algorithm with the highest F-score in the development set. Note that we use the best selection scheme at entity level, not at sentence level. This is because each base algorithm tends to achieve high performance on some specific categories, so if we select the best algorithm for each entity, we will achieve higher performance for the entire sentence.

3 Evaluation

3.1 Data set

We hired seven annotators to create an ENE tagged dataset. Specifically, for each ENE category, the annotators created 100 Japanese sentences, each sentence includes at least one entity in the corresponding category. The annotators then manually tagged the sentences with ENE tags. After filtering out erroneous sentences (sentences with invalid tag format), we obtain totally 19,363 well-formed sentences. We divided the dataset into three subsets: the training set (70% of the total number of sentences), development set (15%) and test set (15%). Table 1 shows some statistics of the dataset.

Dataset	No. sentences	No. tokens	No. entities
Train	13,625	266,454	37,062
Dev	2,869	58,529	7,673
Test	2,869	55,999	7,711

Table 1: Statistics of the datasets

[3]http://nlp.ist.i.kyoto-u.ac.jp/EN/?JUMAN

3.2 Performance of the ENER API

We use the test set to evaluate the precision, recall and F-score of the ENER API. Table 2 shows

Category	Precision (%)	Recall (%)	F-score (%)
Cabinet	100.00	100.00	100.00
Intensity	100.00	100.00	100.00
URL	100.00	100.00	100.00
Phone_Number	100.00	95.25	97.56
Email	100.00	93.33	96.55
Volume	100.00	93.10	96.43
...	...	...	...
Aircraft	80.95	65.38	72.34
Company_Group	68.42	76.47	72.22
Continental_Region	74.29	69.33	71.72
...	...	...	...
Printing_Other	50.00	11.76	19.05
Name_Other	23.08	15.00	18.18
Weapon	9.09	4.17	5.71
Average	**73.47**	**70.50**	**71.95**

Table 2: Precision, Recall, F-score of the ENER API on the test dataset

the Precision, Recall and F-score of the ENER API on some specific categories as well as the average evaluation results of the entire 200 categories (in the last row). We achieved very high performance on the categories with small number of known entities (such as Cabinet) or the categories that the rules can capture almost all entities (such as Intensity, Volume, URL, and Email). For categories with free text names (e.g, printing names) or very short name (e.g., AK-47, a type of weapon) the system can not predict the ENE very well because these names might appear in various contexts. We might prioritize Wikification method in these cases to improve the performance. On average, we achieve an F1-score of 71.95%, which is a reasonable result for 200 categories.

3.3 Response time of the API

As ENER is often used by subsequent NLP tasks, the response speed of the ENER API must be fast enough for the subsequent tasks to achieve a high speed. Consequently, we executed the ENER API with the test dataset (containing 2869 sentences) and evaluated the response time of the API. The average response time of a sentence (a query) is 195 ms (0.195 second). This response speed is fast enough for various tasks such as generating answer for an intelligent chatbot or a search engine session. Figure 5 shows the relation between the response time and the length of the input sentence (calculated by the number of tokens, each token is a word produced by the morphological analyzer). When the input sentence length increases, the response time increases nearly linearly (except when the sentence is too long, as we have a small number of such sentences so the variance is large). The typical sentence length in Japanese is from 10 to 20 tokens so the speed of the ENER is fast in most cases.

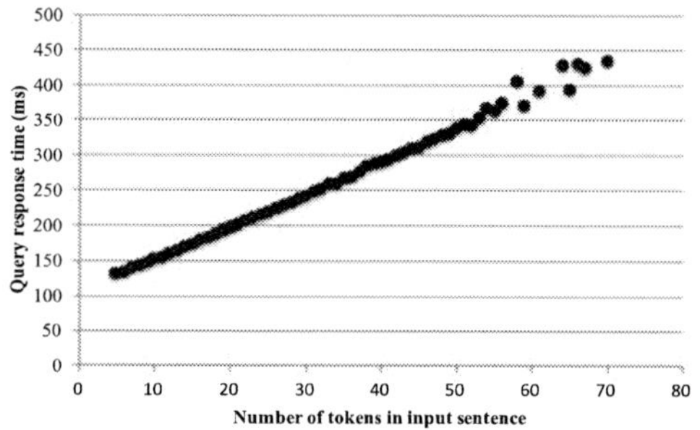

Figure 5: Relation between input sentence length and response time of the API

4 Application of the ENER API

In this section, we present a real-world application of the AL+ ENER API: glossary linking in an online news service.

4.1 Mazii: an online news service for Japanese learners

The Mazii News service[4] is an online news service for Japanese learners. For each sentence in a news article, Mazii automatically analyzes it and creates a link for each word that it recognizes as an ENE or an entry in its dictionary. This will help Japanese learners to quickly reference to the words/entities when they do not understand the meaning of the words/entities. To recognize ENEs in a news article, Mazii inputs each sentence of the article into the AL+ ENER API (sentence boundary detection in Japanese is very simple because Japanese language has a special symbol for sentence boundary mark). Because the AL+ ENER API also returns the position (and the length) of the ENEs, Mazii can easily create a link to underline the ENEs in the sentence. When a user clicks on a link, Mazii will open a popup window to provide details information concerning the entity: the ENE category (with parent categories) of the entity, the definition of the entity (if any). Figure 6

---

[4] http://en.mazii.net/#/news

shows a screenshot of the Mazii ENE linking results.

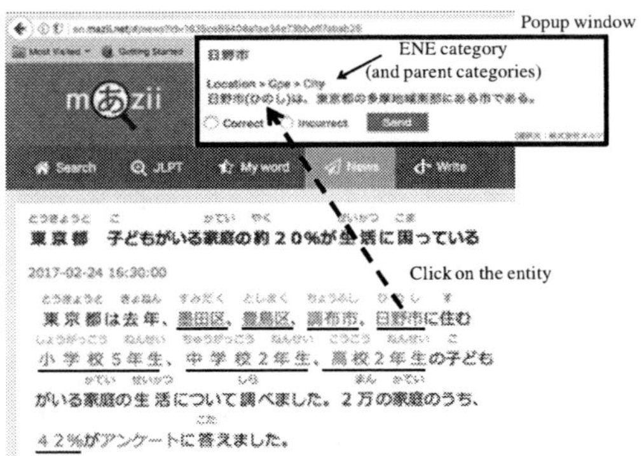

Figure 6: Mazii entity linking with AL+ ENER API, the underlined entities are linked. When a user clicks on a link (as shown in the Figure, a mention to a city in Japan is clicked), a popup window will open and show the ENE category hierarchy of the corresponding ENE.

4.2 Collecting user feedbacks

Mazii has more than 4 thousands daily active users and many users click on the linked ENEs. This provides us a big chance to obtain user feedbacks about the prediction results of the AL+ ENER API. We have implemented two interfaces to collect user feedbacks, as shown in Figure 6 and Figure 7.

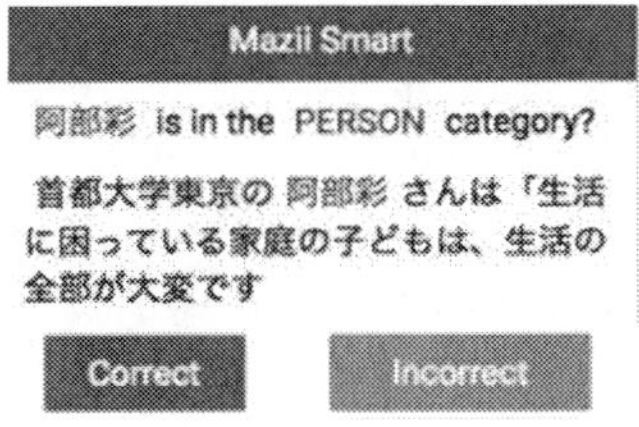

Figure 7: Collecting ENE user feedback from Mazii with playcard game

In Figure 6, when a user clicks on an entity, we display the ENE hierarchy of the entity in a popup window. We also display two radio buttons: **Correct** and **Incorrect** to let the user give us feedbacks. If the user chooses **Incorrect** then we also ask the user the correct category of the entity.

Using the method in Figure 6, we can only collect feedbacks when the users click on the entities. However, the number of clicks is often much smaller than the number of views. To increase the user feedbacks, we invented a playcard game for language learners, as shown in Figure 7. When a user views an article, we show a frame with a question asking about the correct category of an ENE in the article (we also provide the sentence which includes the ENE to gather the context for the CRF-SVM and RNN models). If the user reacts to this frame (by pressing Correct/Incorrect button), we store the feedback and move to the next ENE in our database. This involves the user in a language learning game and helps he/she to study many new words as well as grammatical constructs.

4.3 User feedback statistics

In this section, we show some statistics that we derived from the user feedback log of the Mazii News service. We collected the user feedback log (including the view, click and correct log) in 3 months (from Dec 2016 to Feb 2017). We then count the number of views, clicks and number of feedbacks (number of times the Correct/Incorrect button is pressed) and number of Correct times for each ENE categories. We calculate the correct ratio (%Correct) by the number of corrects divided by number of feedbacks (Correct/Feedback).

Category	View	Click	Feedback	%Correct
Date	360,625	7,100	1,421	95.50
N_Person	139,191	1,934	523	98.47
Province	109,974	9,880	439	94.76
...	...	...	...	...
Animal Part	6,514	637	8	100.00
Broadcast Program	6,121	1,003	21	47.62
Clothing	4,079	632	14	85.71
...	...	...	...	...
Fish	656	474	2	100.00
Fungus	615	106	1	0.00
Religion	614	227	4	100.00
Total	1,582,081	138,404	5,198	88.96

Table 3: Number views, clicks, feedbacks and percentage of correct times from the Mazii feedback log

Table 3 shows the experiment results. The correct ratio (%Correct) is 88.96% on 96 categories with more than 100 views and have at least one user feedback. The table also shows the detailed numbers for some categories, sorted by number of views. The average click-through-rate (CTR=Click/View) is 8.7%, which is very high compared to the average CTR of display ads (about 0.4%) (Zhang et al., 2014). This proves that the users are interested in the linked ENEs. Moreover, the percentage of correct times shows that the ENER API is good enough to provide useful information to the users.

5 Related Work

The ENE hierarchy that we recognize in this paper is proposed in (Sekine et al., 2002). (Sekine and Nobata, 2004) proposed a Japanese rule-based ENER with a precision of 72% and recall of 80%. The performance of the rule-based ENER is good if the ENEs containing in the text are included in the dictionary or the rules can capture the patterns in which the ENEs appeared. However, ENEs often evolve with time, new ENEs are frequently added and their meaning might be changed. Consequently, rule-based systems might not work well after a several years. In the presented system, we re-use the rules and dictionary in (Sekine and Nobata, 2004) but we also add machine learning models to capture the evolution of the ENEs. The proposed model can be retrained at anytime if we have new training data. Iwakura et al. (Iwakura et al., 2011) proposed an ENER based on decomposition/concatenation of word chunks. They evaluated the system with 191 ENE categories and achieved an F-score of 81%. However, in their evaluation, they did not evaluate directly on input sentences, but only on correct chunks. Moreover, they did not deal with word boundaries as stated in their paper. Therefore, we cannot compare our results with theirs.

6 Conclusion

We presented an API for recognition of Extended Named Entities (ENEs). The API takes a sentence as input and outputs a JSON containing a list of ENEs with their categories. The API can recognize named entities at deep level with high accuracy in a timely manner, and has been applied in real-life applications. We described an application of the ENER API to a Japanese online news service. The experimental results showed that the API achieves good performance and is fast enough for practical applications.

Acknowledgments

We would like to thank Yoshikazu Nishimura, Hideyuki Shibuki, Dr. Phuong Le-Hong and Maya Ando for their precious comments and suggestions on this work.

References

Patrice Bellot, Eric Crestan, Marc El-Bèze, Laurent Gillard, and Claude de Loupy. 2002. Coupling Named Entity Recognition, Vector-Space Model and Knowledge Bases for TREC 11 Question Answering Track. In *Proc. of TREC 2002*.

Jenny Rose Finkel, Trond Grenager, and Christopher D. Manning. 2005. Incorporating Non-local Information into Information Extraction Systems by Gibbs Sampling. In *Proc. of ACL 2005*. pages 363–370.

Tomoya Iwakura, Hiroya Takamura, and Manabu Okumura. 2011. A Named Entity Recognition Method based on Decomposition and Concatenation of Word Chunks. In *Proc. of IJCNLP 2011*. pages 828–836.

Andrew McCallum and Wei Li. 2003. Early Results for Named Entity Recognition with Conditional Random Fields, Feature Induction and Web-Enhanced Lexicons. In *Proc. of CoNLL 2003*. pages 188–191.

David Nadeau and Satoshi Sekine. 2007. A Survey of Named Entity Recognition and Classification. *Linguisticae Investigationes* 30(1):3–26.

Ryohei Sasano and Sadao Kurohashi. 2008. Japanese Named Entity Recognition Using Structural Natural Language Processing. In *Proc. of IJCNLP 2008*. pages 607–612.

Satoshi Sekine and Chikashi Nobata. 2004. Definition, Dictionaries and Tagger for Extended Named Entity Hierarchy. In *Proc. of LREC 2004*. pages 1977–1980.

Satoshi Sekine, Kiyoshi Sudo, and Chikashi Nobata. 2002. Extended Named Entity Hierarchy. In *Proc. of LREC 2002*. pages 1818–1824.

Masatoshi Suzuki, Koji Matsuda, Satoshi Sekine, Naoaki Okazaki, and Kentaro Inui. 2016. Fine-Grained Named Entity Classification with Wikipedia Article Vectors. In *Proc. of Int'l Conf. on Web Intelligence (WI 2016)*. pages 483–486.

Koichi Takeuchi and Nigel Collier. 2002. Use of Support Vector Machines in Extended Named Entity Recognition. In *Proc. of CoNLL 2002*.

Hiroyasu Yamada, Taku Kudo, and Yuji Matsumoto. 2002. Japanese Named Entity Extraction Using Support Vector Machine. *Transactions of Information Processing Society of Japan (IPSJ)* 43(1):44–53.

Weinan Zhang, Shuai Yuan, and Jun Wang. 2014. Optimal Real-Time Bidding for Display Advertising. In *Proc. of KDD 2014*. pages 1077–1086.

Guodong Zhou and Jian Su. 2002. Named Entity Recognition Using an HMM-Based Chunk Tagger. In *Proc. of ACL 2002*. pages 473–480.

Hafez: an Interactive Poetry Generation System

Marjan Ghazvininejad*, Xing Shi*, Jay Priyadarshi, and Kevin Knight
[†]Information Sciences Institute & Computer Science Department
University of Southern California
`{ghazvini,xingshi,jpriyada,knight}@isi.edu`

Abstract

Hafez is an automatic poetry generation system that integrates a Recurrent Neural Network (RNN) with a Finite State Acceptor (FSA). It generates sonnets given arbitrary topics. Furthermore, Hafez enables users to revise and polish generated poems by adjusting various style configurations. Experiments demonstrate that such "polish" mechanisms consider the user's intention and lead to a better poem. For evaluation, we build a web interface where users can rate the quality of each poem from 1 to 5 stars. We also speed up the whole system by a factor of 10, via vocabulary pruning and GPU computation, so that adequate feedback can be collected at a fast pace. Based on such feedback, the system learns to adjust its parameters to improve poetry quality.

1 Introduction

Automated poetry generation is attracting increasing research effort. Researchers approach the problem by using grammatical and semantic templates (Oliveira, 2009, 2012) or treating the generation task as a translation/summarization task (Zhou et al., 2009; He et al., 2012; Yan et al., 2013; Zhang and Lapata, 2014; Yi et al., 2016; Wang et al., 2016; Ghazvininejad et al., 2016). However, such poetry generation systems face these challenges:

1. **Difficulty of evaluating poetry quality.** Automatic evaluation methods, like BLEU, cannot judge the rhythm, meter, creativity or syntactic/semantic coherence, and furthermore, there is no test data in most cases. Subjective evaluation requires evaluators to have relatively high literary training, so systems will receive limited feedback during the development phase.[1]

2. **Inability to adjust the generated poem.** When poets compose a poem, they usually need to revise and polish the draft from different aspects (e.g., word choice, sentiment, alliteration, etc.) for several iterations until satisfaction. This is a crucial step for poetry creation. However, given a user-supplied topic or phrase, most existing automated systems can only generate different poems by using different random seeds, providing no other support for the user to polish the generated poem in a desired direction.

3. **Slow generation speed.** Generating a poem may require a heavy search procedure. For example, the system of Ghazvininejad et al. (2016) needs 20 seconds for a four-line poem. Such slow speed is a serious bottleneck for a smooth user experience, and prevents the large-scale collection of feedback for system tuning.

This work is based on our previous poetry generation system called Hafez (Ghazvininejad et al., 2016), which generates poems in three steps: (1) search for related rhyme words given user-supplied topic, (2) create a finite-state acceptor (FSA) that incorporates the rhyme words and controls meter, and (3) use a recurrent neural network (RNN) to generate the poem string, guided by the FSA. We address the above-mentioned challenges with the following approaches:

---

[1]The Dartmouth Turing Tests in the Creative Arts (bit.ly/2OWGLF3), in which human experts are employed to judge the generation quality, is held only once a year.

*equal contributions

Proceedings of the 55th Annual Meeting of the Association for Computational Linguistics-System Demonstrations, pages 43–48
Vancouver, Canada, July 30 - August 4, 2017. ©2017 Association for Computational Linguistics
https://doi.org/10.18653/v1/P17-4008

Topic: Presidential elections

To hear the sound of communist aggression!
I never thought about an exit poll,
At a new Republican convention,
On the other side of gun control.

Table 1: One poem generated in a 15-minute human/computer interactive poetry contest.

1. We build a web interface[2] for our poem generation system, and for each generated poem, the user can rate its quality from 1-star to 5-stars. Our logging system collects poems, related parameters, and user feedback. Such crowd-sourcing enables us to obtain large amounts of feedback in a cheap and efficient way. Once we collect enough feedback, the system learns to find a better set of parameters and updates the system continuously.

2. We add additional weights during decoding to control the style of generated poem, including the extent of words repetition, alliteration, word length, cursing, sentiment, and concreteness.

3. We increase speed by pre-calculation, preloading model parameters, and pruning the vocabulary. We also parallelize the computation of FSA expansion, weight merging, and beam search, and we port them into a GPU. Overall, we can generate a four-line poem within 2 seconds, ten times faster than our previous CPU-based system.

With the web interface's style control and fast generation speed, people can generate creative poems within a short time. Table 1 shows one of the poems generated in a poetry mini-competition where 7 people are asked to use Hafez to generate poems within 15 minutes. We also conduct experiments on Amazon Mechanical Turk, which show: first, through style-control interaction, 71% users can find a better poem than the poem generated by the default configuration. Second, based on users' evaluation results, the system learns a new configuration which generates better poems.

2 System Description

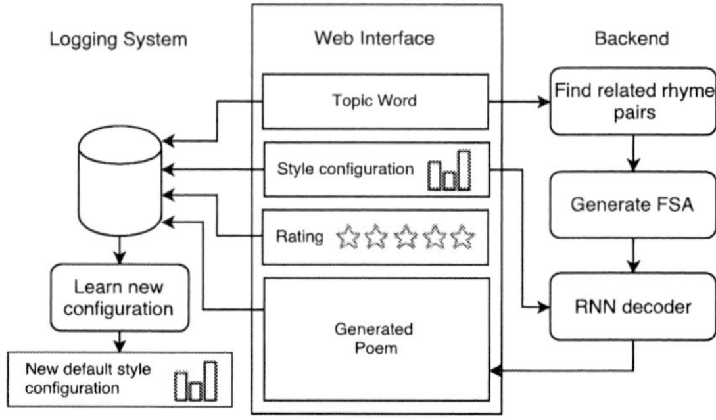

Figure 1: Overview of Hafez

Figure 1 shows an overview of Hafez. In the web interface, a user can input topic words or phrases and adjust the style configuration. This information is then sent to our backend server, which is primarily based on our previously-described work (Ghazvininejad et al., 2016). First, the backend will use the topic words/phrases to find related rhyme word pairs by using a word2vec model and a pre-calculated rhyme-type dictionary. Given these rhyme word pairs, an FSA that encodes all valid word sequences is generated, where a valid word sequence follows certain type of meter and puts the rhyme word at the end of each line. This FSA, together with the user-supplied style configuration, is then used to guide the Recurrent Neural Network (RNN) decoder to generate the rest of the poem. User can rate the generated poem using a 5-star system. Finally, the tuple (topic, style configuration, generated poem, star-rating) is pushed to the logging system. Periodically, a module will analyze the logs, learn a better style configuration and update it as the new default style configuration.

2.1 Example in Action

Figure 2 provides an example in action. The user has input the topic word "love" and left the style configuration as default. After they click the "Generate" button, a four-line poem is generated and displayed. The user may not be satisfied with current generation, and may decide to add more positive sentiment and encourage a little bit of the alliteration. After they move the corresponding slider bars and click the "Re-generate with the same rhyme words" button, a new poem is returned. This poem has more positive sentiment ("A lonely part of you and me tonight" vs. "A lovely dream of you and me tonight") and more alliteration ("My merry little love", "The lucky lady" and "She sings the sweetest song").

2.2 Style Control

During the RNN's beam search, each beam cell records the current FSA state s. Its succeeding state is denoted as s_{suc}. All the words over all the succeeding states forms a vocabulary V_{suc}. To expand the beam state b, we need to calculate a score for each word in V_{suc}:

$$score(w, b) = score(b) + \log P_{RNN}(w)$$
$$+ \sum_i w_i * f_i(w); \forall w \in V_{suc} \quad (1)$$

where $\log P_{RNN}(w)$ is the log-probability of word w calculated by RNN. $score(b)$ is the accumulated score of the already-generated words in beam state b . $f_i(w)$ is ith feature function and w_i is the corresponding weight.

To control the style, we design the following 8 features:

1. Encourage/discourage words. User can input words that they would like in the poem, or words to be banned. $f(w) = I(w, V_{enc/dis})$ where $I(w, V) = 1$ if w is in the word list V, otherwise $I(w, V) = 0$. $w_{enc} = 5$ and $w_{dis} = -5$.

2. Curse words. We pre-build a curse-word list V_{curse}, and $f(w) = I(w, V_{curse})$.

3. Repetition. To control the extent of repeated words in the poem. For each beam, we record the current generated words $V_{history}$, and $f(w) = I(w, V_{history})$.

4. Alliteration. To control how often adjacent *non-function* words start with the same consonant sound. In the beam cell, we also record the previous generated word w_{t-1}, and $f(w_t) = 1$ if w_t and w_{t-1} share the same first consonant sound, otherwise it equals 0.

5. Word length. To control a preference for longer words in the generated poem. $f(w) = length(w)^2$.

6. Topical words. For each user-supplied topic words, we generate a list of related words $V_{topical}$. $f(w) = I(w, V_{topical})$.

7. Sentiment. We pre-build a word list together with its sentiment scores based on Senti-WordNet (Baccianella et al., 2010). $f(w)$ equals to $w's$ sentiment score.

8. Concrete words. We pre-build a word list together with a score to reflect its concreteness based on Brysbaert et al. (2014). $f(w)$ equals to w's concreteness score.

2.3 Speedup

To find the rhyming words related to the topic, we employ a word2vec model. Given a topic word or phrase $w_t \in V$, we find related words w_r based on the cosine distance:

$$w_r = \underset{w_r \in V' \subseteq V}{\mathrm{argmax}}\ cosine(e_{w_r}, e_{w_t}) \quad (2)$$

where e_w is the embedding of word w. Then we calculate the rhyme type of each related word w_r to find rhyme pairs.

To speed up this step, we carefully optimize the computation with these methods:

1. Pre-load all parameters into RAM. As we are aiming to accept arbitrary topics, the vocabulary V of word2vec model is very large (1.8M words and phrases). Pre-loading saves 3-4 seconds.

2. Pre-calculate the rhyme types for all words $w \in V'$. During runtime, we use this dictionary to lookup the rhyme type.

3. Shrink V'. As every rhyme word/phrase pairs must be in the target vocabulary V_{RNN} of the RNN, we further shrink $V' = V \cap V_{RNN}$.

To speedup the RNN decoding step, we use GPU processing for all forward-propagation computations. For beam search, we port to GPU the two most time-consuming parts, calculating scores with Equation 1 and finding the top words based the score:

1. We warp all the computation needed in Equation 1 into a single large GPU kernel launch.

2. With beam size B, to find the top k words, instead of using a heap sort on CPU with complexity $\mathcal{O}(B|V_{suc}|logk)$, we do a global sort on GPU with complexity $\mathcal{O}(B|V_{suc}|log(B|V_{suc}|))$ in one kernel launch. Even though the complexity increases, the computation time in practice reduces quite a bit.

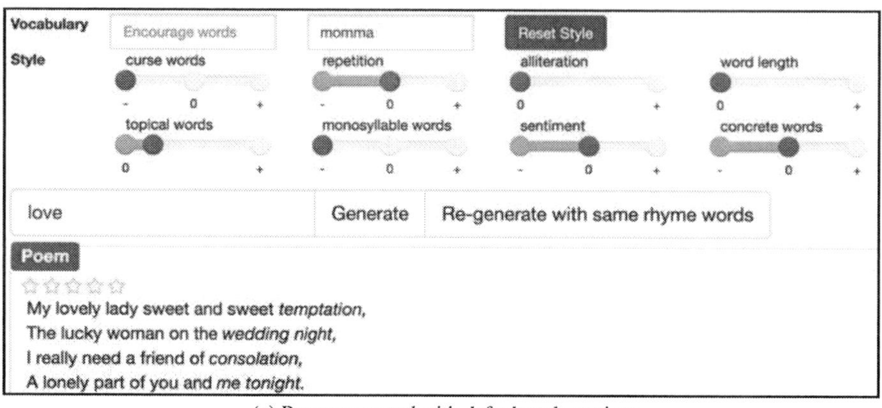

(a) Poem generated with default style settings

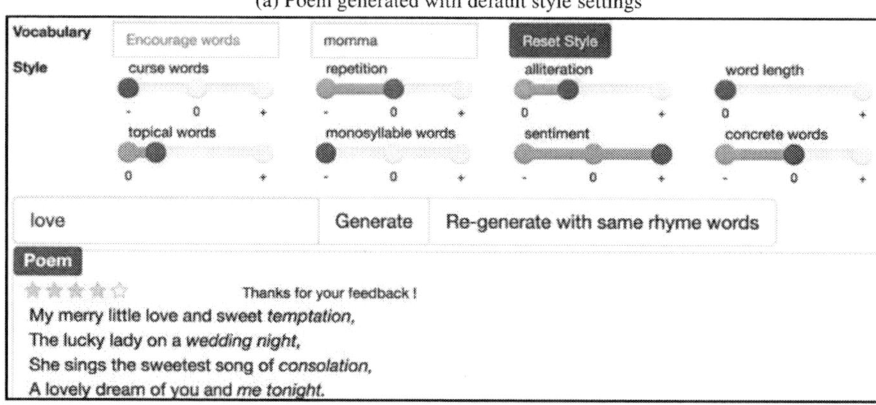

(b) Poem generated with user adjusted style settings

Figure 2: A poem generated with (a) default style configuration and (b) user-adjusted style configuration.

Finally, our system can generate a 4-line poem within 2 seconds, which is 10 times faster than the previous CPU-based version.

2.4 Learn a New Style Configuration

Except the fixed weight for encouragement and discouragement of words, all other 7 weights form our style configuration space:

$$W = \{w_i | i = 1..7\} \qquad (3)$$

and we denote the default configuration as W_d, intuitively selected.

Users will usually start with W_d to generate their first poem p_d, and if they later adjust the style configuration and click "Re-generate with same rhyme words" button, the new poem p_i will change the style accordingly, but still with the same rhyme words as p_d. In the logging system, a unique hash h_r is recorded to distinguish different rhyme word sets in the poem.

After proper processing, our logging system organizes the data points as a dictionary $D = \{h_r : [(p_d, W_d, r_d), (p_1, W_1, r_1), ..., (p_n, W_n, r_n)]\}$. r_d represents user's star rating for the poem with default setting(p_d) while $r_i \in \{1, ..., n\}$ represents user's star rating for $p_1, ..., p_n$.

To learn a new style configuration W_{new}, we construct our training data $D_{train} = \{h_r : [(\Delta W_1, \Delta r_1), ..., (\Delta W_n, \Delta r_n)]\}$, where $\Delta W_i = W_i - W_d$ and $\Delta r_i = r_i - r_d$. Then, we fit a quadratic regression between the rating change Δr and each weight change $\Delta w_j \in \Delta W$ independently:

$$\Delta r = a(\Delta w_j)^2 + b\Delta w_j + c \qquad (4)$$

and the new weight $w_{j,new}$ is

$$w_{j,new} = w_{j,d} + \underset{\Delta w_j}{\operatorname{argmax}} \Delta r \qquad (5)$$

2.5 Alexa Skill

To feel beauty, rhythm, and emotion in poetry, it is better to listen to a spoken version. With this

┌───┐
User: Alexa, start Custom Poetry
Alexa: Welcome to Custom Poetry.
Please give me a topic.
User: Mountains
Alexa:
A hundred thousand Morrison formation,
An ancient crown of gold or mountain chains,
Mountains from the land of elevation,
A northern storm across the hills and plains.
Alexa: Feel free to give me another topic.
User: Lakes
Alexa: ...
Alexa: Feel free to give me another topic.
User: Stop
Alexa: Thank you for trying Custom
Poetry. Have a nice day!
└───┘

Table 2: Spoken onversation between a user and Alexa.

in mind, we also publish our system as an Amazon Alexa Skill ("Custom Poetry"), so that users can ask Alexa to compose and recite a poem on any topic. Table 2 shows a sample conversation between a user and Alexa.

3 Experiments

We design an Amazon Mechanical Turk task to explore the effect of style options. In this task Turkers first use Hafez to generate a *default poem* on an arbitrary topic with the default style configuration, and rate it. Next, they are asked to adjust the style configurations to re-generate at least five different *adjusted poems* with the same rhyme words, and rate them as well. Improving the quality of *adjusted poems* over the *default poem* is not required for finishing the task, but it is encouraged. For each task, Turkers can select the best generated poem, and if subsequent human judges (domain experts) rank that poem as "great", a bonus reward will be assigned to that Turker. We gathered data from 62 completed HITs (Human Intelligence Tasks) for this task.

3.1 Human-Computer Collaboration

This experiment tests whether human collaboration can help Hafez generate better poems.

In only 10% of the HITs, the reported best poem was generated by the default style options, i.e., the *default poem*. Additionally, in 71% of the HITs, users assign a higher star rating to at least one of

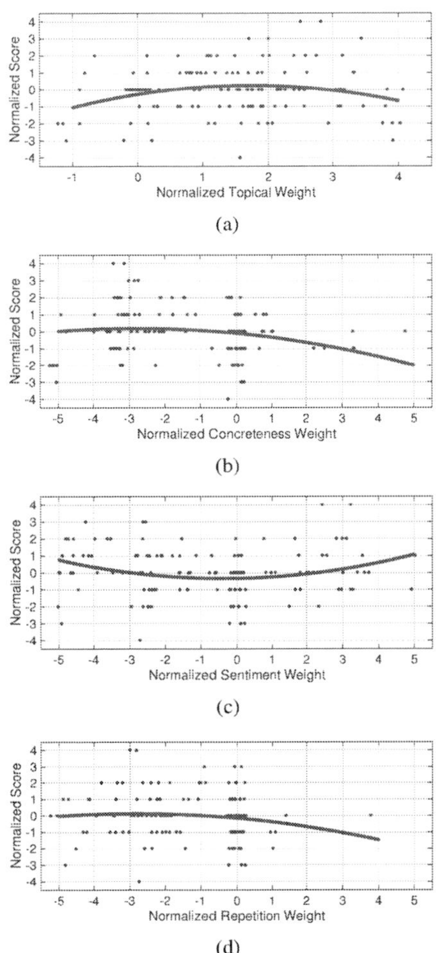

Figure 3: The distribution of poem star-ratings against normalized topical, concreteness, sentiment and repetition weights. Star ratings are computed as an offset from the version of the poem generated from default settings. We normalize all features weights by calculating their offset from the default values. The solid curve represents a quadratic regression fit to the data. To avoid overlapping points, we plot with a small amount of random noise added.

the *adjust poems* than the *default poem*. On average the best poems got $+1.4$ more stars compared to the default one.

However, poem creators might have a tendency to report a higher ranking for poems generated through the human/machine collaboration process. To sanity check the results we designed another task and asked 18 users to compare the default and the reported best poems. This experiment seconded the original rankings in 72% of the cases.

3.2 Automatic tuning for quality

We learn new default configurations using the data gathered from Mechanical Turk. As we explained in section 2.4, we examine the effect of different feature weights like repetition and sentiment on star ranking scores. We aim to cancel out the effect of topic and rhyme words on our scoring function. We achieve this by plotting the score offset from the *default poem* for each topic and set of rhyme words. Figure 3 shows the distribution of scores against topical, concreteness, sentiment and repetition weights. In each plot the zero weight represents the default value. Each plot also shows a quadratic regression curve fit to its data.

In order to alter the style options toward generating better default poems, we re-set each weight to the maximum of each quadratic curve. Hence, the new weights encourage more topical, less concrete, more positive words and less repetition. It is notable that for sentiment, users prefer both more positive and more negative words to the initial neutral setting, but the preference is slightly biased towards positive words.

We update Hafez's default settings based on this analysis. We ask 29 users to compare poems generated on the same topic and rhyme words using both old and new style settings. In 59% of the cases, users prefer the poem generated by the new setting.

We thus improve the default settings for generating a poem, though this does not mean that the poems cannot be further improved by human collaboration. In most cases, a better poem can be generated by collaboration with the system (changing the style options) for the specific topic and set of rhyme words.

4 Conclusion

We demonstrate Hafez, an interactive poetry generation system. It enables users to generate poems about any topic, and revise generated texts through multiple style configurations. We speed up the system by vocabulary pruning and GPU computation. Together with an easily-accessible web interface, we can collect large numbers of human evaluations in a short timespan, making automatic system tuning possible.

References

Stefano Baccianella, Andrea Esuli, and Fabrizio Sebastiani. 2010. Sentiwordnet 3.0: An enhanced lexical resource for sentiment analysis and opinion mining. In *LREC*.

Marc Brysbaert, Amy Beth Warriner, and Victor Kuperman. 2014. Concreteness ratings for 40 thousand generally known english word lemmas. *Behavior research methods* .

Marjan Ghazvininejad, Xing Shi, Yejin Choi, and Kevin Knight. 2016. Generating topical poetry. In *Proc. EMNLP*.

Jing He, Ming Zhou, and Long Jiang. 2012. Generating Chinese classical poems with statistical machine translation models. In *Proc. AAAI*.

Hugo Oliveira. 2009. Automatic generation of poetry: an overview. In *Proc. 1st Seminar of Art, Music, Creativity and Artificial Intelligence*.

Hugo Oliveira. 2012. PoeTryMe: a versatile platform for poetry generation. *Computational Creativity, Concept Invention, and General Intelligence* 1.

Qixin Wang, Tianyi Luo, Dong Wang, and Chao Xing. 2016. Chinese song iambics generation with neural attention-based model. *arXiv:1604.06274* .

Rui Yan, Han Jiang, Mirella Lapata, Shou-De Lin, Xueqiang Lv, and Xiaoming Li. 2013. I, Poet: Automatic Chinese poetry composition through a generative summarization framework under constrained optimization. In *Proc. IJCAI*.

Xiaoyuan Yi, Ruoyu Li, and Maosong Sun. 2016. Generating chinese classical poems with RNN encoder-decoder. *arXiv:1604.01537* .

Xingxing Zhang and Mirella Lapata. 2014. Chinese poetry generation with recurrent neural networks. In *Proc. EMNLP*.

Ming Zhou, Long Jiang, and Jing He. 2009. Generating Chinese couplets and quatrain using a statistical approach. In *Proc. Pacific Asia Conference on Language, Information and Computation*.

Interactive Visual Analysis of Transcribed Multi-Party Discourse

Mennatallah El-Assady[1], Annette Hautli-Janisz[1], Valentin Gold[2],
Miriam Butt[1], Katharina Holzinger[1], and Daniel Keim[1]

[1]University of Konstanz, Germany
[2]University of Göttingen, Germany

Abstract

We present the first web-based Visual Analytics framework for the analysis of multi-party discourse data using verbatim text transcripts. Our framework supports a broad range of server-based processing steps, ranging from data mining and statistical analysis to deep linguistic parsing of English and German. On the client-side, browser-based Visual Analytics components enable multiple perspectives on the analyzed data. These interactive visualizations allow exploratory content analysis, argumentation pattern review and speaker interaction modeling.

1 Introduction

With the increasing availability of large amounts of multi-party discourse data, the breadth and complexity of questions that can be answered with natural language processing (NLP) is expanding. Discourses can be analyzed with respect to what topics are discussed, who contributes to which topic to what extent, how the turn-taking plays out, how speakers convey their opinions and arguments, what Common Ground is assumed and what the speaker stance is. The challenge presented for NLP lies in the automatic identification of relevant cues and in providing assistance towards the analysis of these primarily pragmatic features via the automatic processing of large amounts of discourse data. The challenge is exacerbated by the fact that linguistic data is inherently multidimensional with complex feature interaction being the norm rather than the exception. The problem becomes particularly difficult when one moves on to compare multi-party discourse strategies across different languages.

In this paper we present a novel Visual Analytics framework that encodes various layers of discourse properties and allows for an analysis of multi-party discourse. The system combines discourse features derived from shallow text mining with more in-depth, linguistically-motivated annotations from a discourse processing pipeline. Based on this hybrid technology, users from political science, journalism or digital humanities are able to draw inferences regarding the progress of the debate, speaker behavior and discourse content in large amounts of data at-a-glance, while still maintaining a detailed view on the underlying data. To the best of our knowledge, our *VisArgue* system offers the first web-based, interactive Visual Analytics approach of multi-party discourse data using verbatim text transcripts.[1]

2 Related work

Discourse processing A large amount of work in discourse processing focuses on analyzing discourse relations, annotated in different granularity and style in RST (Mann and Thompson, 1988) or SDRT (Asher and Lascarides, 2003). While a large amount of work is for English and based on landmark corpora such as the Penn Discourse Treebank (Prasad et al., 2008), the parsing of discourse relations in German has only lately received attention (Versley and Gastel, 2012; Stede and Neumann, 2014; Bögel et al., 2014).

Another strand of research is concerned with dialogue act annotation, to which end several annotation schemes have been proposed (Bunt et al., 2010, inter alia). Those have also been applied across a range of German corpora (Jekat et al., 1995; Zarisheva and Scheffler, 2015). Another area deals with the classification of speaker stance (Mairesse et al., 2007; Danescu-Niculescu-Mizil et al., 2013; Sridhar et al., 2015).

Despite the existing variety of previous work in discourse processing, our contribution is novel. For one, we combine different levels of analysis

---

[1]Accessible at `http://visargue.inf.uni.kn/`. Accounts (beyond the demo) are available upon request.

Proceedings of the 55th Annual Meeting of the Association for Computational Linguistics-System Demonstrations, pages 49–54
Vancouver, Canada, July 30 - August 4, 2017. ©2017 Association for Computational Linguistics
https://doi.org/10.18653/v1/P17-4009

and integrate information that has not been dealt with intensively in discourse processing before, for instance regarding rhetorical framing. For another, we provide an innovation with respect to the type of data the system can handle in that the system is designed to deal with noisy transcribed natural speech, a genre underresearched in the area.

Visual Analytics Visualizing the features and dynamics of communication has been gaining interest in information visualization, due to the diversity and ambiguity of this data. Erickson and Kellogg (2000) introduce a general framework for the design of such visualization systems. Other approaches attempt to model the social interactions in chat systems, e.g. Chat Circles (Donath and Viégas, 2002) and GroupMeter (Leshed and et al., 2009). Conversation Clusters (Bergstrom and Karahalios, 2009) and MultiConVis (Hoque and Carenini, 2016) group the content of conversations dynamically. Overall, the majority of these systems are designed to model the dynamics and changes in the content of conversations and do not rely on a rich set of linguistic features.

3 Computational linguistic processing

Our automatic annotation system is based on a linguistically-informed, hand-crafted set of rules that deals with the disambiguation of explicit linguistic markers and the identification of spans and relations in the text. For that, we divide all utterances into smaller units of text in order to work with a more fine-grained structure of the discourse. Although there is no consensus in the literature on what exactly these units have to comprise, it is generally assumed that each discourse unit describes a single event (Polanyi et al., 2004). Following Marcu (2000), we term these units *ele-*

mentary discourse units (EDUs). For German, we approximate the assumption made by Polanyi et al. (2004) by inserting a boundary at every punctuation mark and every clausal connector (conjunctions, complementizers). For English we rely on clause-level splitting of the Stanford PCFG parser (Klein and Manning, 2003) and create EDUs at the SBAR, SBARQ, SINV and SQ clause level. The annotation is performed on the level of these EDUs, therefore relations that span multiple units are marked individually at each unit.

We were not able to use an off the shelf parser for German. For instance, an initial experiment using the German Stanford Dependency parser (Rafferty and Manning, 2008) showed that 60% of parses are incorrect due to interruptions, speech repairs and multiple embeddings. We therefore hand-crafted our own rules on the basis of morphological and POS information from DMOR (Schiller, 1994). For English, the data contained less noise and we were able to use the POS tags from the Stanford parser.

Levels of analysis With respect to *discourse relations*, we annotate spans as to whether they represent: reasons, conclusions, contrasts, concessions, conditions or consequences. For German, we rely on the connectors in the Potsdam Commentary Corpus (Stede and Neumann, 2014), for English we use the PDTP-style parser (Ziheng Lin and Kan, 2014).

In order to identify relevant *speech acts*, we compiled lists of speech act verbs comprising agreement, disagreement, arguing, bargaining and information giving/seeking/refusing. In order to gage *emotion*, we use EmoLex, a crowdsourced emotion lexicon (Mohammad and Turney, 2010) available for a number of languages, plus our own curated lexicon of *politeness* markers. With re-

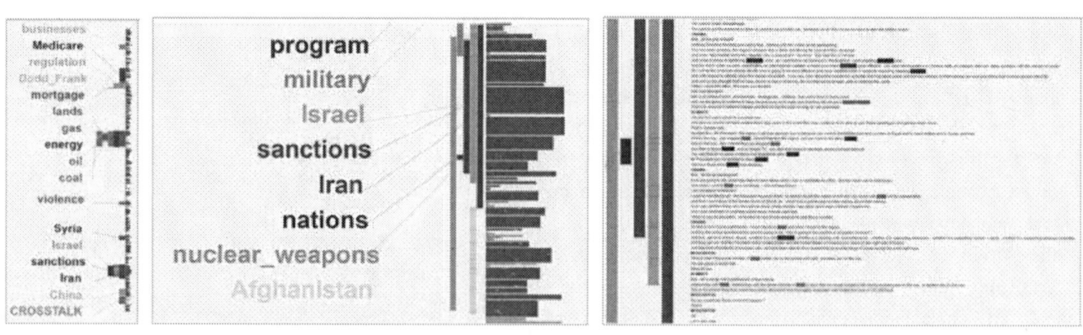

<table>
<tr><td>(a) Overview</td><td>(b) Zooming and Highlighting</td><td>(c) Close-Reading</td></tr>
</table>

Figure 1: Lexical Episode Plots

spect to *event modality*, we take into account all modal verbs and adverbs signaling obligation, permission, volition, reluctance or alternative. Concerning *epistemic modality* and speaker stance we use modal expressions conveying certainty, probability, possibility and impossibility. Finally, we added a category called *rhetorical framing* (Hautli-Janisz and Butt, 2016), which accounts for the illocutionary contribution of German discourse particles. Here we look at different ways of invoking Common Ground, hedging and signaling accommodation in argumentation, for example.

Disambiguation Many of the crucial linguistic markers are ambiguous. We developed handcrafted rules that take into account the surrounding context to achieve disambiguation. Important features include position in the EDU (for instance for lexemes which can be discourse connectors at the beginning of an EDU but not at the end, and vice versa) or the POS of other lexical items in the context. Overall, the German system features 20 disambiguation rules, the English one has 12.

Relation identification After disambiguation is complete, a second set of rules annotates the spans and the relations that the lexical items trigger. In this module, we again take into account the context of the lexical item. An important factor is negation, which in some cases reverses the contribution of the lexical item, e.g. in the case of 'possible' to 'not possible'.

With respect to discourse connectors, for instance the German causal markers *da, denn, darum* and *daher* 'because/thus', we only analyze relations within a single utterance of a speaker, i.e., relations that are expressed in a sequence of clauses which a speaker utters without interference from another speaker. As a consequence, the annotation system does not take into account relations that are split up between utterances of one speaker or utterances of different speakers. For causal relations (reason and conclusion spans), we show in Bögel et al. (2014) that the system performs with an F-score of 0.95.

4 Visual Analytics Framework

The web-based Visual Analytics framework is designed to give analysts multiple perspectives on the same datasets. The transcripts are uploaded through the web interface to undergo the previously discussed linguistic processing and other visualization-dependent processing steps. The visualizations are classified into four categories. (1) **Basic Data Exploration Views**, which enable the user to explore the annotations and dynamically create statistical charts using all computed features. (2) **Content Analysis Views** are designed to allow the user to explore *what* is being said. (3) **Argumentation Analysis Views** rely on the linguistic parsing to address the question of *how* it is being said. (4) **Speaker Analysis Views** are focused on giving an insight into the speaker dynamics to answer the question *by whom* it is being said. In the following, we will discuss a sample of the visualization components using the transcriptions of the three televised US presidential election debates from 2012 between Obama and Romney. In the visualizations, the three speakers in the debate are distinguished through their set colors and icons: Obama as ⚞ **Democrat** (blue); Romney as ⚟ **Republican** (red) and all moderators combined as ⚘ **Moderator** (green).

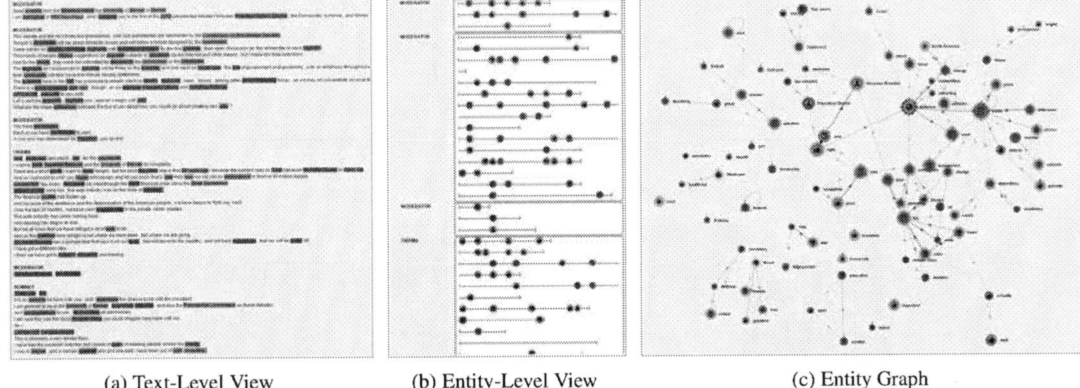

| (a) Text-Level View | (b) Entity-Level View | (c) Entity Graph |

Figure 2: Named-Entity Relationship Explorer

4.1 Content Analysis Views

Lexical Episode Plots This visualization is designed to give a high-level overview of the content of the transcripts, based on the concept of lexical chaining. For this, we compute word chains that appear with a high density in a certain part of the text and determine their importance through the compactness of their appearance. Lexical Episodes (Gold et al., 2015) are defined as a portion of the word sequence where a certain word appears more densely than expected from its frequency in the whole text. These episodes are visualized as bars on the left-hand side of the text (Figure 1). The text is shown on the right and each utterance is abstracted by one box with each sentence as one line. This visualization supports a smooth uniform zooming from the text level to the high-level overview, which enables both a close-reading (Figure 1c) of the text and a distant-reading using the episodes. The user can also select episodes which are then highlighted in the text (Figure 1b). The level of detail is adjusted by changing the significance level of the episode detection. Figure 1a shows an overview of the three presidential debates, with a high significance level selected to achieve a high level of detail.

Named-Entity Relationship Explorer This visualization (El-Assady et al., 2017) enables the analysis of different concepts and their relation in the utterances. We categorize relevant named-entities and concepts from the text and abstract them into ten classes: ● Persons, ● Geo-Locations, ● Organizations, ● Date-Time, ● Measuring Units, ● Measures, ● Context-Keywords, ● Positive- and ● Negative-Emotion Indicators, and ● Politeness-Keywords. We then abstract the text from the Text-Level View (Figure 2a) to the Entity-Level View (Figure 2b) to allow a high-level overview of the entity distribution across utterances.

 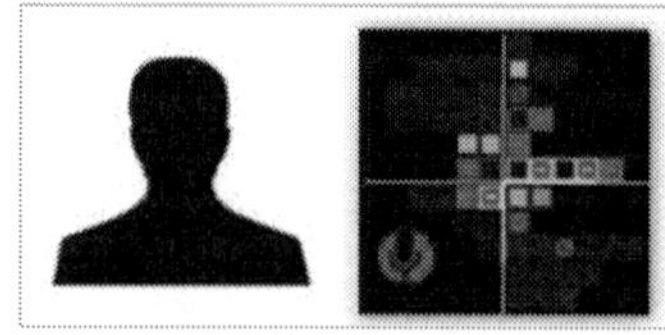  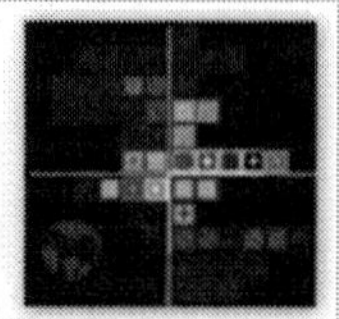

(a) Binary   (b) Numerical   (c) Bi-Polar

Figure 4: Data-type color mapping for glyphs.

In order to extract their relations, we devise a tailored distance-restricted entity-relationship model to comply with the often ungrammatical structure of verbatim transcriptions. This model relates two entities if they are present in the same sentence within a small distance window defined by a user-selected threshold. The concept map of the conversations, which builds up as the discourse progresses, can then be explored in the Entity Graph (Figure 2c). All views support a rich set of interactions, e.g., linking, brushing, selection, querying and interactive parameter adjustment.

4.2 Argumentation Analysis Views

Argumentation Feature Fingerprinting In an attempt to measure the deliberative quality of discourse (Gold and Holzinger, 2015), we use the annotations discussed in Section 3 and create a fingerprint of all utterances, the Argumentation Glyph. The glyph maps the four theoretic dimensions of deliberation in its four quadrants which are separated by the axes: NW (Accommodation), NE (Atmosphere & Respect), SE (Participation), SW (Argumentation & Justification). In each row, we group features that are thematically related, e.g. speech acts of information-giving/seeking/refusing. Each feature is represented as a small rectangular box. The strength of each value is encoded via a divergent color mapping, with each type of data (binary, numerical, bipolar) having a different color scale (Figure 4). The small circular icon at the bottom left shows the average length of each utterance.

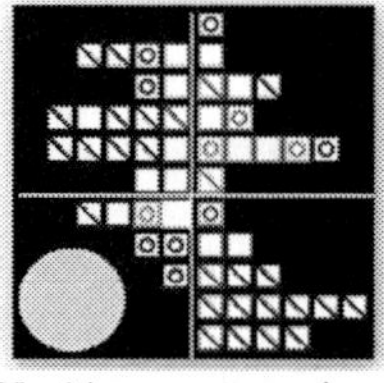

This glyph-based fingerprinting of discourse features can be used to analyze sets of aggregated utterances, e.g. Figure 3 displays one glyph for every speaker representing the average of all their utterances. These speaker profiles are used for the identification of individual behavior patterns. In addition, the glyphs can be aggregated for topics, speaker parties, and combinations of these.

Figure 3: Speaker Profiles with Argumentation Glyphs

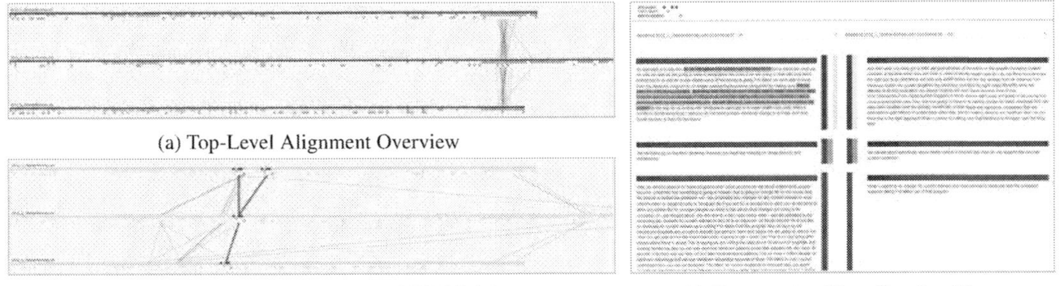

(a) Top-Level Alignment Overview

(b) Interactive Pattern Selection and Highlighting

(c) Comparative Close-Reading View

Figure 5: Argumentation Feature Alignment for Discourse Pattern Detection

Argumentation Feature Alignment The user can also form hypotheses about the occurrences of these discourse features in the data. To facilitate their verification across multiple conversations we use sequential pattern mining to create feature alignment views (Jentner et al., 2017) based on selected features. Figure 5 shows alignment views created using the following three features: **Speakers** (● Obama, ● Romeny, ● Moderator); **Topic Shift** (● Progressive, ● Recurring); and **Arrangement** (● Agreement, ● Disagreement). The sidefigure shows the pattern of Obama making a statement, followed by a topic shift and a turn of Romney and the moderator, fol-

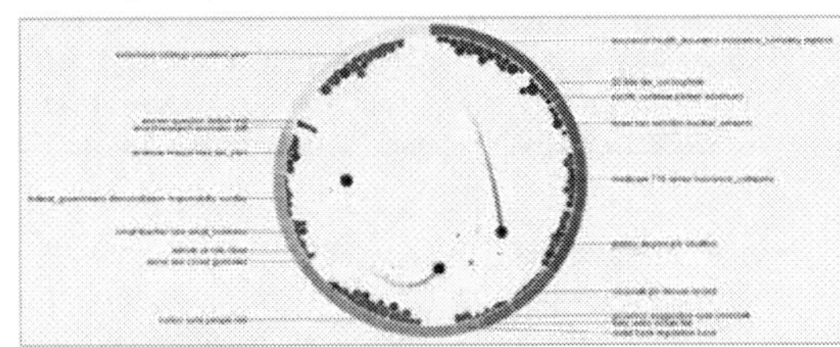

lowed by an agreement. This pattern can be found across all three presidential debates, shown in Figure 5b. For further analysis, the user can switch to a comparative close-reading view to investigate two occurrences of the found pattern on the text level, as shown in Figure 5c.

4.3 Speaker Analysis Views

Topic-Space Views In this visualization, we model the interactions between speakers using the metaphor of a closed discussion floor. We designed a radial plot, the topic space, in which the speakers interact over the course of a discussion. Using this metaphor, we created a set of different (static and animated) views to highlight the various aspects of the speaker interactions. Figure 6 displays one time-frame of the utterance sedimentation view (El-Assady et al., 2016) of the accumulated presidential debates. In this animation, all discussed topics (ordered by their similarity to a selected base-topic at 12 o'clock) span the radial topic space. The length of the arch representing a topic is mapped to the size of the topic. All currently active speakers are displayed as moving dots with motion chart trails. A gradual visual-decay function blends out non-active speakers over time. Using a sedimentation metaphor, all past utterances are pulled to their top topic by a radial gravitation.

Figure 6: Topic Space View

5 Summary

The VisArgue framework provides a novel visual analytics toolbox for exploratory and confirmatory analyses of multi-party discourse data. Overall, each of the presented visualizations support disentangling speaker and discourse patterns.

Acknowledgments

The research carried out in this paper was supported by the Bundesministerium für Bildung und Forschung (BMBF) under grant no. 01461246 (eHumanities VisArgue project).

References

Nick Asher and Alex Lascarides. 2003. *Logics of Conversation*. Cambridge: Cambridge University Press.

Tony Bergstrom and Karrie Karahalios. 2009. Conversation clusters: grouping conversation topics through human-computer dialog. In *Proc. of the SIGCHI Conf. on Human Factors in Computing Systems*. pages 2349–2352.

Tina Bögel, Annette Hautli-Janisz, Sebastian Sulger, and Miriam Butt. 2014. Automatic Detection of Causal Relations in German Multilogs. In *Proc. of the EACL 2014 CAtCL Workshop*. pages 20–27.

Harry Bunt, Jan Alexandersson, and Jean Carletta et al. 2010. Towards an ISO standard for dialogue act annotation. In *Proc. of LREC'10*. pages 2548–2555.

Cristian Danescu-Niculescu-Mizil, Moritz Sudhof, Dan Jurafsky, Jure Leskovec, and Christopher Potts. 2013. A computational approach to politeness with application to social factors. In *Proc. of ACL'13*. pages 250–259.

Judith Donath and Fernanda B Viégas. 2002. The chat circles series: explorations in designing abstract graphical communication interfaces. In *Proc. of the 4th conference on Designing interactive systems*. pages 359–369.

Mennatallah El-Assady, Valentin Gold, Carmela Acevedo, Christopher Collins, and Daniel Keim. 2016. ConToVi: Multi-Party Conversation Exploration using Topic-Space Views. *Computer Graphics Forum* 35(3):431–440.

Mennatallah El-Assady, Rita Sevastjanova, Bela Gipp, Daniel Keim, and Christopher Collins. 2017. NEREx: Named-Entity Relationship Exploration in Multi-Party Conversations. *Computer Graphics Forum* .

Thomas Erickson and Wendy A Kellogg. 2000. Social translucence: an approach to designing systems that support social processes. *ACM transactions on computer-human interaction (TOCHI)* 7(1):59–83.

Valentin Gold and Katharina Holzinger. 2015. An Automated Text-Analysis Approach to Measuring Deliberative Quality. Annual Meeting of the Midwest Political Science Association (Chicago).

Valentin Gold, Christian Rohrdantz, and Mennatallah El-Assady. 2015. Exploratory Text Analysis using Lexical Episode Plots. In E. Bertini, J. Kennedy, and E. Puppo, editors, *Eurographics Conference on Visualization (EuroVis) - Short Papers*.

Annette Hautli-Janisz and Miriam Butt. 2016. On the role of discourse particles for mining arguments in German dialogs. In *Proc. of the COMMA 2016 FLA workshop*. pages 10–17.

Enamul Hoque and Giuseppe Carenini. 2016. Multiconvis: A visual text analytics system for exploring a collection of online conversations. In *Proc. of Intelligent User Interfaces*. ACM, IUI, pages 96–107.

Susanne Jekat, Alexandra Klein, Elisabeth Maier, Ilona Maleck, Marion Mast, and J. Joachim Quantz. 1995. Dialgue acts in verbmobil. Technical report, Saarländische Universitäts- und Landesbibliothek.

Wolfgang Jentner, Mennatallah El-Assady, Bela Gipp, and Daniel Keim. 2017. Feature Alignment for the Analysis of Verbatim Text Transcripts. *EuroVis Workshop on Visual Analytics (EuroVA)* .

Dan Klein and Christopher D. Manning. 2003. Accurate unlexicalized parsing. In *Proc. of ACL 2003*. pages 423–430.

Gilly Leshed and Diego Perez et al. 2009. Visualizing real-time language-based feedback on teamwork behavior in computer-mediated groups. In *Proc. of the SIGCHI Conf. on Human Factors in Computing Systems*. pages 537–546.

Francois Mairesse, Marilyn A. Walker, Matthias R. Mehl, and Roger K. Moore. 2007. Using Linguistic Cues for the Automatic Recognition of Personality in Conversation and Text. *Journal of Artificial Intelligence Research* 30:457–500.

William C. Mann and Sandra A. Thompson. 1988. Rhetorical structure theory: Towards a theory of text organization. *Text* 8(3):243–281.

Daniel Marcu. 2000. *The Theory and Practice of Discourse Parsing and Summarization*. MIT Press, Cambridge, Mass.

Saif M. Mohammad and Peter D. Turney. 2010. Emotions evoked by common words and phrases: Using mechanical turk to create and emotion lexicon. In *Proc. of the NAACL 2015 WASSA Workshop*. pages 26–34.

Livia Polanyi, Chris Culy, Martin van den Berg, Gian Lorenzo Thione, and David Ahn. 2004. Sentential structure and discourse parsing. In *Proc. of the ACL'04 Workshop on Discourse Annotation*. pages 80–87.

Rashmi Prasad, Nikhil Dinesh, Alan Lee, Eleni Miltsakaki, Livio Robaldo, Aravind Joshi, and Bonnie Webber. 2008. The Penn Discourse Treebank 2.0. In *Proc. of LREC'08*. pages 2961–2968.

Anne N. Rafferty and Christopher D. Manning. 2008. Parsing three german treebanks: Lexicalized and unlexicalized baselines. In *Proc. of the ACL-08 PaGe-08 workshop*. pages 40–46.

Anne Schiller. 1994. DMOR - User's Guide. Technical report, IMS, Universität Stuttgart.

Dhanya Sridhar, James Foulds, Marilyn Walker, Bert Huang, and Lise Getoor. 2015. Joint models of disagreement and stance in online debate. In *Proc. of ACL 2015*. pages 26–31.

Manfred Stede and Arne Neumann. 2014. Potsdam commentary corpus 2.0: Annotation for discourse research. In *Proc. of LREC'14*. pages 925–929.

Yannick Versley and Anna Gastel. 2012. Linguistic Tests for Discourse Relations in the Tüba-D/Z Corpus of Written German. *Dialogue and Discourse* 1(2):1–24.

Elina Zarisheva and Tatjana Scheffler. 2015. Dialogue act annotation for twitter data. In *Proc. of SIGDIAL 2015*. pages 114–123.

Hwee Tou Ng Ziheng Lin and Min-Yen Kan. 2014. A PDTB-Styled End-to-End Discourse Parser. *Natural Language Engineering* 20:151–184.

Life-iNet: A Structured Network-Based Knowledge Exploration and Analytics System for Life Sciences

Xiang Ren[1], Jiaming Shen[1], Meng Qu[1], Xuan Wang[1], Zeqiu Wu[1], Qi Zhu[1], Meng Jiang[1]
Fangbo Tao[1], Saurabh Sinha[1,2], David Liem[3], Peipei Ping[3], Richard Weinshilboum[4], Jiawei Han[1]

[1] Department of Computer Science, University of Illinois Urbana-Champaign, IL, USA

[2] Institute of Genomic Biology, University of Illinois at Urbana-Champaign, IL, USA

[3] School of Medicine, University of California, Los Angeles, CA, USA

[4] Department of Pharmacology, Mayo Clinic, MN, USA

[1,2] {xren7, js2, xwang174, mengqu2, zeqiuwu1, qiz3, mjiang89, ftao2, sinhas, hanj}@illinois.edu

[3] {dliem, pping}@mednet.ucla.edu   [4] weinshilboum.richard@mayo.edu

Abstract

Search engines running on scientific literature have been widely used by life scientists to find publications related to their research. However, existing search engines in the life-science domain, such as PubMed, have limitations when applied to exploring and analyzing factual knowledge (*e.g.*, disease-gene associations) in massive text corpora. These limitations are mainly due to the problems that factual information exists as an unstructured form in text, and also keyword and MeSH term-based queries cannot effectively imply semantic relations between entities. This demo paper presents the Life-iNet system to address the limitations in existing search engines on facilitating life sciences research. Life-iNet automatically constructs structured networks of factual knowledge from large amounts of background documents, to support efficient exploration of structured factual knowledge in the unstructured literature. It also provides functionalities for finding distinctive entities for given entity types, and generating hypothetical facts to assist literature-based knowledge discovery (*e.g.*, drug target prediction).

1 Introduction

Scientific literature is an important resource in facilitating life science research, and a primary medium for communicating novel research results. However, even though vast amounts of biomedical textual information are available online (*e.g.*, publications in PubMed, encyclopedic articles in Wikipedia, ontologies on genes, drugs, etc.), there exists only limited support of exploring and analyzing relevant factual knowledge in the massive

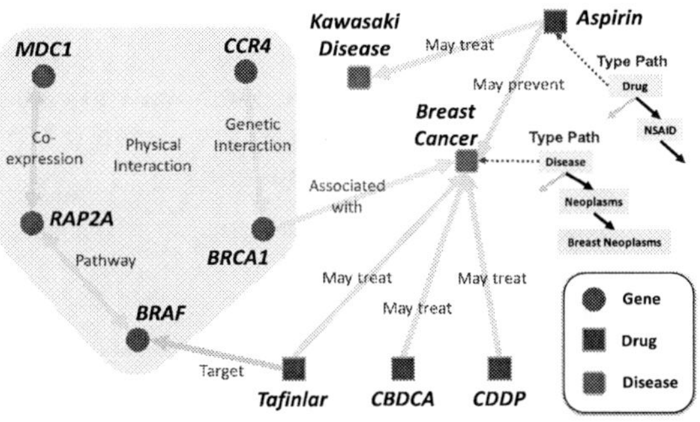

Figure 1: A snapshot of the structured network in Life-iNet.

literature (Tao et al., 2014), or of gaining new insights from the existing factual information (McDonald et al., 2005; Riedel and McCallum, 2011). Users typically search PubMed using keywords and Medical Subject Headings (MeSH) terms, and then rely on Google and external biomedical ontologies for everything else. Such an approach, however, might not work well on capturing different entity relationships (*i.e.*, facts), or identifying publications related to facts of interest.

For example, a biologist who is interested in `cancer` might need to check what specific diseases belong to the category of `breast_neoplasms` (*e.g.*, *breast cancer*) and what genes (*e.g.*, *BRCA1*) and drugs (*e.g.*, *Aspirin*, *Tafinlar*) are related to *breast cancer*, and might need a list of related papers which study and discuss about these disease-gene relations. For cancer experts, they might want to learn about what genes are distinctively associated with `breast_neoplasms` (as compared to other kinds of cancers), whether there exists other genes that are potentially associated with `breast_neoplasms` entities, and whether there exist other drugs that can also treat *breast cancer*.

• **Previous Efforts and Limitations.** In life sciences domain, recent studies (Ernst et al., 2016; Szklarczyk et al., 2014; Thomas et al., 2012;

55

Proceedings of the 55th Annual Meeting of the Association for Computational Linguistics-System Demonstrations, pages 55–60
Vancouver, Canada, July 30 - August 4, 2017. ©2017 Association for Computational Linguistics
https://doi.org/10.18653/v1/P17-4010

Kim et al., 2008) rely on biomedical entity information associated with the documents to support entity-centric literature search. Most existing information retrieval systems exploit either the MeSH terms manually annotated for each PubMed article (Kim et al., 2008) or textual mentions of biomedical entities automatically recognized within the documents (Thomas et al., 2012), to capture the entity-document relatedness. Compared with traditional keyword-based systems, current entity-centric retrieval systems can identify and index entity information for documents in a more accurate way (to enable effective literature exploration), but encounter several challenges, as shown below, in supporting exploration and analysis of factual knowledge (*i.e.*, entities and their relationships) in a given corpus.

- **Lack of Factual Structures:** Most existing entity-centric systems compute the document/corpus-level co-occurrence statistics between two biomedical entities to capture the relations between them, but cannot identify the semantic relation types between two entities based on the textual evidence in a specific sentence. For example, in Fig. 1, relations between `gene` entities should be categorized as `CoExpression`, `GeneticInteraction`, `PhysicalInteraction`, `Pathway`, etc. Extracting typed entity relationships from unstructured text corpus enables: (1) structured search over the factual information in the given corpus; (2) fine-grained exploration of the documents at the sentence level; and (3) more accurate identification of entity relationships.

- **Limited Diversity and Coverage:** There exist several biomedical knowledge bases (KBs) (*e.g.*, Gene Ontology, UniProt, STRING (Szklarczyk et al., 2014), Literome (Poon et al., 2014)) that support search and data exploration functionality. However, each of these KBs is highly specialized and covers only a relatively narrow topic within life sciences (Ernst et al., 2016). Also, there is limited inter-linkage between entities in these KBs (*e.g.*, between `drug`, `disease` and `gene` entities). An integrative view on all aspects of life sciences knowledge is still missing. Moreover, many newly emerged entities are not covered in current KBs, as the manual curation process is time-consuming and costly.

- **Restricted Analytic Functionality:** Due to the lack of notion for factual structures, current retrieval and exploration systems have restricted functionality at analyzing entity relationships—

they mainly focus on entity-centric literature search (Ernst et al., 2016; Thomas et al., 2012) and exploring entity co-occurrences (Kim et al., 2008). In practice, analytic functionality over factual information (*e.g.*, drug-disease targeting prediction and distinctive disease-gene association identification) is highly desirable.

Proposed Approach. This paper presents a novel system, called Life-iNet, which transforms an *unstructured* corpus into a *structured* network of factual knowledge, and supports multiple exploratory and analytic functions over the constructed network for knowledge discovery. Life-iNet automatically detects token spans of entities mentioned from text, labels entity mentions with semantic categories, and identifies relationships of various relation types between the detected entities. These inter-related pieces of information are integrated to form a unified, structured network, where nodes represent different types of entities and edges denote relationships of different relation types between the entities (see Fig. 1 for example). To address the issue of limited diversity and coverage, Life-iNet relies on the external knowledge bases to provide seed examples (*i.e.*, *distant supervision*), and identifies additional entities and relationships from the given corpus (*e.g.*, using multiple text resources such as scientific literature and encyclopedia articles) to construct a structured network. By doing so, we integrate the factual information in the existing knowledge bases with those extracted from the corpus. To support analytic functionality, Life-iNet implements link prediction functions over the constructed network and integrates a distinctive summarization function to provide insight analysis (*e.g.*, answering questions such as "*which genes are distinctively related to the given disease type under* `GeneDiseaseAssociation` *relation?*").

To systematically incorporate these ideas, Life-iNet leverages the novel distantly-supervised information extraction techniques (Ren et al., 2017, 2016a, 2015) to implement an *effort-light network construction framework* (see Fig. 2). Specially, it relies on distant supervision in conjunction with external knowledge bases to (1) detect quality entity mentions (Ren et al., 2015), (2) label entity mentions with fine-grained entity types in a given type hierarchy (Ren et al., 2016a), and (3) identify relationships of different types between entities (Ren et al., 2017). In particular, we design specialized loss functions to faithfully model "*appropriate*" labels and remove "*false positive*" la-

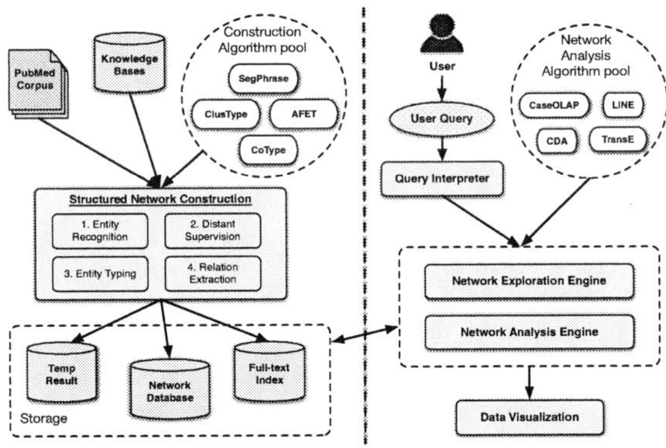

Figure 2: System Architecture of Life-iNet.

Background corpora	Cancer	Heart Disease
#PubMed publications	2,936,615	2,105,257
#PMC full-text papers	95,008	38,205
#Wikipedia articles	37,128	25,577
#Sentences in total	38M	23M
#Entity types	1,116	1,086
#Relation types	414	384
#KB-mapped (seed) entity mentions	59M	33M
#KB-mapped (seed) relation mentions	47M	23M
#Nodes in Life-iNet (*i.e.*, entities)	64M	39M
#Edges in Life-iNet (*i.e.*, facts)	186M	82M

Table 1: Data statistics of corpora and networks in Life-iNet.

bels for the training instances (heuristically generated by distant supervision), regarding the specific context where an instance is mentioned (Ren et al., 2017, 2016a). By doing so, we can construct *corpus-specific* information extraction models by using distant supervision in a noise-robust way. The proposed network construction framework is domain-independent—it can be quickly ported to other disciplines and sciences without additional human labeling effort. With the constructed network, Life-iNet further applies link prediction algorithms (Tang et al., 2015; Bordes et al., 2013) to infer new entity relationships, and distinctive summarization algorithm (Tao et al., 2016) to find other entities that are distinctively related to the query entity (or the given entity types).

Contributions. The contributions and features of the Life-iNet system are summarized as follows.

1. A novel knowledge exploration and analysis system for life sciences that integrates existing knowledge bases and factual information extracted from massive literature.

2. An *effort-light* framework that leverages distant supervision in a *robust* way to automatically construct a structured network of factual knowledge from the given unstructured text corpus.

3. Capabilities for exploration and analysis over the constructed structured network to facilitate life sciences research.

The Life-iNet demo system will be made available online for interactive use after its demonstration in the conference.

2 The Life-iNet System

At a high level, Life-iNet consists of two major components: a structured network construction pipeline and a network exploration and analysis engine. The former (*i.e.*, the network construction pipeline) includes four functional modules: (1) entity mention detection, (2) distant supervision generation, (3) entity typing, and (4) relation extraction; whereas the latter (*i.e.*, the network exploration and analysis engine) implements network exploratory functions, relationship prediction algorithms (*e.g.*, LINE (Tang et al., 2015)) and network-based distinctive summarization algorithms (*e.g.*, CaseOLAP (Tao et al., 2016)), and operates on the constructed network to support answering different user queries. Fig. 2 shows its system architecture. The functional modules are presented in detail as follows.

2.1 Structured Network Construction

The network construction pipeline automatically extracts factual structures (*i.e.*, entities, relations) from given corpora with (potentially noisy) distant supervision, and integrates them with existing knowledge bases to build a unified structured network. In particular, to extract high-quality, typed entities and relations, we design *noise-robust objective functions* to select the "*most appropriate*" training labels when constructing models from labeled data (heuristically obtained by distant supervision) (Ren et al., 2016b,a, 2017).

Data Collection. To obtain background text corpora for network construction, we consider two kinds of textual resources, *i.e.*, scientific publications and encyclopedia articles. For scientific publications, we collect titles and abstracts of 26M papers from the entire PubMed[1] dump, and full-text paper content of 2.2M papers from PubMed Central (PMC)[2]. For encyclopedia articles, we collect 62,705 related articles through Wikipedia Health Portal[3]. For demonstration purpose, we select documents related to two kinds of important diseases, *i.e.*, cancer and heart diseases to form the background corpora for Life-iNet. Table 1 summarizes the statistics of the background corpora.

Entity Mention Detection. The entity mention detection module in Life-iNet runs a data-driven

---

[1]https://www.ncbi.nlm.nih.gov/pubmed/
[2]https://www.ncbi.nlm.nih.gov/pmc/
[3]https://en.wikipedia.org/wiki/Portal:Health_and_fitness

text segmentation algorithm, SegPhrase (Liu et al., 2015), to extract high-quality words/phrases as entity candidates. SegPhrase uses entity names from KBs as positive examples to train a quality classifier, and then efficiently segments the corpus by maximizing the joint probability based on the trained classifier. Table 1 shows the statistics of detected entity mentions for the corpora.

Distant Supervision Generation.. Distant supervisions (Mintz et al., 2009; Ren et al., 2017, 2016a) leverages the information overlap between external KBs and given corpora to automatically generate large amounts of training data. A typical workflow is as follows: (1) map detected entity mentions to entities in KB, (2) assign, to the entity type set of each entity mention, KB types of its KB-mapped entity, and (3) assign, to the relation type set of each entity mention pair, KB relations between their KB-mapped entities. Such a label generation process may introduce noisy type labels (Ren et al., 2017). Our network construction pipeline faithfully incorporates the noisy labels in training to learn effective extraction models. In Life-iNet, we use a publicly-available KB, UMLS (Unified Medical Language System)[4], and further enrich its entity type ontology with MeSH tree structures[5]. This yields a KB with 6.7M unique entities, 10M entity relationships, 56k entity types, and 581 relation types. Table 1 shows the data statistics of distant supervision.

Entity Typing. The entity typing module is concerned with predicting a single type-path in the given entity type hierarchy for each *unlinkable* entity mention (*i.e.*, mentions that cannot be mapped to entities in KB) based on its local context (*e.g.*, sentence). Life-iNet adopts a two-step entity typing process, which first identifies the coarse type label for each mention (*e.g.*, `disease`, `gene`, `protein`, `drug`, `symptom`), then refines the coarse label into a more fine-grained type-path (*e.g.*, `disease::heart_disease::arrhythmias`). Specifically, we first run ClusType (Ren et al., 2015) to predict coarse type label for each unlinkable mention. Then, using coarse type label as constraints, we apply AFET (Ren et al., 2016a) to estimate a single type path for each mention. AFET models the noisy candidate type set generated by distant supervision to learn a predictive typing model for unseen entity mentions.

Relation Extraction. The task of relation extrac-

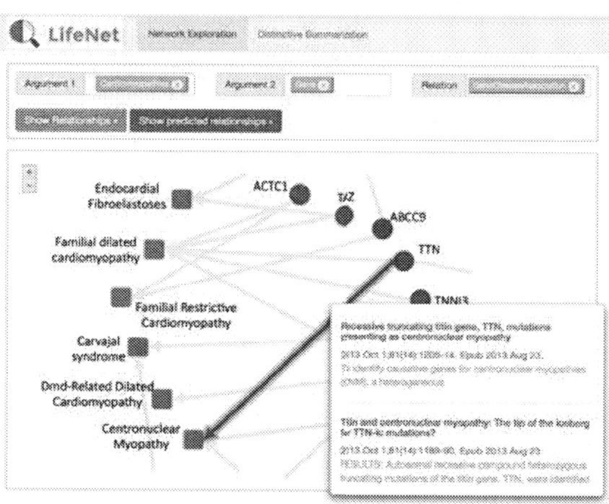

Figure 3: Screen shot of the user interface for relation-based exploration and relationship prediction in Life-iNet.

tion focuses on determining whether a relationship of interest (*i.e.*, in given relation type set) is expressed between a pair of entity mentions in a specific sentence, and label them with the appropriate relation type if a specific relation is expressed. Life-iNet relies on a distantly-supervised relation extraction framework, CoType (Ren et al., 2017), to extract typed relation mentions from text. CoType leverages a variety of text features extracted from the local context of a pair of entity mentions, and jointly embeds relation mentions, text features and relation type labels into a low-dimensional space, where, in that space, objects with similar type semantics are also close to each other. It then performs nearest neighbor search to estimate the relation type for a relation mention.

Performance of Network Construction. Performance comparisons with state-of-the-art (distantly-supervised) information extraction systems demonstrate the effectiveness of the proposed pipeline (Ren et al., 2017)—CoType achieves a 25% F1 score improvement on relation extraction and a 6% enhancement in F1 score for entity recognition and typing, on the public BioInfer corpus (manually labeled biomedical papers). Table 1 summarizes the statistics of the constructed structures networks—Life-iNet discovers over 250% more facts compared to those generated by distant supervision.

2.2 Network Exploration and Analysis

The network exploration and analysis engine indexes the network structures and their related textual evidence to support fast exploration. It also implements several network mining algorithms to facilitate knowledge discovery.

---

[4]https://www.nlm.nih.gov/research/umls/
[5]https://www.nlm.nih.gov/mesh/intro_trees.html

Network Exploration. For each entity e_i, we index its entity types $\mathcal{T}_i$, and sentences $\mathcal{S}_i$ (and documents $\mathcal{D}_i$) where it is mentioned. For each relation mention $z_i = (e_1, e_2; s)$, we index its sentence s and relation type r_i. With this data model, Life-iNet can support several structured search queries: (1) find entities of a given entity type, (2) find entities that have a specific relation to a given entity (entity type), and (3) find papers related to given entities, entity types, relationships, or relation types. We use raw frequency discounted by object popularity to rank the results.

Relationship Prediction. We adopt state-of-the-art heterogeneous network-based link prediction algorithms, LINE (Tang et al., 2015) and TransE (Bordes et al., 2013), to discover new relationships in the network. The intuition behind these algorithms is straightforward: if two nodes share similar neighbors in the network, they should be related. Following this idea, the algorithms embed the network into a low-dimensional space based on distributional assumption. A new edge will be formed if the similarity between the embedding vectors of the corresponding entity arguments are larger than a pre-defined threshold δ, *i.e.*, $\mathrm{sim}(\mathrm{vec}(e1), \mathrm{vec}(e2)) > \delta$. The prediction can be further interpreted using existing network structures, by retrieving indirect paths between the two entities (if there exists).

Distinctive Summarization. In biomedical domain, some high-popularity entities may form relationships with many other entities simultaneously. For example, some genes may be associated with multiple heart disease types. It is desirable to find genes that are distinctively associated with *each* heart disease type. This motivates us to apply CaseOLAP (Tao et al., 2016), a context-aware, multi-dimensional summarization algorithm to generate distinctive entities. The basic idea is that: an entity is *distinctively* related to the target entity type if it is relevant to entities of the *target* entity type but relatively irrelevant to entities of the *other* entity types. We pre-compute the distinctive summarization results between different entity types and materialize the temporary results for efficient user query answering.

3 Demo Scenarios

3.1 Relation-Based Exploration

Life-iNet indexes the extracted factual structures along with their support documents. Our demo provides an exploration interface (see Fig. 3), where users can enter an argument triple to specify the entity and relation types they want to explore (user will be prompted with type candidates). Suppose a biologist is interested in finding genes associated with `cardiomyopathies`, he/she can enter type `gene` as argument 1, `cardiomyopathies` as argument 2, and `GeneDiseaseAssociation` as the relation. Life-iNet will then retrieve and visualize a sub-network to show different `cardiomyopathies` entities (*e.g.*, *Endocardial Fibroelastoses*, *Centronuclear Myopathy*, *Carvajal syndrome*), and their associated `gene` entities (*e.g.*, *TAZ*, *BIN1*, *DSC2*). When a user moves his/her mouse cursor to an edge (or node) in the sub-network, Life-iNet will return a ranked list of supporting papers (also linked to PubMed) related to the target relationship (or entity), based on the pre-computed relevance measures. Note that Life-iNet also supports specific entities as input for arguments 1 and 2 in the interface.

3.2 Hypothetical Relationship Generation

In life sciences, some entity relationships (*e.g.*, of type `DrugTargetGene`, `GeneDiseaseAssociation`) may not be explicitly expressed in the existing literature. However, indirect connections between two isolated entities in the constructed network may provide good hints on predicting whether a specific relation exists between them. Life-iNet generates high-confidence predictions of new edges for the constructed network and forms hypothetical entity relationships to facilitate scientific research (*e.g.*, discovering a new drug that can target a specific gene). We integrate this analysis function into our relation-exploration interface. For example, when exploring the sub-network for gene-heart disease associations, users can click on the "*Show Predicted Relationships*" to see hypothetical relationships that Life-iNet generates (highlighted as dash-line edges in the network). In particular, Life-iNet provides explanation of the prediction, using the existing network structures—the indirect paths between two isolated entities will be highlighted when a user clicks on the predicted edge. Thus, a user can further retrieve papers related to the edges on the indirect paths to gain better understanding about the hypothetical relationships.

3.3 Distinctive Entity Summarization

Life-iNet provides a separate user interface for distinctive summarization function (see Fig. 4). In many cases, a user would need to

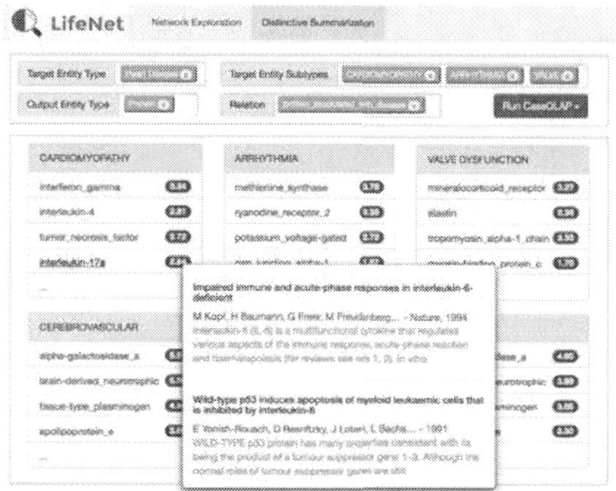

Figure 4: Screen shot for distinctive summarization function.

compare sets of entities (*e.g.*, proteins) related to several entity types (*e.g.*, different types of heart diseases), to discover the distinctive entities related to each entity type. For example, she may want to know what genes are often associated with `arrhythmia` but are unlikely associated with other kinds of heart diseases such as `cardiomyopathy` and `heart_valve_disease`. Life-iNet allows a user to enter: (1) an entity type to specify the target domain (*e.g.*, `heart_disease`), (2) several sub-types of the target entity type for comparison (*e.g.*, `cardiomyopathy`, `arrhythmia`, `heart_valve_disease`), (3) an entity type to specify the list of related entities (*e.g.*, `protein`), and (4) a relation type (*e.g.*, `protein_associated_with_disease`). With user input queries, Life-iNet produces a structured table to summarize the distinctive entities for each entity sub-type. It also shows the distinctiveness score for each entity. A user can click on each distinctive entity to find documents related to the relationship (similar to the use case in relation-based exploration). An example output of the distinctive summarization for `heart_disease` is shown in Fig. 4.

Acknowledgement

Research was sponsored in part by the U.S. Army Research Lab. under Cooperative Agreement No. W911NF-09-2-0053 (NSCTA), National Science Foundation IIS-1320617 and IIS 16-18481, and grant 1U54GM114838 awarded by NIGMS through funds provided by the trans-NIH Big Data to Knowledge (BD2K) initiative. The views and conclusions contained in this paper are those of the authors and should not be interpreted as representing any funding agencies.

References

Antoine Bordes, Nicolas Usunier, Alberto Garcia-Duran, Jason Weston, and Oksana Yakhnenko. 2013. Translating embeddings for modeling multi-relational data. In *NIPS*.

Patrick Ernst, Amy Siu, Dragan Milchevski, Johannes Hoffart, and Gerhard Weikum. 2016. Deeplife: An entity-aware search, analytics and exploration platform for health and life sciences. In *ACL*.

Jung-jae Kim, Piotr Pezik, and Dietrich Rebholz-Schuhmann. 2008. Medevi: retrieving textual evidence of relations between biomedical concepts from medline. *Bioinformatics* .

Jialu Liu, Jingbo Shang, Chi Wang, Xiang Ren, and Jiawei Han. 2015. Mining quality phrases from massive text corpora. In *SIGMOD*.

Ryan McDonald, Fernando Pereira, Seth Kulick, Scott Winters, Yang Jin, and Pete White. 2005. Simple algorithms for complex relation extraction with applications to biomedical ie. In *ACL*.

Mike Mintz, Steven Bills, Rion Snow, and Dan Jurafsky. 2009. Distant supervision for relation extraction without labeled data. In *ACL*.

Hoifung Poon, Chris Quirk, Charlie DeZiel, and David Heckerman. 2014. Literome: Pubmed-scale genomic knowledge base in the cloud. *Bioinformatics* .

Xiang Ren, Ahmed El-Kishky, Chi Wang, Fangbo Tao, Clare R Voss, and Jiawei Han. 2015. ClusType: effective entity recognition and typing by relation phrase-based clustering. In *KDD*.

Xiang Ren, Wenqi He, Meng Qu, Lifu Huang, Heng Ji, and Jiawei Han. 2016a. AFET: Automatic fine-grained entity typing by hierarchical partial-label embedding. In *EMNLP*.

Xiang Ren, Wenqi He, Meng Qu, Clare R Voss, Heng Ji, and Jiawei Han. 2016b. Label noise reduction in entity typing by heterogeneous partial-label embedding. In *KDD*.

Xiang Ren, Zeqiu Wu, Meng Qu, Clare R. Voss, Heng Ji, Tarek F. Abdelzaher, and Jiawei Han. 2017. CoType: Joint extraction of typed entities and relations with knowledge bases. In *WWW*.

Sebastian Riedel and Andrew McCallum. 2011. Fast and robust joint models for biomedical event extraction. In *EMNLP*.

Damian Szklarczyk, Andrea Franceschini, Stefan Wyder, Kristoffer Forslund, Davide Heller, Milan Simonovic, Alexander Roth, Alberto Santos, Kalliopi P Tsafou, et al. 2014. String v10: protein–protein interaction networks, integrated over the tree of life. *Nucleic acids research* .

Jian Tang, Meng Qu, Mingzhe Wang, Ming Zhang, Jun Yan, and Qiaozhu Mei. 2015. Line: Large-scale information network embedding. In *WWW*.

Fangbo Tao, George Brova, Jiawei Han, Heng Ji, Chi Wang, Brandon Norick, Ahmed El-Kishky, Jialu Liu, Xiang Ren, and Yizhou Sun. 2014. Newsnetexplorer: automatic construction and exploration of news information networks. In *SIGMOD*.

Fangbo Tao, Honglei Zhuang, Chi Wang Yu, Qi Wang, Taylor Cassidy, Lance Kaplan, Clare Voss, and Jiawei Han. 2016. Multi-dimensional, phrase-based summarization in text cubes. *Data Engineering* page 74.

Philippe Thomas, Johannes Starlinger, Alexander Vowinkel, Sebastian Arzt, and Ulf Leser. 2012. Geneview: a comprehensive semantic search engine for pubmed. *Nucleic acids research* 40(1):585–591.

Olelo: A Question Answering Application for Biomedicine

**Mariana Neves, Hendrik Folkerts, Marcel Jankrift, Julian Niedermeier,
Toni Stachewicz, Sören Tietböhl, Milena Kraus, Matthias Uflacker**
Hasso Plattner Institute at University of Potsdam
August-Bebel-Strasse 88, Potsdam 14482 Germany
`mariana.neves@hpi.de, milena.kraus@hpi.de`

Abstract

Despite the importance of the biomedical domain, there are few reliable applications to support researchers and physicians for retrieving particular facts that fit their needs. Users typically rely on search engines that only support keyword- and filter-based searches. We present Olelo, a question answering system for biomedicine. Olelo is built on top of an in-memory database, integrates domain resources, such as document collections and terminologies, and uses various natural language processing components. Olelo is fast, intuitive and easy to use. We evaluated the systems on two use cases: answering questions related to a particular gene and on the BioASQ benchmark.

Olelo is available at: `http://hpi.de/plattner/olelo`.

1 Introduction

Biomedical researchers and physicians regularly query the scientific literature for particular facts, e.g., a syndrome caused by mutations on a particular gene or treatments for a certain disease. For this purposes, users usually rely on the PubMed search engine[1], which indexes millions of publications available in the Medline database. Similar to classical information retrieval (IR) systems, input to PubMed is usually in the form of keywords, and alternatively MeSH concepts, and output is usually a list of documents.

For instance, when searching for diseases which could be caused by mutations on the CFTR gene, the user would simply write the gene name in PubMed's input field. For this example, he would

be presented with a list of 9227 potentially relevant publications (as of February/2017).

There are plenty of other Web applications for searching and navigating through the scientific biomedical literature, as surveyed in (Lu, 2011). However, most of these systems rely on simple natural language processing (NLP) techniques, such as tokenization and named-entity recognition (NER). Their functionalities are restricted to ranking documents with the support of domain terminologies, enriching publications with concepts and clustering similar documents.

Question answering (QA) can support biomedical professionals by allowing input in the form of natural questions and by providing exact answers and customized short summaries in return (Athenikos and Han, 2010; Neves and Leser, 2015). We are aware of three of such systems for biomedicine (cf. Section 2), however, current solutions still fail to fulfill the needs of users: (i) In most of them, no question understanding is carried out on the questions. (ii) Those that do make use of more complex NLP techniques (e.g., HONQA (Cruchet et al., 2009)) cannot output answers in real time. (iii) The output is usually in the form of a list of documents, instead of short answers. (iv) They provide no innovative or NLP-based means to further explore the scientific literature.

We present Olelo, a QA system for the biomedical domain. It indexes biomedical abstracts and full texts, relies on a fast in-memory database (IMDB) for storage and document indexing and implements various NLP procedures, such as domain-specific NER, question type detection, answer type detection and answer extraction. We evaluated the methods behind Olelo in the scope of the BioASQ challenge (Tsatsaronis et al., 2015), the most comprehensive shared task on biomedical QA. We participated in the last three challenges and obtained top results for snippets retrieval and

---

[1] `http://www.ncbi.nlm.nih.gov/pubmed`

61

Proceedings of the 55th Annual Meeting of the Association for Computational Linguistics-System Demonstrations, pages 61–66
Vancouver, Canada, July 30 - August 4, 2017. ©2017 Association for Computational Linguistics
`https://doi.org/10.18653/v1/P17-4011`

ideal answers (customized summaries) in the last two editions (Neves, 2014, 2015; Schulze et al., 2016).

Olelo provides solutions for the shortcomings listed above: (i) It detects both the question type and answer type. (ii) It includes various NLP components and outputs answers in real time (cf. Section 5). (iii) It always outputs a short answer, either exact answers or short summaries, while also allowing users to explore the corresponding documents. (iv) Users can navigate through the answers and their corresponding semantic types, check MeSH definition for terms, create document collections, generate customized summaries and query for similar documents, among other tasks. Finally, Olelo is an open-access system and no login is required. We tested it in multiple Web browsers, but we recommend Chrome for optimal results.

2 Related Work

MEDIE[2] was one of the first QA-inspired system for biomedicine (Miyao et al., 2006). It allows users to pose questions in the form of subject-object-verb (SOV) structures. For instance, the question "What does p53 activate?" needs to be split into its parts: "p53" (subject), "activate" (verb), and no object (i.e., the expected answer). MEDIE relies on domain ontologies, parsing and predicate-argument structures (PAS) to search Medline. However, SOV structures are not a user-friendly input, given that many of the biomedical users have no advanced knowledge on linguistics.

We are only aware of three other QA systems for biomedicine: AskHermes[3], EAGLi[4] and HONQA[5]. All of them support input in the form of questions but present result in a different ways.

AskHermes (Cao et al., 2011) outputs lists of snippets and clusters of terms, but the result page is often far too long. Their methods involve regular expressions for question understanding, question target classification, concept recognition and passage ranking based on the BM25 model. The document collection includes Medline articles and Wikipedia documents.

EAGLi (Gobeill et al., 2015) provides answers

based on concepts from the Gene Ontology (GO). Even when no answers are found for a question, EAGLi always outputs a list of relevant publications. It indexes Medline documents locally in the Terrier IR platform and uses Okapi BM25 to rank documents.

HONQA (Cruchet et al., 2009) considers documents from certified websites from the Health On the Net (HON) and supports French and Italian, besides the English language. The answer type detection is based on the UMLS database and the architecture of the systems seems to follow the typical QA workflow. However, no further details are described in their publication.

3 System Architecture

The architecture of Olelo follows the usual components of a QA system (Athenikos and Han, 2010), i.e., document indexing, question processing, passage retrieval and answer processing (cf. Figure 1). In this section we present a short overview of the many tasks inside each of these components. We previously published our methods for multi-document summarization (Schulze and Neves, 2016), which we applied not only for biomedical QA but also for gene-specific summaries. Finally, our participations on the BioASQ challenges also provide insights on previous and current methods behind our system (Neves, 2014, 2015; Schulze et al., 2016).

Document Indexing. We index the document collection and the questions into an IMDB (Plattner, 2013), namely, the SAP HANA database. This database stores data in the main memory and includes other desirable features for on-line QA systems, such as multi-core processing, parallelization, lightweight compression and partitioning. Our document collection currently consists of abstracts from Medline[6] and full text publications from PubMed Central Open Access subset[7]. The document collection is regularly updated to account for new publications.

When indexed in the database, documents and questions are processed using built-in text analysis procedures from the IMDB, namely, sentence splitting, tokenization, stemming, part-of-speech (POS) tagging and NER (cf. Table 1). The latter is

---

[2]http://www.nactem.ac.uk/medie/

[3]http://www.askhermes.org/

[4]http://eagl.unige.ch/EAGLi

[5]http://www.hon.ch/QA/

[6]https://www.nlm.nih.gov/bsd/pmresources.html

[7]https://www.ncbi.nlm.nih.gov/pmc/tools/openftlist/

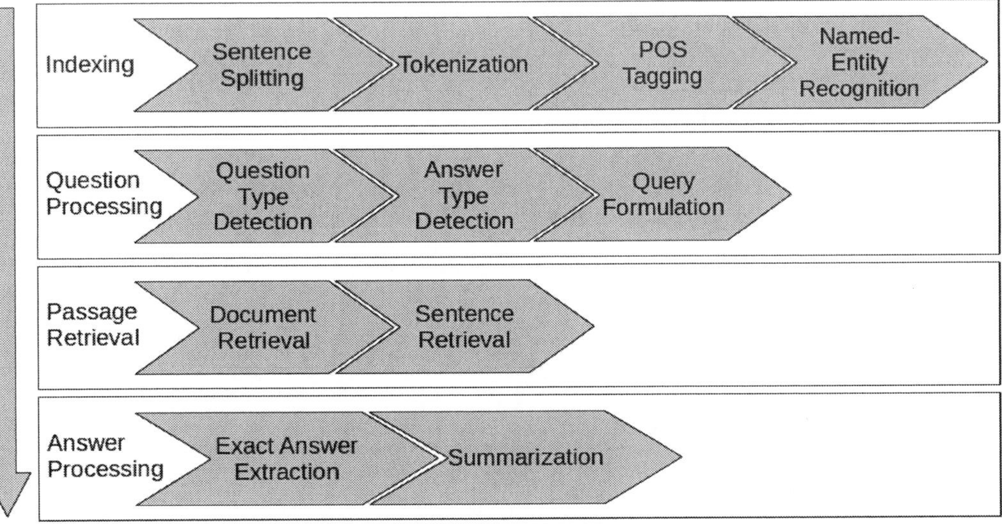

Figure 1: Natural language processing components of Olelo question answering system.

Totals	Abstracts	Full text
Documents	8,335,584	1,116,645
MeSH all	335,174,549	48,455,036
MeSH distinct	54,313	56,587
UMLS all	1,773,195,457	6,209,018,977
UMLS distinct	387,110	392,932

Table 1: Statistics on documents, sentences and named entities (as of February/2017).

based on customized dictionaries for the biomedical domain, which we compiled based on two domain resources: the Medical Subject Headings (MeSH)[8] and the Unified Medical Language System (UMLS)[9].

Question Processing. Olelo currently supports three types of questions: (i) factoid; (ii) definition; and (iii) summary. A factoid question requires one or more short answers in return, such as a list of disease names, definition questions query for a particular definition of a concept, while summary questions expect a short summary about a topic. Components in this step include the detection of the question type via simple regular expressions, followed by the detection of the answer type, in the case of factoid questions. This step also comprises the detection of the headword via regular expression and the identification of its semantic types with the support of the previously detected named entities. The semantic types correspond to

the ones defined by UMLS semantic types (Bodenreider, 2004). Finally, a query is built based on surface forms of tokens, as well as previously detected MeSH and UMLS terms.

Passage Retrieval. The system ranks documents and passages based on built-in features of the IMDB. It matches keywords from the query to the documents in an approximate way, including linguistic variations. We start by considering all keywords in the query and we drop some of them later if no document match is found.

Answer Processing. An answer is produced depending on the question type. In case of a definition question, the system simply shows the corresponding MeSH term along with its definition, as originally included in the MeSH terminology. In the case of factoid questions, Olelo returns MeSH terms which belong to the corresponding semantic type that was previously detected. Lastly, the system builds a customized summary for summary questions, based on the retrieved documents and on the query.

4   Use Cases

In this section we show two use cases of obtaining precise answers for particular questions. The examples include a question related to a specific gene and two questions from the BioASQ benchmark. We also present a preliminary comparison of our systems to three others on-line biomedical QA applications.

---

[8] https://www.nlm.nih.gov/mesh/
[9] https://www.nlm.nih.gov/research/umls/

The "Tutorial" page in Olelo contains more details on the various functionalities of the system. Some few parameters can be set on the "Setting" page, such as the minimal year of publication, the size of the summary (in terms of number of sentence, default value is 5) and the number of documents considered when generating a summary (default value is 20).

Gene-related question. This use case focuses on the gene CFTR, which was one of the chosen #GeneOfTheWeek in a campaign promoted in Twitter by the Ensembl database of genes. Mutations on genes are common causes of diseases, therefore, a user could post the following question to Olelo: "What are the diseases related to mutations on the CFTR gene?". Olelo returns a list of potential answers to the question (cf. Figure 2), and indeed, "cystic fibrosis" is associated to the referred gene[10]. By clicking on "cystic fibrosis", its definition in MeSH is shown, and Olelo informs that 349 relevant document were found (blue button on the bottom). By clicking on this button, a document is shown and this is indeed relevant, as we can confirm by reading the first sentence of its abstract. At this point, the user has many ways to navigate further on the topic, for instance: (a) flick through the rest of the documents; (b) create a summary for this document collection; (c) click on a term (in blue) to learn more about it; (d) visualize full details on the publication (small icon besides its title); (e) navigate through the semantic types listed for cystic fibrosis; or (f) click on another disease name, i.e., "asthma".

BioASQ benchmark questions. Currently, BioASQ (Tsatsaronis et al., 2015) is the most comprehensive benchmark for QA systems in biomedicine. We selected one summary and one factoid question to illustrate the results returned by Olelo for different question types. For the question "What is the Barr body?" (identifier 55152c0a46478f2f2c000004), the system returns a short summary whose first sentence indeed contains the answer to the question: "The Barr body is the inactive X chromosome in a female somatic cell." (PubMed article 21416650). On the other hand, for the factoid question "List chromosomes that have been linked to Arnold Chiari syndrome in the literature.", Olelo presents

a list of chromosome names. Indeed, the following are the official answers in the BioASQ benchmark: "1", "3", "5", "6", "8", "9", "12", "13", "15", "16", "18", "22", "X", "Y". For this particular example, Olelo outputs an even more comprehensive answer than BioASQ, as the MeSH terms include the word "chomosome".

Preliminary evaluation. We recently compared Olelo to the three other biomedical QA systems (cf. Section 2) by manually posing 10 randomly selected factoid questions from BioASQ. We manually recorded the response time of each system and the experiments were carried out outside of the network of our institute. HONQA did not provide results for any of the questions because an error occurred in the system. Olelo found correct answers for four questions (in the returned summaries), EAGLi for two of them (in the titles of the returned documents) and AskHermes for one of them (among the many returned sentences). Regarding the response time, Olelo was the fastest one (average of 8.8 seconds), followed by AskHermes (average of 10.1 seconds) and EAGLi (average of 58.6 seconds).

5 Conclusions and Future Work

We presented our Olelo QA system for the biomedical domain. Olelo relies on built-in NLP procedures of an in-memory database and SQL procedures for the various QA components, such as multi-document summarization and detection of answer type. We have shown examples of the output provided by Olelo when obtaining information for a particular gene and for checking the answers for two questions from the BioASQ benchmark.

Nevertheless, the methods behind Olelo still present room for improvement: (a) The system does not always detect factoid questions correctly given the simple rules it uses for question type detection. In these cases, Olelo generates a short summary from the corresponding relevant documents. (b) Answers are limited to existing MeSH terms, which also support our system for further navigation (cf. Figures 2 and 3). Indeed, our experiments show that we cannot provide answers for many of the questions which expect a gene or protein name, both weakly supported in MeSH, but very frequent in BioASQ (Neves and Kraus, 2016). (c) Our document and passage retrieval components currently rely on approximate match-

---

[10]`http://www.ensembl.org/Homo_sapiens/ Gene/Summary?g=ENSG00000001626`

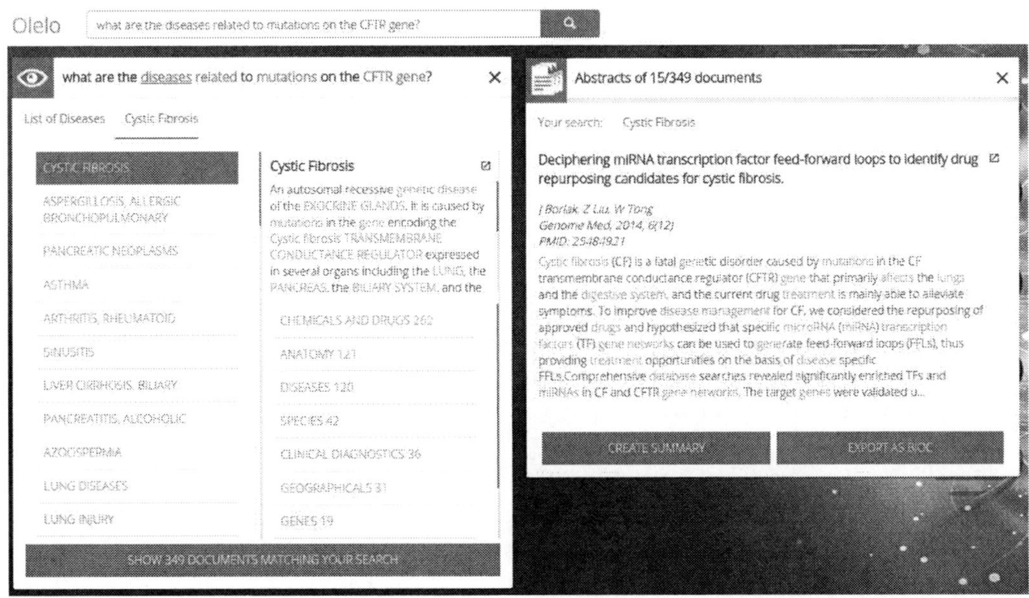

Figure 2: List of answers (disease names) potentially caused by the CFTR gene (on the left) and an overview of one of the relevant publications which contains the answer (on the right).

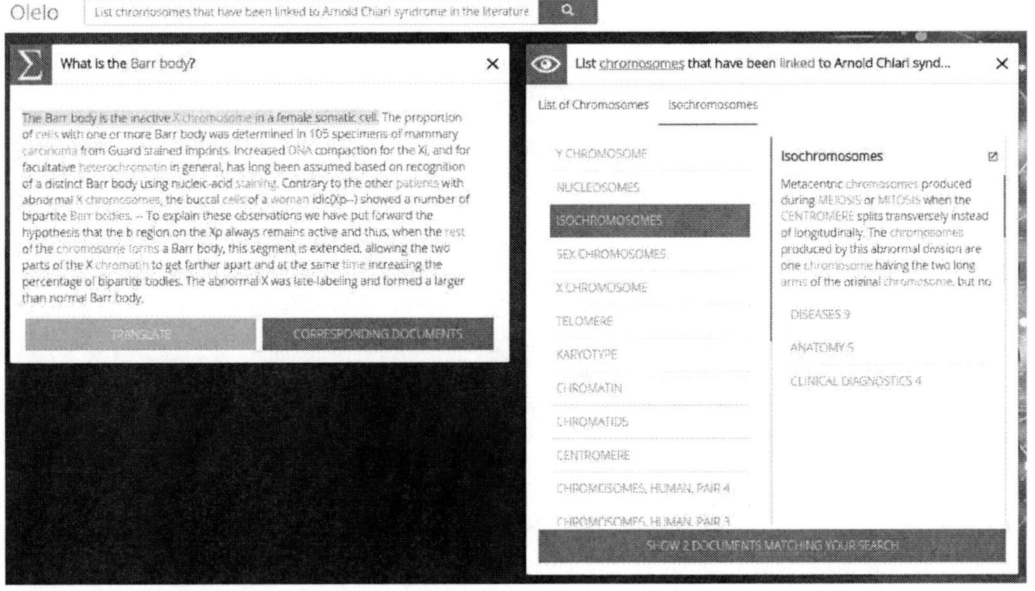

Figure 3: Short paragraph for a summary question (on the left) and list of answers (chromosome names) for a factoid question (on the right), both from the BioASQ dataset.

ing of tokens and named entities but do not consider state-of-the-art IR methods, such as TF-IDF. (d) The sentences that belong to a summary could have been better arranged. The fluency of the summaries is not optimal and we do not deal with coreferences, such as pronouns (e.g., "we") which frequently occur in the original sentences. However, when compared to other biomedical QA systems, Olelo performs faster and provides focused answers for most of the questions, instead of a long list of documents. Finally, it provides means to further explore the biomedical literature.

Olelo is under permanent development and improvements are already being implemented on multiple levels: (a) integration of more advanced NLP components, such as chunking and semantic role labeling; (b) support for yes/no questions and improvement of the extraction of exact answers based on deep learning; (c) integration of additional biomedical documents, e.g., clinical trials, as well as documents in other languages.

Finally, in its current state, adaptation of our methods to a new domain would not require major changes. Minor changes are necessary on the question processing step, which relies on specific ontologies, as well as creating new dictionaries for the NER component. In summary, adaptation of the system would mainly consist on the integration of new document collections and specific terminologies.

References

Sofia J. Athenikos and Hyoil Han. 2010. Biomedical question answering: A survey. *Computer Methods and Programs in Biomedicine* 99(1):1 – 24. https://doi.org/10.1016/j.cmpb.2009.10.003.

Olivier Bodenreider. 2004. The unified medical language system (umls): integrating biomedical terminology. *Nucleic Acids Res* 32(Database issue):D267–D270. https://doi.org/10.1093/nar/gkh061.

Yonggang Cao, Feifan Liu, Pippa Simpson, Lamont D. Antieau, Andrew S. Bennett, James J. Cimino, John W. Ely, and Hong Yu. 2011. Askhermes: An online question answering system for complex clinical questions. *Journal of Biomedical Informatics* 44(2):277–288. https://www.ncbi.nlm.nih.gov/pubmed/21256977.

Sarah Cruchet, Arnaud Gaudinat, Thomas Rindflesch, and Celia Boyer. 2009. What about trust in the question answering world? In *Proceedings of the AMIA Annual Symposium*. San Francisco, USA, pages 1–5.

Julien Gobeill, Arnaud Gaudinat, Emilie Pasche, Dina Vishnyakova, Pascale Gaudet, Amos Bairoch, and Patrick Ruch. 2015. Deep question answering for protein annotation. *Database* 2015:bav081. https://doi.org/10.1093/database/bav081.

Zhiyong Lu. 2011. Pubmed and beyond: a survey of web tools for searching biomedical literature. *Database* 2011. https://www.ncbi.nlm.nih.gov/pubmed/21245076.

Yusuke Miyao, Tomoko Ohta, Katsuya Masuda, Yoshimasa Tsuruoka, Kazuhiro Yoshida, Takashi Ninomiya, and Jun'ichi Tsujii. 2006. Semantic retrieval for the accurate identification of relational concepts in massive textbases. In *Proceedings of the 21st International Conference on Computational Linguistics and the 44th Annual Meeting of the Association for Computational Linguistics*. Association for Computational Linguistics, Stroudsburg, PA, USA, ACL-44, pages 1017–1024. https://doi.org/10.3115/1220175.1220303.

Mariana Neves. 2014. Hpi in-memory-based database system in task 2b of bioasq. In *Working Notes for CLEF 2014 Conference, Sheffield, UK, September 15-18*. pages 1337–1347. http://ceur-ws.org/Vol-1180/CLEF2014wn-QA-Neves2014.pdf.

Mariana Neves. 2015. Hpi question answering system in the bioasq 2015 challenge. In *Working Notes for CLEF 2015 Conference, Toulouse, France, September 8-11*. http://ceur-ws.org/Vol-1391/59-CR.pdf.

Mariana Neves and Milena Kraus. 2016. Biomedlat corpus: Annotation of the lexical answer type for biomedical questions. In *Proceedings of the Open Knowledge Base and Question Answering Workshop (OKBQA 2016)*. The COLING 2016 Organizing Committee, Osaka, Japan, pages 49–58. http://aclweb.org/anthology/W16-4407.

Mariana Neves and Ulf Leser. 2015. Question answering for biology. *Methods* 74:36 – 46. Text mining of biomedical literature. https://doi.org/10.1016/j.ymeth.2014.10.023.

Hasso Plattner. 2013. *A Course in In-Memory Data Management: The Inner Mechanics of In-Memory Databases*. Springer, 1st edition.

Frederik Schulze and Mariana Neves. 2016. Entity-supported summarization of biomedical abstracts. In *Proceedings of the Fifth Workshop on Building and Evaluating Resources for Biomedical Text Mining (BioTxtM2016)*. The COLING 2016 Organizing Committee, Osaka, Japan, pages 40–49. http://aclweb.org/anthology/W16-5105.

Frederik Schulze, Ricarda Schüler, Tim Draeger, Daniel Dummer, Alexander Ernst, Pedro Flemming, Cindy Perscheid, and Mariana Neves. 2016. Hpi question answering system in bioasq 2016. In *Proceedings of the Fourth BioASQ workshop at the Conference of the Association for Computational Linguistics*. pages 38–44. http://aclweb.org/anthology/W/W16/W16-3105.pdf.

George Tsatsaronis, Georgios Balikas, Prodromos Malakasiotis, Ioannis Partalas, Matthias Zschunke, Michael R Alvers, Dirk Weissenborn, Anastasia Krithara, Sergios Petridis, Dimitris Polychronopoulos, et al. 2015. An overview of the bioasq large-scale biomedical semantic indexing and question answering competition. *BMC bioinformatics* 16(1):138. https://www.ncbi.nlm.nih.gov/pubmed/25925131.

OpenNMT: Open-Source Toolkit for Neural Machine Translation

Guillaume Klein[†], Yoon Kim[*], Yuntian Deng[*], Jean Senellart[†], Alexander M. Rush[*]
SYSTRAN [†], Harvard SEAS[*]

Abstract

We describe an open-source toolkit for neural machine translation (NMT). The toolkit prioritizes efficiency, modularity, and extensibility with the goal of supporting NMT research into model architectures, feature representations, and source modalities, while maintaining competitive performance and reasonable training requirements. The toolkit consists of modeling and translation support, as well as detailed pedagogical documentation about the underlying techniques.

1 Introduction

Neural machine translation (NMT) is a new methodology for machine translation that has led to remarkable improvements, particularly in terms of human evaluation, compared to rule-based and statistical machine translation (SMT) systems (Wu et al., 2016; Crego et al., 2016). Originally developed using pure sequence-to-sequence models (Sutskever et al., 2014; Cho et al., 2014) and improved upon using attention-based variants (Bahdanau et al., 2014; Luong et al., 2015), NMT has now become a widely-applied technique for machine translation, as well as an effective approach for other related NLP tasks such as dialogue, parsing, and summarization.

As NMT approaches are standardized, it becomes more important for the machine translation and NLP community to develop open implementations for researchers to benchmark against, learn from, and extend upon. Just as the SMT community benefited greatly from toolkits like Moses (Koehn et al., 2007) for phrase-based SMT and CDec (Dyer et al., 2010) or travatar (Neubig, 2013) for syntax-based SMT, NMT toolkits can provide a foundation to build upon. A toolkit

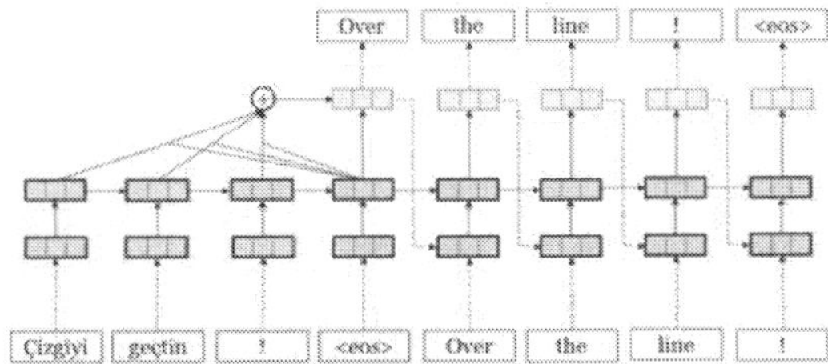

Figure 1: Schematic view of neural machine translation. The red source words are first mapped to word vectors and then fed into a recurrent neural network (RNN). Upon seeing the ⟨eos⟩ symbol, the final time step initializes a target blue RNN. At each target time step, *attention* is applied over the source RNN and combined with the current hidden state to produce a prediction $p(w_t|w_{1:t-1}, x)$ of the next word. This prediction is then fed back into the target RNN.

should aim to provide a shared framework for developing and comparing open-source systems, while at the same time being efficient and accurate enough to be used in production contexts.

Currently there are several existing NMT implementations. Many systems such as those developed in industry by Google, Microsoft, and Baidu, are closed source, and are unlikely to be released with unrestricted licenses. Many other systems such as *GroundHog*, *Blocks*, *neuralmonkey*, *tensorflow-seq2seq*, *lamtram*, and our own *seq2seq-attn*, exist mostly as research code. These libraries provide important functionality but minimal support to production users. Perhaps most promising is University of Edinburgh's *Nematus* system originally based on NYU's NMT system. Nematus provides high-accuracy translation, many options, clear documentation, and has been used in several successful research projects. In the development of this project, we aimed to build upon the strengths of this system, while providing additional documentation and functionality to provide a useful open-source NMT framework

Proceedings of the 55th Annual Meeting of the Association for Computational Linguistics-System Demonstrations, pages 67–72
Vancouver, Canada, July 30 - August 4, 2017. ©2017 Association for Computational Linguistics
https://doi.org/10.18653/v1/P17-4012

for the NLP community in academia and industry.

With these goals in mind, we introduce *OpenNMT* (`http://opennmt.net`), an open-source framework for neural machine translation. OpenNMT is a complete NMT implementation. In addition to providing code for the core translation tasks, OpenNMT was designed with three aims: (a) prioritize fast training and test efficiency, (b) maintain model modularity and readability, (c) support significant research extensibility.

This engineering report describes how the system targets these criteria. We begin by briefly surveying the background for NMT, describing the high-level implementation details, and then describing specific case studies for the three criteria. We end by showing benchmarks of the system in terms of accuracy, speed, and memory usage for several translation and translation-like tasks.

2 Background

NMT has now been extensively described in many excellent tutorials (see for instance `https://sites.google.com/site/acl16nmt/home`). We give only a condensed overview.

NMT takes a conditional language modeling view of translation by modeling the probability of a target sentence $w_{1:T}$ given a source sentence $x_{1:S}$ as $p(w_{1:T}|x) = \prod_1^T p(w_t|w_{1:t-1}, x; \theta)$. This distribution is estimated using an attention-based encoder-decoder architecture (Bahdanau et al., 2014). A source encoder recurrent neural network (RNN) maps each source word to a word vector, and processes these to a sequence of hidden vectors $\mathbf{h}_1, \ldots, \mathbf{h}_S$. The target decoder combines an RNN hidden representation of previously generated words $(w_1, \ldots w_{t-1})$ with source hidden vectors to predict scores for each possible next word. A softmax layer is then used to produce a next-word distribution $p(w_t|w_{1:t-1}, x; \theta)$. The source hidden vectors influence the distribution through an attention pooling layer that weights each source word relative to its expected contribution to the target prediction. The complete model is trained end-to-end to maximize the likelihood of the training data. An unfolded network diagram is shown in Figure 1.

In practice, there are also many other important aspects that improve the effectiveness of the base model. Here we briefly mention four areas: (a) It is important to use a gated RNN

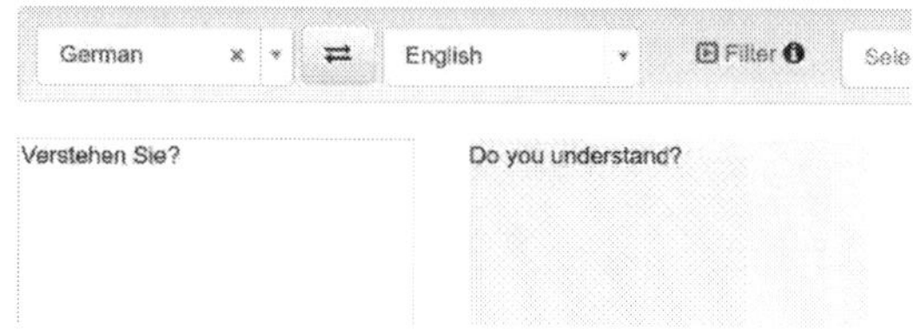

Figure 2: Live demo of the OpenNMT system across dozens of language pairs.

such as an LSTM (Hochreiter and Schmidhuber, 1997) or GRU (Chung et al., 2014) which help the model learn long-distance features within a text. (b) Translation requires relatively large, stacked RNNs, which consist of several vertical layers (2-16) of RNNs at each time step (Sutskever et al., 2014). (c) Input feeding, where the previous attention vector is fed back into the input as well as the predicted word, has been shown to be quite helpful for machine translation (Luong et al., 2015). (d) Test-time decoding is done through *beam search* where multiple hypothesis target predictions are considered at each time step. Implementing these correctly can be difficult, which motivates their inclusion in an NMT framework.

3 Implementation

OpenNMT is a complete library for training and deploying neural machine translation models. The system is successor to *seq2seq-attn* developed at Harvard, and has been completely rewritten for ease of efficiency, readability, and generalizability. It includes vanilla NMT models along with support for attention, gating, stacking, input feeding, regularization, beam search and all other options necessary for state-of-the-art performance.

The main system is implemented in the Lua/Torch mathematical framework, and can be easily be extended using Torch's internal standard neural network components. It has also been extended by Adam Lerer of Facebook Research to support Python/PyTorch framework, with the same API.

The system has been developed completely in the open on GitHub at (`http://github.com/opennmt/opennmt`) and is MIT licensed. The first version has primarily (intercontinental) contributions from SYSTRAN Paris and the Harvard NLP group. Since official beta release, the project has been starred by over 1000 users, and there have been active development by those outside of these two organizations. The project has an active forum for community feedback with over five hundred posts in the last two months. There is also a live demonstration available of the system in use (Figure 3).

One nice aspect of NMT as a model is its relative compactness. When excluding Torch framework code, the Lua OpenNMT system including preprocessing is roughly 4K lines of code, and the Python version is less than 1K lines (although slightly less feature complete). For comparison the Moses SMT framework including language modeling is over 100K lines. This makes the system easy to completely understand for newcomers. The project is fully self-contained depending on minimal number of external Lua libraries and including also a simple language independent reversible tokenization and detokenization tools.

4 Design Goals

As the low-level details of NMT have been covered previously (see for instance (Neubig, 2017)), we focus this report on the design goals of Open-NMT: system efficiency, code modularity, and model extensibility.

4.1 System Efficiency

As NMT systems can take from days to weeks to train, training efficiency is a paramount concern. Slightly faster training can make be the difference between plausible and impossible experiments.

Memory Sharing When training GPU-based NMT models, memory size restrictions are the most common limiter of batch size, and thus directly impact training time. Neural network toolkits, such as Torch, are often designed to trade-off extra memory allocations for speed and declarative simplicity. For OpenNMT, we wanted to have it both ways, and so we implemented an external memory sharing system that exploits the known time-series control flow of NMT systems and aggressively shares the internal buffers between clones. The potential shared buffers are dynamically calculated by exploration of the network graph before starting training. In practical use, aggressive memory reuse in OpenNMT provides a saving of 70% of GPU memory with the default model size.

Multi-GPU OpenNMT additionally supports multi-GPU training using data parallelism. Each GPU has a replica of the master parameters and process independent batches during training phase. Two modes are available: synchronous and asynchronous training. In synchronous training, batches on parallel GPU are run simultaneously and gradients aggregated to update master parameters before resynchronization on each GPU for the following batch. In asynchronous training, batches are run independent on each GPU, and independent gradients accumulated to the master copy of the parameters. Asynchronous SGD is known to provide faster convergence (Dean et al., 2012). Experiments with 8 GPUs show a $6\times$ speed up in per epoch, but a slight loss in training efficiency. When training to similar loss, it gives a $3.5\times$ total speed-up to training.

C/Mobile/GPU Translation Training NMT systems requires some code complexity to facilitate fast back-propagation-through-time. At deployment, the system is much less complex, and only requires (i) forwarding values through the network and (ii) running a beam search that is much simplified compared to SMT. OpenNMT includes several different translation deployments specialized for different run-time environments: a batched CPU/GPU implementation for very quickly translating a large set of sentences, a simple single-instance implementation for use on mobile devices, and a specialized C implementation. The first implementation is suited for research use, for instance allowing the user to easily include constraints on the feasible set of sentences and ideas such as pointer networks and copy mechanisms. The last implementation is particularly suited for industrial use as it can run on CPU in standard production environments; it reads the structure of the network and then uses the *Eigen* package to implement the basic linear algebra necessary for decoding. Table 4.1 compares the performance of the different implementations based on batch size, beam size, showing significant speed ups due to batching on GPU and when using the CPU/C implementation.

4.2 Modularity for Research

A secondary goal was a desire for code readability for non-experts. We targeted this goal by explicitly separating out many optimizations from the core model, and by including tutorial documenta-

Batch	Beam	GPU	CPU	CPU/C
1	5	209.0	24.1	62.2
1	1	166.9	23.3	84.9
30	5	646.8	104.0	116.2
30	1	535.1	128.5	392.7

Table 1: Translation speed in source tokens per second for the Torch CPU/GPU implementations and for the multi-threaded CPU C implementation. (Run with Intel i7/GTX 1080)

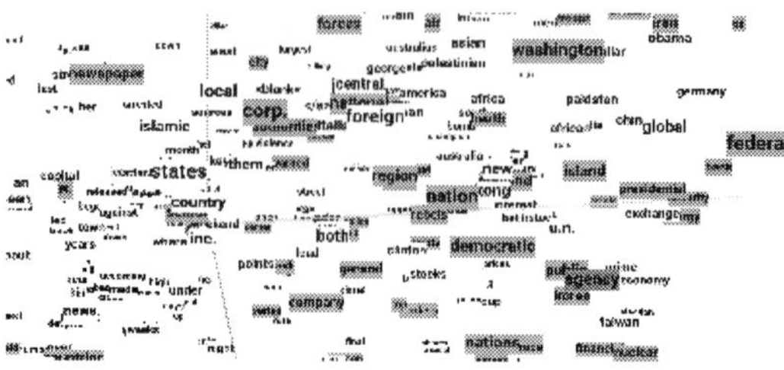

Figure 3: 3D Visualization of OpenNMT source embedding from the TensorBoard visualization system.

tion within the code. To test whether this approach would allow novel feature development we experimented with two case studies.

Case Study: Factored Neural Translation In feature-based factored neural translation (Sennrich and Haddow, 2016), instead of generating a word at each time step, the model generates both word and associated features. For instance, the system might include words and separate case features. This extension requires modifying both the inputs and the output of the decoder to generate multiple symbols. In OpenNMT both of these aspects are abstracted from the core translation code, and therefore factored translation simply modifies the input network to instead process the feature-based representation, and the output generator network to instead produce multiple conditionally independent predictions.

Case Study: Attention Networks The use of attention over the encoder at each step of translation is crucial for the model to perform well. The default method is to utilize the global attention mechanism. However there are many other types of attention that have recently proposed including local attention (Luong et al., 2015), sparse-max attention (Martins and Astudillo, 2016), hierarchical attention (Yang et al., 2016) among others. As this is simply a module in OpenNMT it can easily be substituted. Recently the Harvard group developed a *structured* attention approach, that utilizes graphical model inference to compute this attention. The method is quite computationally complex; however as it is modularized by the Torch interface, it can be used in OpenNMT to substitute for standard attention.

4.3 Extensibility

Deep learning is a quickly evolving field. Recently work such as variational seq2seq auto-encoders (Bowman et al., 2016) or memory networks (Weston et al., 2014), propose interesting extensions to basic seq2seq models. We next discuss a case study to demonstrate that OpenNMT is extensible to future variants.

Multiple Modalities Recent work has shown that NMT-like systems are effective for image-to-text generation tasks (Xu et al., 2015). This task is quite different from standard machine translation as the source sentence is now an image. However, the future of translation may require this style of (multi-)modal inputs (e.g. `http://www.statmt.org/wmt16/multimodal-task.html`).

As a case study, we adapted two systems with non-textual inputs to run in OpenNMT. The first is an image-to-text system developed for mathematical OCR (Deng et al., 2016). This model replaces the source RNN with a deep convolution over the source input. Excepting preprocessing, the entire adaptation requires less than 500 lines of additional code and is also open-sourced as `github.com/opennmt/im2text`. The second is a speech-to-text recognition system based on the work of Chan et al. (2015). This system has been implemented directly in OpenNMT by replacing the source encoder with a Pyrimidal source model.

4.4 Additional Tools

Finally we briefly summarize some of the additional tools that extend OpenNMT to make it more beneficial to the research community.

Tokenization We aimed for OpenNMT to be a standalone project and not depend on commonly used tools. For instance the Moses tokenizer has language specific heuristics not necessary in NMT. We therefore include a simple reversible tokenizer that (a) includes markers seen by the model that allow simple deterministic deto-

	ES	FR	IT	PT	RO
ES	-	32.7 (+5.4)	28.0 (+4.6)	34.4 (+6.1)	28.7 (+6.4)
FR	32.9 (+3.3)	-	26.3 (+4.3)	30.9 (+5.2)	26.0 (+6.6)
IT	31.6 (+5.3)	31.0 (+5.8)	-	28.0 (+5.0)	24.3 (+5.9)
PT	35.3 (+10.4)	34.1 (+4.7)	28.1 (+5.6)	-	28.7 (+5.0)
RO	35.0 (+5.4)	31.9 (+9.0)	26.4 (+6.3)	31.6 (+7.3)	-

Table 2: 20 language pair single translation model. Table shows BLEU(Δ) where Δ compares to only using the pair for training.

Vocab	System	Speed tok/sec		BLEU
		Train	Trans	
V=50k	Nematus	3393	284	17.28
	ONMT	4185	380	17.60
V=32k	Nematus	3221	252	18.25
	ONMT	5254	457	19.34

Table 3: Performance Results for EN→DE on WMT15 tested on *newstest2014*. Both system 2x500 RNN, embedding size 300, 13 epochs, batch size 64, beam size 5. We compare on a 50k vocabulary and a 32k BPE setting. OpenNMT shows improvements in speed and accuracy compared to Nematus.

kenization, (b) has extremely simple, language-independent tokenization rules. The tokenizer can also perform Byte Pair Encoding (BPE) which has become a popular method for sub-word tokenization in NMT systems (Sennrich et al., 2015).

Word Embeddings OpenNMT includes tools for simplifying the process of using pretrained word embeddings, even allowing automatic download of embeddings for many languages. This allows training in languages or domain with relatively little aligned data. Additionally OpenNMT can export the word embeddings from trained models to standard formats, allowing analysis in external tools such as TensorBoard (Figure 3).

5 Benchmarks

We now document some runs of the model. We expect performance and memory usage to improve with further development. Public benchmarks are available at `http://opennmt.net/Models/`, which also includes publicly available pre-trained models for all of these tasks and tutorial instructions for all of these tasks. The benchmarks are run on a Intel(R) Core(TM) i7-5930K CPU @ 3.50GHz, 256GB Mem, trained on 1 GPU GeForce GTX 1080 (Pascal) with CUDA v. 8.0 (driver 375.20) and cuDNN (v. 5005).

The comparison, shown in Table 3, is on English-to-German (EN→DE) using the WMT 2015[1] dataset. Here we compare, BLEU score, as well as training and test speed to the publicly available *Nematus* system. [2]

We additionally trained a multilingual translation model following Johnson (2016). The model translates from and to French, Spanish, Portuguese, Italian, and Romanian. Training data is 4M sentences and was selected from the open parallel corpus[3], specifically from Europarl, GlobalVoices and Ted. Corpus was selected to be multi-source, multi-target: each sentence has its translation in the 4 other languages. Corpus was tokenized using shared Byte Pair Encoding of 32k. Comparative results between multi-way translation and each of the 20 independent training are presented in Table 2. The systematically large improvement shows that language pair benefits from training jointly with the other language pairs.

Additionally we have found interest from the community in using OpenNMT for non-standard MT tasks like sentence document summarization dialogue response generation (chatbots), among others. Using OpenNMT, we were able to replicate the sentence summarization results of Chopra et al. (2016), reaching a ROUGE-1 score of 33.13 on the Gigaword data. We have also trained a model on 14 million sentences of the OpenSubtitles data set based on the work Vinyals and Le (2015), achieving comparable perplexity.

6 Conclusion

We introduce *OpenNMT*, a research toolkit for NMT that prioritizes efficiency and modularity. We hope to further develop OpenNMT to maintain strong MT results at the research frontier, providing a stable and framework for production use.

---

[1] `http://statmt.org/wmt15`

[2] `https://github.com/rsennrich/nematus`. Comparison with OpenNMT/Nematus github revisions `907824/75c6ab1`.

[3] `http://opus.lingfil.uu.se`

References

Dzmitry Bahdanau, Kyunghyun Cho, and Yoshua Bengio. 2014. Neural Machine Translation By Jointly Learning To Align and Translate. In *ICLR*. pages 1–15. https://doi.org/10.1146/annurev.neuro.26.041002.131047.

Samuel R. Bowman, Luke Vilnis, Oriol Vinyals, Andrew M. Dai, Rafal Józefowicz, and Samy Bengio. 2016. Generating sentences from a continuous space. In *Proceedings of the 20th SIGNLL Conference on Computational Natural Language Learning, CoNLL 2016, Berlin, Germany, August 11-12, 2016.* pages 10–21. http://aclweb.org/anthology/K/K16/K16-1002.pdf.

William Chan, Navdeep Jaitly, Quoc V. Le, and Oriol Vinyals. 2015. Listen, attend and spell. *CoRR* abs/1508.01211. http://arxiv.org/abs/1508.01211.

Kyunghyun Cho, Bart van Merrienboer, Caglar Gulcehre, Dzmitry Bahdanau, Fethi Bougares, Holger Schwenk, and Yoshua Bengio. 2014. Learning Phrase Representations using RNN Encoder-Decoder for Statistical Machine Translation. In *Proc of EMNLP*.

Sumit Chopra, Michael Auli, Alexander M Rush, and SEAS Harvard. 2016. Abstractive sentence summarization with attentive recurrent neural networks. *Proceedings of NAACL-HLT16* pages 93–98.

Junyoung Chung, Caglar Gulcehre, KyungHyun Cho, and Yoshua Bengio. 2014. Empirical evaluation of gated recurrent neural networks on sequence modeling. *arXiv preprint arXiv:1412.3555* .

Josep Crego, Jungi Kim, and Jean Senellart. 2016. Systran's pure neural machine translation system. *arXiv preprint arXiv:1602.06023* .

Jeffrey Dean, Greg Corrado, Rajat Monga, Kai Chen, Matthieu Devin, Mark Mao, Andrew Senior, Paul Tucker, Ke Yang, Quoc V Le, et al. 2012. Large scale distributed deep networks. In *Advances in neural information processing systems*. pages 1223–1231.

Yuntian Deng, Anssi Kanervisto, and Alexander M. Rush. 2016. What you get is what you see: A visual markup decompiler. *CoRR* abs/1609.04938. http://arxiv.org/abs/1609.04938.

Chris Dyer, Jonathan Weese, Hendra Setiawan, Adam Lopez, Ferhan Ture, Vladimir Eidelman, Juri Ganitkevitch, Phil Blunsom, and Philip Resnik. 2010. cdec: A decoder, alignment, and learning framework for finite-state and context-free translation models. In *Proc ACL*. Association for Computational Linguistics, pages 7–12.

Sepp Hochreiter and Jürgen Schmidhuber. 1997. Long short-term memory. *Neural computation* 9(8):1735–1780.

Mike Schuster Quoc V. Le Maxim Krikun Yonghui Wu Zhifeng Chen Nikhil Thorat Fernanda Vigas Martin Wattenberg Greg Corrado Macduff Hughes Jeffrey Dean Johnson. 2016. Google's multilingual neural machine translation system: Enabling zero-shot translation .

Philipp Koehn, Hieu Hoang, Alexandra Birch, Chris Callison-Burch, Marcello Federico, Nicola Bertoldi, Brooke Cowan, Wade Shen, Christine Moran, Richard Zens, et al. 2007. Moses: Open source toolkit for statistical machine translation. In *Proc ACL*. Association for Computational Linguistics, pages 177–180.

Minh-Thang Luong, Hieu Pham, and Christopher D. Manning. 2015. Effective Approaches to Attention-based Neural Machine Translation. In *Proc of EMNLP*.

André FT Martins and Ramón Fernandez Astudillo. 2016. From softmax to sparsemax: A sparse model of attention and multi-label classification. *arXiv preprint arXiv:1602.02068* .

G. Neubig. 2017. Neural Machine Translation and Sequence-to-sequence Models: A Tutorial. *ArXiv e-prints* .

Graham Neubig. 2013. Travatar: A forest-to-string machine translation engine based on tree transducers. In *Proc ACL*. Sofia, Bulgaria.

Rico Sennrich and Barry Haddow. 2016. Linguistic input features improve neural machine translation. *arXiv preprint arXiv:1606.02892* .

Rico Sennrich, Barry Haddow, and Alexandra Birch. 2015. Neural machine translation of rare words with subword units. *CoRR* abs/1508.07909. http://arxiv.org/abs/1508.07909.

Ilya Sutskever, Oriol Vinyals, and Quoc V. Le. 2014. Sequence to Sequence Learning with Neural Networks. In *NIPS*. page 9. http://arxiv.org/abs/1409.3215.

Oriol Vinyals and Quoc Le. 2015. A neural conversational model. *arXiv preprint arXiv:1506.05869* .

Jason Weston, Sumit Chopra, and Antoine Bordes. 2014. Memory networks. *CoRR* abs/1410.3916. http://arxiv.org/abs/1410.3916.

Yonghui Wu, Mike Schuster, Zhifeng Chen, Quoc V Le, Mohammad Norouzi, Wolfgang Macherey, Maxim Krikun, Yuan Cao, Qin Gao, Klaus Macherey, et al. 2016. Google's neural machine translation system: Bridging the gap between human and machine translation. *arXiv preprint arXiv:1609.08144* .

Kelvin Xu, Jimmy Ba, Ryan Kiros, Kyunghyun Cho, Aaron C. Courville, Ruslan Salakhutdinov, Richard S. Zemel, and Yoshua Bengio. 2015. Show, attend and tell: Neural image caption generation with visual attention. *CoRR* abs/1502.03044. http://arxiv.org/abs/1502.03044.

Zichao Yang, Diyi Yang, Chris Dyer, Xiaodong He, Alex Smola, and Eduard Hovy. 2016. Hierarchical attention networks for document classification. In *Proc ACL*.

PyDial: A Multi-domain Statistical Dialogue System Toolkit

Stefan Ultes, Lina Rojas-Barahona, Pei-Hao Su, David Vandyke[*], Dongho Kim[†], Iñigo Casanueva, Paweł Budzianowski, Nikola Mrkšić, Tsung-Hsien Wen, Milica Gašić and Steve Young
Cambridge University Engineering Department, Trumpington Street, Cambridge, UK
`{su259,lmr46,phs26,ic340,pfb30,nm480,thw28,mg436,sjy11}@cam.ac.uk`

Abstract

Statistical Spoken Dialogue Systems have been around for many years. However, access to these systems has always been difficult as there is still no publicly available end-to-end system implementation. To alleviate this, we present PyDial, an open-source end-to-end statistical spoken dialogue system toolkit which provides implementations of statistical approaches for all dialogue system modules. Moreover, it has been extended to provide multi-domain conversational functionality. It offers easy configuration, easy extensibility, and domain-independent implementations of the respective dialogue system modules. The toolkit is available for download under the Apache 2.0 license.

1 Introduction

Designing speech interfaces to machines has been a focus of research for many years. These Spoken Dialogue Systems (SDSs) are typically based on a modular architecture consisting of input processing modules speech recognition and semantic decoding, dialogue management modules belief tracking and policy, and output processing modules language generation and speech synthesis (see Fig. 1).

Statistical SDS are speech interfaces where all SDS modules are based on statistical models learned from data (in contrast to hand-crafted rules). Examples of statistical approaches to various components of a dialogue system can be found in (Levin and Pieraccini, 1997; Jurafsky and Martin, 2008; De Mori et al., 2008; Thomson and Young, 2010; Lemon and Pietquin, 2012; Young

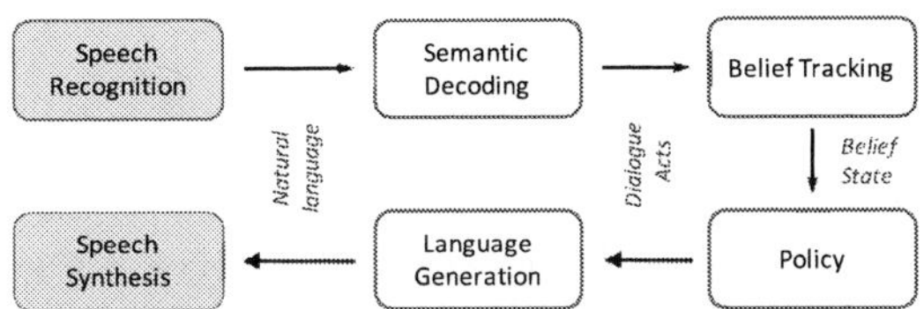

Figure 1: Architecture of a modular Spoken Dialoug System.

et al., 2013; Wen et al., 2015; Su et al., 2016; Wen et al., 2017; Mrkšić et al., 2017).

Despite the rich body of research on statistical SDS, there is still no common platform or open toolkit available. Other toolkit implementations usually focus on single modules (e.g. (Williams et al., 2010; Ultes and Minker, 2014) or are not full-blown statistical systems (e.g. (Lison and Kennington, 2016; Bohus and Rudnicky, 2009)). The availability of a toolkit targetted specifically at statistical dialogue systems would enable people new to the field would be able to get involved more easily, results to be compared more easily, and researchers to focus on their specific research questions instead of re-implementing algorithms (e.g., evaluating understanding or generation components in an interaction).

Hence, to stimulate research and make it easy for people to get involved in statistical spoken dialogue systems, we present PyDial, a multi-domain statistical spoken dialogue system toolkit. PyDial is implemented in Python and is actively used by the Cambridge Dialogue Systems Group.

PyDial supports multi-domain applications in which a conversation may range over a number of different topics. This introduces a variety of new research issues including generalised belief tracking (Mrkšić et al., 2015; Lee and Stent, 2016) rapid policy adaptation and parallel learning (Gašić et al., 2015a,b) and natural language generation (Wen et al., 2016).

---

[*] now with Apple Inc., Cambridge, UK
[†] now with PROWLER.io Limited, Cambridge, UK

Proceedings of the 55th Annual Meeting of the Association for Computational Linguistics-System Demonstrations, pages 73–78
Vancouver, Canada, July 30 - August 4, 2017. ©2017 Association for Computational Linguistics
https://doi.org/10.18653/v1/P17-4013

The remainder of the paper is organized as follows: in Section 2, the general architecture of PyDial is presented along with the extension of the SDS architecture to multiple domains and PyDial's key application principles. Section 3 contains details of the implemented dialogue system modules. The available domains are listed in Section 4 out of which two are used for the example interactions in Section 5. Finally, Section 6 summarizes the key contributions of this toolkit.

2 PyDial Architecture

This section presents the architecture of PyDial and the way it interfaces to its environment. Subsequently, the extension of single-domain functionality to enable conversations over multiple domains is described. Finally, we discuss the three key principles underlying PyDial design.

2.1 General System Architecture

The general architecture of PyDial is shown in Figure 2. The main component is called Agent which resides at the core of the system. It encapsulates all dialogue system modules to enable text-based interaction, i.e. typed (as opposed to spoken) input and output. The dialogue system modules rely on the domain specification defined by an Ontology. For interacting with its environment, PyDial offers three interfaces: the Dialogue Server, which allows spoken interaction, the Texthub, which allows typed interaction, and the User Simulation system. The performance of the interaction is monitored by the Evaluation component.

The **Agent** is responsible for the dialogue interaction. Hence, the internal architecture is similar to the architecture presented in Figure 1. The pipeline contains the dialogue system modules semantic parser, which transforms textual input to a semantic representation, the belief tracker, which is responsible for maintaining the internal dialogue state representation called the belief state, the policy, which maps the belief state to a suitable system dialogue act, and the semantic output, which transforms the system dialogue act to a textual representation. For multi-domain functionality, a topic tracker is needed whose functionality will be explained in Section 2.2. The Agent also maintains the dialogue sessions, i.e., ensures that each input is routed to the correct dialogue. Thus, multiple dialogues may be supported by instantiating multiple agents.

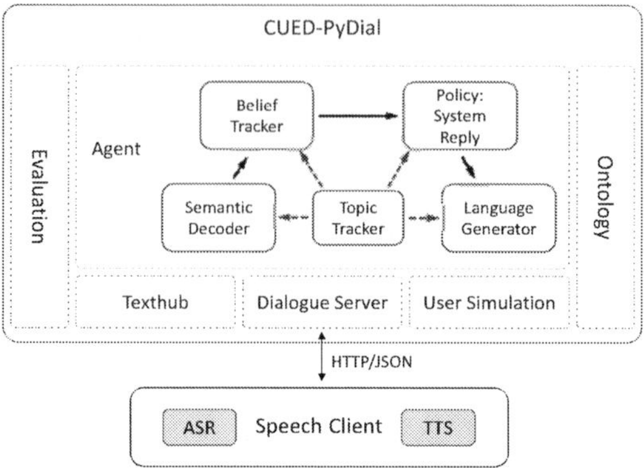

Figure 2: The general architecture of PyDial: the Agent resides at the core and the interfaces Texthub, Dialogue Server and User Simulation provide the link to the environment.

The **User Simulation** component provides simulation of dialogues on the semantic level, i.e., not using any semantic parser or language generation. This is a widely used technique for training and evaluating reinforcement learning-based algorithms since it avoids the need for costly data collection exercises and user trials. It does of course provide only an approximation to real user behaviour, so results obtained through simulation should be viewed with caution!

To enable the Agent to communicate with its environment, PyDial offers two modes: speech and text. As the native interface of the PyDial is text-based, the **Texthub** simply connects the Agent to a terminal. To enable speech-based dialogue, the **Dialogue Server** allows connecting to an external speech client. This client is responsible for mapping the input speech signal to text using Automatic Speech Recognition (ASR) and for mapping the output text to speech (TTS) using speech synthesis. The speech client connects to the Dialogue Server via HTTP exchanging JSON messages. Note that the speech client is not part of PyDial. Cloud-based services for ASR and TTS are widely available from providers like Google[1], Microsoft[2], or IBM[3]. PyDial is currently connected to DialPort (Zhao et al., 2016) allowing speech-based interaction.

Alongside the agent and the interface compo-

-----

[1] https://cloud.google.com/speech
[2] https://www.microsoft.com/cognitive-services/en-us/speech-api
[3] http://www.ibm.com/watson/developercloud/speech-to-text.html

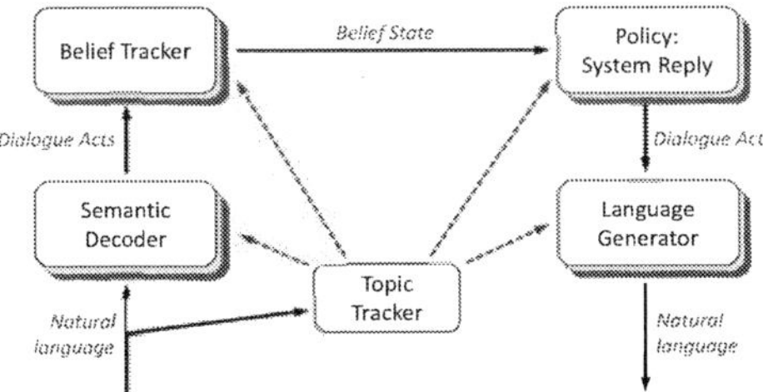

Figure 3: The multi-domain dialogue system architecture: for each module there is an instance for each domain. During runtime, a topic tracker identifies the domain of the current input which is then delegated to the respective domain-pipeline.

nents resides the **Ontology** which encapsulates the dialogue domain specification as well as the access to the back-end data base, e.g., set of restaurants and their properties. Modelled as a global object, it is used by most dialogue system modules and the user simulator for obtaining the relevant information about user actions, slots, slot values, and system actions.

The **Evaluation** component is used to compute evaluation measures for the dialogues, e.g., Task Success. For dialogue modules based on Reinforcement Learning, the Evaluation component is also responsible for providing the reward.

2.2 Multi-domain Dialogue System Architecture

One of the main aims of PyDial is to enable conversations ranging over multiple domains. To achieve this, modifications to the single-domain dialogue system pipeline are necessary. Note that the current multi-domain architecture as shown in Figure 3 assumes that each user input belongs to exactly one domain and that only the user is allowed to switch domains.

To identify the domain the user input or the current sub-dialogue belongs to, a module called the **Topic Tracker** is provided. Based on the identified domain, domain-specific instances of each dialogue module are loaded. For example, if the domain *CamRestaurants* is found, the dialogue pipeline consists of the *CamRestaurants*-instances of the semantic decoder, the belief tracker, the policy, and the language generator.

To handle the various domain instances, every module type has a Manager which stores all of the domain-specific instances in a dictionary-like structure. These instances are only created once

for each domain (and each agent). Subsequent inquiries to the same domain are then handled by the same instances.

2.3 Key Principles

To allow PyDial to be applied to new problems easily, the PyDial architecture is designed to support three key principles:

Domain Independence Wherever possible, the implementation of the dialogue modules is kept separate from the domain specification. Thus, the main functionality is domain independent, i.e., by simply using a different domain specification, simulated dialogues using belief tracker and policy are possible. To achieve this, the Ontology handles all domain-related functionality and is accessible system-wide.

While this is completely true for the belief tracker, the policy, and the user simulator, the semantic decoder and the language generator inevitably have some domain-dependency and each needs domain-specific models to be loaded.

Easy Configurability To use PyDial, all relevant functionality can be controlled via a configuration file. This specifies the domains of the conversation, the variant of each domain module, which is used in the pipeline, and its parameters. For example, to use a hand-crafted policy in the domain *CamRestaurants*, a configuration section `[policy_CamRestaurants]` with the entry `policytype = hdc` is used. The configuration file is then loaded by Pydial and the resulting configuration object is globally accessible.

Extensibility One additional benefit of introducing the manager concept described in Sec. 2.2 is to allow for easy extensibility. As shown with the example in Figure 4, each manager contains a set of D domain instances. The class of each domain instance inherits from the interface class and must implement all of its interface methods.

To add a new module, the respective class simply needs to adhere to the required interface definition. To use it in the running system, the configuration parameter may simply point to the new class, e.g., `policytype = policy.HDCPolicy.HDCPolicy`. The following modules and components support this functionality: Topic Tracker, Semantic Decoder, Belief Tracker, Policy, Language Generator, and Evaluation. Since the configuration file is a simple text file, new entries can be added easily using

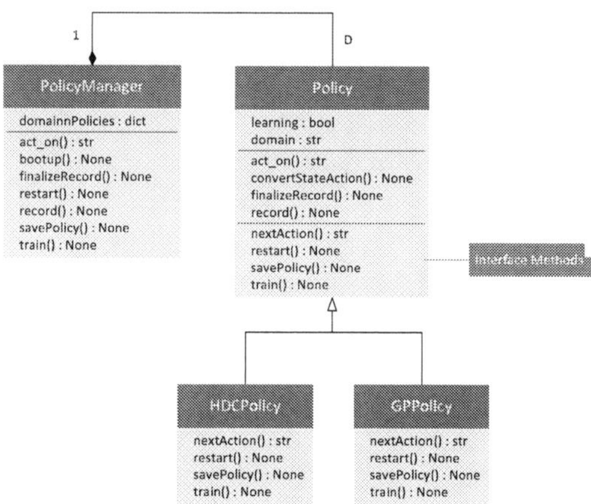

Figure 4: The UML diagram of the policy module. The interface class defines the interface methods for each policy implementation as well as general behaviour relevant for all types of policies. The sub-classes only have to implement the required interface methods. All other modules of the agent have a similar manager-interface architecture.

a convenient text editor and any special configuration options can easily be added.

To add a new domain, a simulated interaction is already possible simply by defining the ontology along with the database. For text-based interaction, an additional understanding and generation component is necessary.

3 Implementation

The PyDial toolkit is a research system under continuous development. It is available for free download from http://pydial.org under the Apache 2.0 license[4]. The following implementations of the various system modules are available in the initial release, however, more will appear in due course.

Semantic Decoder To semantically decode the input sentence (or n-best-list of sentences), PyDial offers a rule-based implementation using regular expressions and a statistical model based on Support Vector Machines, the Semantic Tuple Classifier (Mairesse et al., 2009). For the latter, a model for the *CamRestaurants* domain is provided.

Belief Tracker For tracking the belief state, the rule-based focus tracker is available (Henderson et al., 2014). The implementation is domain-independent. All domain-specific information is drawn from the ontology.

Policy The decision making module responsible for the policy has two implementations: a hand-crafted policy (which should work with any domain) and a Gaussian process (GP) reinforcement-learning policy (Gašić and Young, 2014). For multi-domain dialogue, the policy may be handled like all other modules by a policy manager. Given the domain of each user input, the respective domain policy will be selected.

Additionally, a Bayesian committee machine (BCM) as proposed in Gašić et al. (2015b) is available as an alternative handler: when processing the belief state of one domain, the policies of other domains are consulted to select the final system action. For this to work, the belief state is mapped to an abstract representation which then allows all policies to access it. Within PyDial, trained policies may be moved between the committee-based handler and the standard policy manager handler, i.e., policies trained outside of the committee (in a single- or multi-domain setting) may be used within the committee and vice versa.

Language Generator For mapping the semantic system action to text, PyDial offers two module implementations. For all domains, rule definitions for a template-based language generation are provided. In addition, the LSTM-based language generator as proposed by Wen et al. (2015) is included along with a pre-trained model for the *CamRestaurants* domain.

Topic Tracker PyDial provides an implementation of a keyword-based topic tracker. If the topic tracker has identified a domain for some user input, it will continue with that domain until a new domain is identified. Hence not every user input must contain relevant keywords. If the topic tracker is not able to initially identify the domain, it creates its own meta-dialogue with the user until the initial domain has been identified or a maximum of number of retries has been reached.

Evaluation To evaluate the dialogues, there are currently two success-based modules implemented. The objective task success evaluator compares the constraints and requests the system identifies with the true values. The latter may either be derived from the user simulator or, in real dialogues, by specifying a predefined task. For real dialogues, a subjective task success evaluator may also be applied which queries the user about the outcome of the dialogue.

---

[4]`www.apache.org/licenses/LICENSE-2.0`

User Simulation The implementation of the simulated user uses the agenda-based user simulator (Schatzmann et al., 2006). The simulator contains the user model and an error model thus creating a n-best-list of user acts to simulate the noisy speech channel. By using a set of generally applicable parameters, the simulator may be applied for all domains. The domain-specific information is taken from the ontology.

4 Domains

The main focus of PyDial is task-oriented dialogue where the user has to find a matching entity based on a number of constraints. Once the entity is found, the user can request additional information. For this scenario, PyDial is pre-loaded with a total of ten domains of differing complexity:

Domain	Constraints*	Requests†	Entities
CamRestaurants	3	9	110
CamHotels	5	11	33
CamAttractions	3	9	79
CamShops	2	6	21
CamTransport	2	6	5
SFRestaurants	6	11	271
SFHotels	6	10	182
Laptops6	6	10	123
Laptops11	11	21	123
TV	6	14	94

** # data base search constraints, † # information the user can request*

As earlier stated, all policy implementations as well as the belief tracker and the user simulator implementations are independent of the domain. Thus, simulated interactions are possible over all domains. Furthermore, the semantic decoder and the language generator depend to some degree on domain-specific implementations. PyDial contains rule-based semantic decoders for all domains and a statistical decoder for *CamRestaurants*. Also, PyDial comprises template-based language generation for most domains and a statistical LSTM-based generator for *CamRestaurants*. Thus, a fully statistical conversation is possible in the *CamRestaurants* domain.

5 Examples

To illustrate the functionality of PyDial, a GP policy in the *CamRestaurants* and one in the *SFRestaurants* domain is trained in simulation using the objective success evaluator. The final reward is +20 if the dialogue was successful minus the total number of dialogue turns. After 1,000 training dialogues, the policies achieve a task success rate of 95.4% for *CamRestaurants* and 92.0% for *SFRestaurants* when evaluated with 1,000 additional dialogues.

An example multi-domain text-based interaction in the domains *SFRestaurants* and *SFHotels* is shown in the following:

S:	Hello, welcome to the San Francisco restaurant and hotel dialogue system. How may I help you?
U:	I am looking for a hotel where dogs are not allowed
S:	Would you like a hotel that has internet?
U:	i don't care
S:	Where would you like it to be near to?
U:	a cheap hotel in the area of downtown
S:	Would you like a hotel that accepts credit cards?
U:	i don't care
S:	grant hotel is a nice place, it is in the area of downtown , where no dogs are allowed , it is in the inexpensive price range , it has internet and it accepts credit cards .
U:	I am also looking for a cheap vegetarian restaurant
S:	What part of town do you have in mind?
U:	I don't care but it should be for lunch
S:	Would you like something in the cheap, moderate, or expensive price range?
U:	cheap
S:	What kind of food would you like?
U:	vegetarian
S:	What part of town do you have in mind?
U:	I don't care
S:	Lucky creation restaurant is a nice place, it is good for lunch , it is in the cheap price range , it serves vegetarian food and it is in the area of chinatown .
U:	bye
S:	Goodbye.

6 Conclusion

We have presented PyDial, an open-source multi-domain statistical dialogue system toolkit implemented in Python. To facilitate research on statistical dialogue systems, it aims to provide a simple and accessible programming environment for implementing and evaluating new algorithms. Following the key principles of domain-independence, configurability and extensibility, PyDial is built around a modular architecture enabling end-to-end interaction using text or speech input. The toolkit offers example implementations of state-of-the-art statistical dialogue modules and the capability for conversing over multiple domains within a single dialogue.

Source code and documentation

The PyDial source code, step-by-step tutorials and the latest updates can be found on http://pydial.org. This research was funded by the EPSRC grant EP/M018946/1 *Open Domain Statistical Spoken Dialogue Systems*.

References

Dan Bohus and Alexander I Rudnicky. 2009. The ravenclaw dialog management framework: Architecture and systems. *Computer Speech & Language* 23(3):332–361.

R De Mori, F Bechet, D Hakkani-Tur, M McTear, G Riccardi, and G Tur. 2008. Spoken language understanding. *IEEE Signal Processing Magazine* 25(3):50–58.

Milica Gašić, Dongho Kim, Pirros Tsiakoulis, and Steve Young. 2015a. Distributed dialogue policies for multi-domain statistical dialogue management. In *Proceedings of ICASSP*. IEEE, pages 5371–5375.

Milica Gašić, Nikola Mrkšić, Pei-Hao Su, David Vandyke, Tsung-Hsien Wen, and Steve J. Young. 2015b. Policy committee for adaptation in multi-domain spoken dialogue systems. In *Proceedings of ASRU*. pages 806–812. https://doi.org/10.1109/asru.2015.7404871.

Milica Gašić and Steve J. Young. 2014. Gaussian processes for POMDP-based dialogue manager optimization. *IEEE/ACM Transactions on Audio, Speech, and Language Processing* 22(1):28–40.

Matthew Henderson, Blaise Thomson, and Jason Williams. 2014. The second dialog state tracking challenge. In *Proceedings of SIGDial.*

Daniel Jurafsky and James H. Martin. 2008. *Speech and Language Processing*. Prentice Hall, 2 edition.

Sungjin Lee and Amanda Stent. 2016. Task lineages: Dialog state tracking for flexible interaction. In *Proceedings of SIGDial*. ACL, Los Angeles, pages 11–21. http://www.aclweb.org/anthology/W16-3602.

Oliver Lemon and Olivier Pietquin. 2012. *Data-Driven Methods for Adaptive Spoken Dialogue Systems*. Springer New York. https://doi.org/10.1007/978-1-4614-4803-7.

Esther Levin and Roberto Pieraccini. 1997. A stochastic model of computer-human interaction for learning dialogue strategies. In *Eurospeech*. volume 97, pages 1883–1886.

Pierre Lison and Casey Kennington. 2016. Opendial: A toolkit for developing spoken dialogue systems with probabilistic rules. In *Proceedings of ACL.*

François Mairesse, Milica Gasic, Filip Jurcícek, Simon Keizer, Blaise Thomson, Kai Yu, and Steve Young. 2009. Spoken language understanding from unaligned data using discriminative classification models. In *Proceedings of ICASSP*. IEEE, pages 4749–4752.

Nikola Mrkšić, Diarmuid Ó Séaghdha, Blaise Thomson, Milica Gašić, Pei-Hao Su, David Vandyke, Tsung-Hsien Wen, and Steve Young. 2015. Multi-domain dialog state tracking using recurrent neural networks. In *Proceedings of ACL.* http://www.aclweb.org/anthology/P15-2130.

Nikola Mrkšić, Diarmuid Ó Séaghdha, Blaise Thomson, Tsung-Hsien Wen, and Steve Young. 2017. Neural Belief Tracker: Data-driven dialogue state tracking. In *Proceedings of ACL.*

Jost Schatzmann, Karl Weilhammer, Matt N. Stuttle, and Steve J. Young. 2006. A survey of statistical user simulation techniques for reinforcement-learning of dialogue management strategies. *The Knowledge Engineering Review* 21(2):97–126.

Pei-Hao Su, Milica Gašić, Nikola Mrkšić, Lina Rojas-Barahona, Stefan Ultes, David Vandyke, Tsung-Hsien Wen, and Steve Young. 2016. On-line active reward learning for policy optimisation in spoken dialogue systems. In *Proceedings of ACL.*

Blaise Thomson and Steve J. Young. 2010. Bayesian update of dialogue state: A POMDP framework for spoken dialogue systems. *Computer Speech & Language* 24(4):562–588.

Stefan Ultes and Wolfgang Minker. 2014. Managing adaptive spoken dialogue for intelligent environments. *Journal of Ambient Intelligence and Smart Environments* 6(5):523–539. https://doi.org/10.3233/ais-140275.

Tsung-Hsien Wen, Milica Gašić, Nikola Mrkšić, Lina M. Rojas-Barahona, Pei-Hao Su, David Vandyke, and Steve Young. 2016. Multi-domain neural network language generation for spoken dialogue systems. In *Proceedings of NAACL-HLT.* http://www.aclweb.org/anthology/N16-1015.

Tsung-Hsien Wen, Milica Gašić, Nikola Mrkšić, Pei-Hao Su, David Vandyke, and Steve Young. 2015. Semantically conditioned lstm-based natural language generation for spoken dialogue systems. In *Proceedings of EMNLP*. ACL, Lisbon, Portugal, pages 1711–1721. https://aclweb.org/anthology/D/D15/D15-1199.

Tsung-Hsien Wen, David Vandyke, Nikola Mrkšić, Milica Gašić, Lina M. Rojas-Barahona, Pei-Hao Su, Stefan Ultes, and Steve Young. 2017. A network-based end-to-end trainable task-oriented dialogue system. In *Proceedings of EACL.*

Jason D Williams, Iker Arizmendi, and Alistair Conkie. 2010. Demonstration of at&t let's go: A production-grade statistical spoken dialog system. In *Proceedings of SLT*. IEEE, pages 157–158.

Steve J. Young, Milica Gašić, Blaise Thomson, and Jason D. Williams. 2013. POMDP-based statistical spoken dialog systems: A review. *Proceedings of the IEEE* 101(5):1160–1179.

Tiancheng Zhao, Kyusong Lee, and Maxine Eskenazi. 2016. Dialport: Connecting the spoken dialog research community to real user data. In *IEEE Workshop on Spoken Language Technology.*

RelTextRank: An Open Source Framework for Building Relational Syntactic-Semantic Text Pair Representations

Kateryna Tymoshenko[†] and **Alessandro Moschitti** and **Massimo Nicosia**[†] and **Aliaksei Severyn**[†]
[†]DISI, University of Trento, 38123 Povo (TN), Italy
Qatar Computing Research Institute, HBKU, 34110, Doha, Qatar
`{kateryna.tymoshenko,massimo.nicosia}@unitn.it`
`{amoschitti,aseveryn}@gmail.com`

Abstract

We present a highly-flexible UIMA-based pipeline for developing structural kernel-based systems for relational learning from text, i.e., for generating training and test data for ranking, classifying short text pairs or measuring similarity between pieces of text. For example, the proposed pipeline can represent an input question and answer sentence pairs as syntactic-semantic structures, enriching them with relational information, e.g., links between question class, focus and named entities, and serializes them as training and test files for the tree kernel-based reranking framework. The pipeline generates a number of dependency and shallow chunk-based representations shown to achieve competitive results in previous work. It also enables easy evaluation of the models thanks to cross-validation facilities.

1 Introduction

A number of recent works (Severyn et al., 2013; Tymoshenko et al., 2016b,a; Tymoshenko and Moschitti, 2015) show that tree kernel methods produce state-of-the-art results in many different relational tasks, e.g., Textual Entailment Recognition, Paraphrasing, question, answer and comment ranking, when applied to syntactico-semantic representations of the text pairs.

In this paper, we describe **RelTextRank**, a flexible Java pipeline for converting pairs of raw texts into structured representations and enriching them with semantic information about the relations between the two pieces of text (e.g., lexical exact match). The pipeline is based on the Apache UIMA technology[1], which allows for the creation of highly modular applications and analysis of large volumes of unstructured information.

RelTextRank is an open-source tool available at `https://github.com/iKernels/RelTextRank`. It contains a number of generators for shallow and dependency-based structural representations, UIMA wrappers for multi-purpose linguistic annotators, e.g., Stanford CoreNLP (Manning et al., 2014), question classification and question focus detection modules, and a number of similarity feature vector extractors. It allows for: (i) setting experiments with the new structures, also introducing new types of relational links; (ii) generating training and test data both for kernel-based classification and reranking, also in a cross-validation setting; and (iii) generating predictions using a pre-trained classifier.

In the remainder of the paper, we describe the structures that can be generated by the system (Sec 2), the overall RelTextRank architecture (Sec 3) and the specific implementation of its components (Sec 4). Then, we provide some examples of how to run the pipeline from the command line (Sec 5)[2]. Finally, in Sec 6, we report some results using earlier versions of RelTextRank.

2 Background

Recent work in text pair reranking and classification, e.g., answer sentence selection (AS) and community question answering (cQA), has studied a number of structures for representing text pairs along with their relational links, which provide competitive results when used in a standalone system and the state of the art when combined with feature vectors (Severyn et al., 2013; Tymoshenko et al., 2016b; Tymoshenko and Moschitti, 2015) and embeddings learned by the neural networks (Tymoshenko et al., 2016a). In this sec-

---

[1] `https://uima.apache.org/`

[2] The detailed documentation is available on the related GitHub project.

Proceedings of the 55th Annual Meeting of the Association for Computational Linguistics-System Demonstrations, pages 79–84
Vancouver, Canada, July 30 - August 4, 2017. ©2017 Association for Computational Linguistics
https://doi.org/10.18653/v1/P17-4014

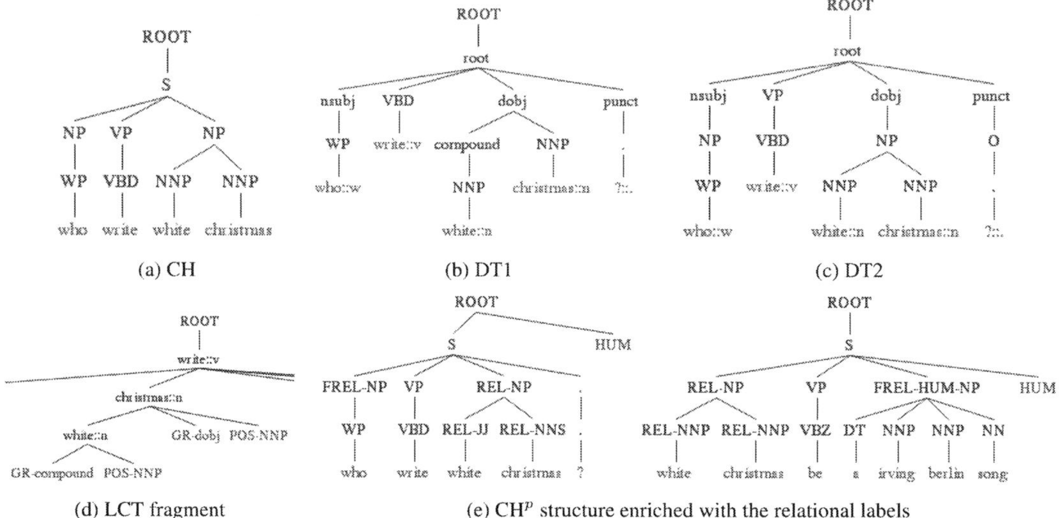

(a) CH   (b) DT1   (c) DT2

(d) LCT fragment   (e) CH^p structure enriched with the relational labels

Figure 1: Structures generated by *RelTextRank*

tion, we provide an overview of the structures and relational links that can be generated by RelTextRank (specific details are in the above papers).

2.1 RelTextRank Structures

RelTextRank can generate the following structural representations for a text pair $\langle T_1, T_2 \rangle$, where, e.g., T_1 can be a question and T_2 a candidate answer passage for an AS task.

Shallow pos-chunk tree representation (CH and CH^p). Here, T_1 and T_2 are both represented as shallow tree structures with lemmas as leaves, their POS-tags as their parent nodes. The POS-tag nodes are further grouped under chunk and sentence nodes. We provide two versions of this structure: CH^p (Fig. 1e), which keeps all information while CH (Fig. 1a) excludes punctuation marks and words outside of any chunk.

Constituency tree representation (CONST). Standard constituency tree representation.

Dependency tree representations. We provide three dependency-based relational structures: DT1, DT2 and LCT. DT1 (Fig. 1b) is a dependency tree in which grammatical relations become nodes and lemmas are located at the leaf level. DT2 (Fig. 1c) is DT1 modified to include the chunking information, and lemmas in the same chunk are grouped under the same chunk node. Finally, LCT (Fig. 1d) is a lexical-centered dependency tree (Croce et al., 2011) with the grammatical relation $REL(head, child)$ represented as *(head (child **GR-REL POS**-pos(head))*. Here REL

is a grammatical relation, *head* and *child* are the head and child lemmas in the relation, respectively, and *pos (head)* is the POS-tag of the head lemma. *GR-* and *POS-* tags in the node name indicate that the node is a grammar relation or part-of-speech node, respectively.

2.2 RelTextRank relational links

Experimental results on multiple datasets (Severyn et al., 2013; Severyn and Moschitti, 2012) show that encoding information about the relations between T_1 and T_2 is crucial for obtaining the state of the art in text pair ranking and classification. RelTextRank provides two kinds of links: hard string match, REL, and semantic match, FREL.

REL. If some lemma occurs both in T_1 and T_2, we mark the respective POS-tag nodes and their parents in the structural representations of T_1 and T_2 with REL labels for all the structures, except for LCT. In LCT, we mark with REL- the POS (POS-) and grammar relation (GR-) nodes.

FREL. When working in the question answering setting, i.e., when T_1 is a question and T_2 is a candidate answer passage, we encode the question focus and question class information into the structural representations. We use FREL-<QC> tag to mark question focus in T_1. Then, in T_2, we mark all the named entities T_2 of type compatible with the question class[3]. Here, <QC> is substituted

---

[3]We use the following mappings to check for compatibility(*Stanford named entity type → UIUC question class (Li and Roth, 2002)*): Person, Organization → HUM ,ENTY; Misc → ENTY; Location →LOC; Date, Time, Money, Percentage, Set, Duration →NUM

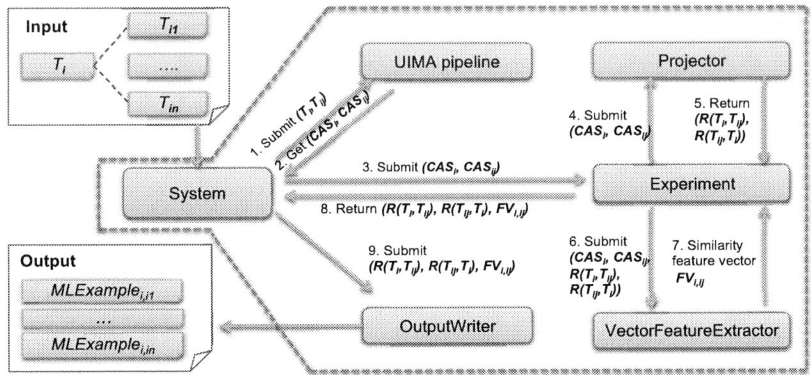

Figure 2: Overall framework

with an actual question class. For all structures in Sec. 2.1, except LCT, we prepend the `FREL-<QC>` tag to the grand-parents of the lemma nodes. In case of LCT, we mark the child grammatical (`GR-`) and POS-tag (`POS-`) nodes of the lemma nodes. Finally, only in case of CH^p structure we also add `<QC>` to the `ROOT` tree node as its rightmost child, and mark the question focus node simply as `FREL`. Fig. 1e shows an example of a CH^p enriched with `REL` and `FREL` links.[4]

3   System Architecture

RelTextRank has a modular architecture easy to adjust towards new structures, features and relational links (see Fig. 2). The basic input of *RelTextRank* is a text T_i, and a list of n texts, $T_{i1}, ..., T_{in}$ to be classified or reranked as relevant or not for T_i. For example, in the QA setting, T_i would be a question and $T_{ij}, j = 1, ..., n$ would be a list of n candidate answer passages. The output of the system is a file in the SVMLight-TK[5] format containing the relational structures and feature vectors generated from the $\langle T_i, (T_{i1}, ..., T_{in}) \rangle$ tuples.

When launched, the *RelTextRank* **System** module first initializes the other modules, such as the **UIMA** text analysis pipeline responsible for linguistic annotation of input texts, the **Experiment** module responsible for generating the structural representations enriched with the relational labels, and, finally, the **OutputWriter** module, which generates the output in the SVMLight-TK format.

At runtime, given an input $\langle T_i, (T_{i1}, ..., T_{in}) \rangle$ tuple, *RelTextRank* generates (T_i, T_{ij}) pairs ($j = 1, ..., n$), and performs the following steps:

Step 1. Linguistic annotation. It runs a pipeline of UIMA Analysis Engines (AEs), which wrap linguistic annotators, e.g., Sentence Splitters, Tokenizers, Syntactic parsers, to convert the input text pairs (T_i, T_{ij}) into the UIMA Common Analysis Structures (CASes), i.e., (CAS_i and CAS_{ij}). CASes contain the original texts and all the linguistic annotations produced by AEs. These produce linguistic annotations defined by a UIMA Type System. In addition, there is an option to persist the produced CASes, and not to rerun the annotators when re-processing a specific document.

Step 2. Generation of structural representations and feature vectors. The **Experiment** module is the core architectural component of the system, which takes CASes as input and generates the relational structures for T_i and T_{ij} along with their feature vector representation, $FV_{i,ij}$. $R(T_i, T_{ij})$ is the relational structure for T_i enriched with the relational links towards T_{ij}, while $R(T_{ij}, T_i)$ is the opposite, i.e., the relational structure for T_{ij} with respect to T_i. Here, the **Projector** module generates $(R(T_i, T_{ij}), R(T_{ij}, T_i))$ and the **VectorFeatureExtractor** module generates $FV_{i,ij}$. In Sec. 4, we provide a list of Experiment modules that implement the representations described in Sec. 2.1, and a list of feature extractors to generate $FV_{i,ij}$.

Step 3. Generation of the output files. Once, all the pairs generated from the $\langle T_i, (T_{i1}, ..., T_{in}) \rangle$ tuple have been processed, the **OutputWriter** module writes them into training/test files. We provide several output strategies described in Sec. 4.

4   Architecture Components

In order to generate the particular configuration of train/test data, one must specify which *System*, *Experiment* and *VectorFeatureExtractor* modules

---

[4]Note that the structures in Fig. 1a- 1d here are depicted without REL and FREL links, however, at runtime the classes described in Sec. 4 do enrich them with the links

[5]http://disi.unitn.it/moschitti/Tree-Kernel.htm

Structure/previous usage	Class Name
CH (Severyn et al., 2013; Tymoshenko et al., 2016b)	`CHExperiment`
DT1 (Severyn et al., 2013; Tymoshenko and Moschitti, 2015)	`DT1Experiment`
DT2 (Tymoshenko and Moschitti, 2015)	`DT2Experiment`
LCT$_Q$-DT2$_A$ (Tymoshenko and Moschitti, 2015)	`LCTqDT2aExperiment`
CONST	`ConstExperiment`
CH^P (Tymoshenko et al., 2016a)	`CHpExperiment`
CH-cQA (Barrón-Cedeño et al., 2016)	`CHcQaExperiment`
CONST-cQA (Tymoshenko et al., 2016b)	`ConstQaExperiment`

Table 1: List of experimental configurations

Algorithm 1 Generating training data for reranking

Require: S_{q+}, S_{q-} - (T_i, T_{ij}) pairs with positive and negative labels, respectively
1: $E_+ \leftarrow \emptyset, E_- \leftarrow \emptyset, flip \leftarrow$ **true**
2: **for all** $s_+ \in S_{q+}$ **do**
3:     **for all** $s_- \in S_{q-}$ **do**
4:         **if** $flip ==$ **true then**
5:             $E_+ \leftarrow E_+ \cup (s_+, s_-)$
6:             $flip \leftarrow$ **false**
7:         **else**
8:             $E_- \leftarrow E_- \cup (s_-, s_+)$
9:             $flip \leftarrow$ **true**
10: **return** E_+, E_-

---

to be used. In this section, we describe the implementations of the architectural modules currently available within RelTextRank.

System modules. These are the entry point to the pipeline, they initialize the specific structure and feature vector generation strategies (*Experiment* and *VectorFeatureExtractor*) and define the type (classification or reranking) and the format of the output file. Currently, we provide the system modules for generating classification (`ClassTextPairConversion`) and reranking training (`RERTextPairConversion`) files. Then, we provide a method to generate the cross-validation experimental data (`ClassCVTextPairConversion` and `CVRERTextPairConversion`). Additionally, we provide a method for generating training/test data for the answer comment reranking in cQA, `CQASemevalTaskA`. Finally, we provide a prediction module for classifying and reranking new text pairs with a pre-trained classifier (`TextPairPrediction`).

Every System module uses a single OutputWriter module, whose type of Experiment and FeatureVectorExtractor to be used are specified with command line parameters (see Sec. 5.)

UIMA pipeline. We provide the UIMA AEs (see `it.unitn.nlpir.annotators`), wrapping the components of the Stanford pipeline (Manning et al., 2014) and Illinois Chunker (Punyakanok and Roth, 2001). The UIMA pipeline takes a pair of texts, (T_i, T_{ij}) as input, and outputs their respective CASes, (CAS_i, CAS_{ij}).

RelTextRank also includes AEs for question classification (`QuestionClassifier`) and question focus detection (`QuestionFocusAnnotator`). Focus classification module employs a model pre-trained as in (Severyn et al., 2013). `QuestionClassifier` can be run with coarse- and fine-grained question classification models trained on the UIUC corpus by (Li and Roth, 2002) as described in (Severyn et al., 2013). The coarse-grained classier uses the following categories, HUMan, ENTitY, LOCation, ABBR, DESCription, NUMber classes, whereas the fine-grained classifier splits the NUM class into DATE, CURRENCY and QUANTITY.

Currently, we use a custom UIMA type system defined for our pipeline, however, in future we plan to use the type systems used in other widely used UIMA pipelines, e.g., DKPro (de Castilho and Gurevych, 2014).

Experiment modules. All the Experiment module implementations are available as classes in the `it.unitn.nlpir.experiment.*` package. Tab. 1 provides an overview of the structures currently available within the system. Here LCT$_Q$-DT2$_A$ represents T_i and T_{ij} as LCT and DT2 structures, respectively. CH-cQA and CONST-cQA are the CH and CONST structures adjusted for cQA (see (Tymoshenko et al., 2016b)).

OutputWriter modules. In the `it.unitn.nlpir.system.datagen` package, we provide the OutputWriters, which output the data in the SVMLight-TK format in the classification (`ClassifierDataGen`) and the reranking (`RerankingDataGenTrain` and `RerankingDataGenTest`) modes. Currently, the type of the OutputWriter can only be specified in the code of the System module. It is possible to create a new System module starting from the existing one and code a different OutputWriter.

In the classification mode, one OutputWriter generates one example for each text pair (T_i, T_{ij}). Another OutputWriter implementation generates input data for kernel-based reranking (Shen et al., 2003) using the strategy described in Alg. 1.

VectorFeatureExtractors. RelTextRank contains feature extractors to compute: (i) *cosine similarity* over the text pair: $sim_{COS}(T_1, T_2)$, where the input vectors are composed of word lemmas, bi-, three- an four-grams, POS-tags; *similarity based on the PTK score* computed for the structural rep-

Command 1. Generate training data
java -Xmx5G -Xss512m it.unitn.nlpir.system.core.RERTextPairConversion -questionsPath data/wikiQA/WikiQA-train.questions.txt
-answersPath data/wikiQA/WikiQA-train.tsv.resultset **-outputDir** data/examples/wikiqa **-filePersistence** CASes/wikiQA
-candidatesToKeep 10 **-mode** train **-expClassName** it.unitn.nlpir.experiment.fqa.CHExperiment
-featureExtractorClass it.unitn.nlpir.features.presets.BaselineFeatures

Command 2. Use pre-trained model to do classification
java -Xmx5G -Xss512m it.unitn.nlpir.system.core.TextPairPrediction -svmModel data/wikiQA/wikiqa-ch-rer-baselinefeats.model
-featureExtractorClass it.unitn.nlpir.features.presets.BaselineFeatures **-questionsPath** data/wikiQA/WikiQA-test.questions.txt
-answersPath data/wikiQA/WikiQA-test.tsv.resultset **-outputFile** data/examples/wikiqa/wikiqa-ch-rer-baselinefeats.pred
-expClassName it.unitn.nlpir.experiment.fqa.CHExperiment **-mode** reranking **-filePersistence** CASes/wikiQA/test

Table 2: Example commands to launch the pipeline

resentations of T_1 and T_2: $sim_{PTK}\,(T_1, T_2) = PTK(T_1, T_2)$, where the input trees can both be the dependency trees and/or the shallow chunk trees; (ii) *IR score*, which is a normalized score assigned to the answer passage by an IR engine, if available; (iii) *question class* as a binary feature.

Then, RelTextRank includes feature extractors based on the DKPro Similarity tool (Bär et al., 2013) for extracting (iv) *longest common substring/subsequence measure*; (v) *Jaccard similarity* coefficient on 1,2,3,4-grams; (vi) *word containment measure* (Broder, 1997); (vii) *greedy string tiling* (Wise, 1996); and (viii) *ESA similarity* based on Explicit Semantic Analysis (ESA) (Gabrilovich and Markovitch, 2007),

We provide several predefined VectorFeature-Extractors: `BaselineFeatures`, `AllFeatures` and `NoESAAllFeatures`[6], which incorporate feature groups: (i)-(iii), (i)-(viii) and (i)-(vii), respectively. Finally, we provide a feature extractor that reads the pre-extracted features from file, `FromFileVectorFeature`. The full list of features can be found by exploring the contents and documentation of the `it.unitn.nlpir.features` package.

5 Running the pipeline

Documentation on the RelTextRank GitHub explains how to install and run the pipeline with the various reranking and classification configurations. Due to the space limitations, here we only provide the sample commands for running the training file generation for the reranking mode (Tab. 2, Command 1) and using a pretrained model to rank the produced data (Tab. 2, Command 2).

Command 1 runs the RERTextPairConversion system (see Sec. 4), using the files specified as *-questionsPath* and *-answersPath* parameters to read the questions (T_i in Fig 2) and their corre-

sponding candidate answers (T_{ij}, in Fig 2 with $j = 1, ..., n$; *-candidatesToKeep* parameter specifies the value of n), respectively. *-outputDir* is a path to the folder that will contain the resulting training file, while *-filePersistence* indicates where to persist the UIMA CASes containing the linguistic annotations produced by the UIMA pipeline (this is optional). *-mode train* indicates that we are generating the training file. *-expClassName* is a mandatory parameter, which indicates the Experiment module (Fig. 2) we want to invoke, i.e., which structure we wish to generate. In this specific example, we build a CH structure (see Tab. 1). Finally, *-featureExtractorClass* specifies which features to include into the feature vector.

Command 2 runs a pipeline that uses a pre-trained SVMLight-TK model (*-svmModel* parameter) to rerank the candidate answers (*-answerPath*) for the input questions (*-questionsPath*), and stores them into a prediction file (*-outputFile*). Here, we also indicate which structure generator and feature extractors to be used (*-expClassName* and *-featureExtractorClass*). Note that *-expClassName* and *-featureExtractorClass* must be exactly the same as the ones used when generating the data for training the model specified by *svmModel*.

6 Previous uses of RelTextRank

Tab. 3 reports the results of some of the state-of-the-art AS and cQA systems that employ `RelTextRank` as a component and combine the structures produced by it with the feature vectors of different nature, V. Here feature vectors are either manually handcrafted thread-level features, V_t, or word and phrase vector features, V_b, for cQA; or embeddings of T_i, T_{ij} learned by Convolutional Neural Networks, V_{CNN}, for the AS task.

Due to space limitations, we do not describe every system in detail, but provide link to a reference paper with the detailed setup description, and

---

[6]The motivation behind this feature extractor is that ESA feature extraction process is time-consuming

83

Corpus	Reference paper	Struct.	Feat.	V		+ Rel.Structures	
				MRR	MAP	MRR	MAP
WikiQA	(Tymoshenko et al., 2016a)*	CHp	V_{CNN}	67.49	66.41	73.88	71.99
TREC13	(Tymoshenko et al., 2016a)	CH	V_{CNN}	79.32	73.37	85.53*	75.18*
SemEval-2016, 3.A, English	(Tymoshenko et al., 2016b)	CONST	V_t	82.98	73.50	86.26	78.78
SemEval-2016, 3.D, Arabic	(Barrón-Cedeño et al., 2016)	CONST	V_b	43.75	38.33	52.55	45.50

Table 3: Previous uses of RelTextRank

mention which of the structures described in Sec. 2 they employ. (Tymoshenko et al., 2016a)* is a new structure and embedding combination approach.

We show the results on two AS corpora, WikiQA (Yang et al., 2015) and TREC13 (Wang et al., 2007). Then, we report the results obtained when using `RelTextRank` in a cQA system for English and Arabic comment selection tasks in the SemEval-2016 competition, Tasks 3.A and 3.D (Nakov et al., 2016).

V column reports the performance of the systems that employ feature vectors only, while $+Rel.Structures$ corresponds to the systems using a combination of relational structures generated by the earlier versions of `RelTextRank` and feature vectors. The numbers marked by * were obtained using relational structures only, since combining features and trees decreased the overall performance in that specific case. *Rel.Structures* always improves the performance.

7 Conclusions

In this demonstration paper we have provided an overview of the architecture and the particular components of the RelTextRank pipeline for generating structural relational representations of text pairs. In previous work, these representations have shown to achieve the state of the art for factoid QA and cQA. In the future, we plan to further evolve the pipeline, improving its code and usability. Moreover, we plan to expand the publicly available code to include more relational links, e.g., Linked Open Data-based relations described in (Tymoshenko et al., 2014). Finally, in order to enable better compatibility with publicly available tools, we plan to adopt the DKPro type system (de Castilho and Gurevych, 2014).

Acknowledgments

This work has been partially supported by the EC project CogNet, 671625 (H2020-ICT-2014-2, Research and Innovation action).

References

D. Bär, T. Zesch, and I. Gurevych. 2013. Dkpro similarity: An open source framework for text similarity. In *ACL: System Demonstrations*.

A. Barrón-Cedeño, G. Da San Martino, S. Joty, A. Moschitti, F. Al-Obaidli, S. Romeo, K. Tymoshenko, and A. Uva. 2016. Convkn at semeval-2016 task 3: Answer and question selection for question answering on arabic and english fora. In *SemEval-2016*.

A. Z Broder. 1997. On the resemblance and containment of documents. In *SEQUENCES*.

D. Croce, A. Moschitti, and R. Basili. 2011. Structured lexical similarity via convolution kernels on dependency trees. In *EMNLP*.

R. Eckart de Castilho and I. Gurevych. 2014. A broad-coverage collection of portable NLP components for building shareable analysis pipelines. In *OIAF4HLT Workshop (COLING)*.

E. Gabrilovich and S. Markovitch. 2007. Computing semantic relatedness using wikipedia-based explicit semantic analysis. In *IJCAI*.

X. Li and D. Roth. 2002. Learning question classifiers. In *COLING*.

C. D. Manning, M. Surdeanu, J. Bauer, J. Finkel, S. J. Bethard, and D. McClosky. 2014. The Stanford CoreNLP natural language processing toolkit. In *ACL*.

P. Nakov, L. Màrquez, A. Moschitti, W. Magdy, H. Mubarak, A. Freihat, J. Glass, and B. Randeree. 2016. Semeval-2016 task 3: Community question answering. In *SemEval*.

V. Punyakanok and D. Roth. 2001. The use of classifiers in sequential inference. In *NIPS*.

A. Severyn and A. Moschitti. 2012. Structural relationships for large-scale learning of answer re-ranking. In *SIGIR*.

A. Severyn, M. Nicosia, and A. Moschitti. 2013. Learning adaptable patterns for passage reranking. In *CoNLL*.

L. Shen, A. Sarkar, and A. Joshi. 2003. Using LTAG Based Features in Parse Reranking. In *EMNLP*.

K. Tymoshenko, D. Bonadiman, and A. Moschitti. 2016a. Convolutional neural networks vs. convolution kernels: Feature engineering for answer sentence reranking. In *NAACL-HLT*.

K. Tymoshenko, D. Bonadiman, and A. Moschitti. 2016b. Learning to rank non-factoid answers: Comment selection in web forums. In *CIKM*.

K. Tymoshenko and A. Moschitti. 2015. Assessing the impact of syntactic and semantic structures for answer passages reranking. In *CIKM*.

K. Tymoshenko, A. Moschitti, and A. Severyn. 2014. Encoding semantic resources in syntactic structures for passage reranking. In *EACL*.

Mengqiu Wang, Noah A. Smith, and Teruko Mitaura. 2007. What is the Jeopardy model? A quasi-synchronous grammar for QA. In *EMNLP-CoNLL*.

Michael J. Wise. 1996. Yap3: improved detection of similarities in computer program and other texts. In *ACM SIGCSE Bulletin*.

Y. Yang, W. Yih, and C. Meek. 2015. Wikiqa: A challenge dataset for open-domain question answering. In *EMNLP*.

Scattertext: a Browser-Based Tool for Visualizing how Corpora Differ

Jason S. Kessler
CDK Global
`jason.kessler@gmail.com`

Abstract

Scattertext is an open source tool for visualizing linguistic variation between document categories in a language-independent way. The tool presents a scatterplot, where each axis corresponds to the rank-frequency a term occurs in a category of documents. Through a tie-breaking strategy, the tool is able to display thousands of visible term-representing points and find space to legibly label hundreds of them. Scattertext also lends itself to a query-based visualization of how the use of terms with similar embeddings differs between document categories, as well as a visualization for comparing the importance scores of bag-of-words features to univariate metrics.

1 Introduction

Finding words and phrases that discriminate categories of text is a common application of statistical NLP. For example, finding words that are most characteristic of a political party in congressional speeches can help political scientists identify means of partisan framing (Monroe et al., 2008; Grimmer, 2010), while identifying differences in word usage between male and female characters in films can highlight narrative archetypes (Schofield and Mehr, 2016). Language use in social media can inform understanding of personality types (Schwartz et al., 2013), and provides insights into customers' evaluations of restaurants (Jurafsky et al., 2014).

A wide range of visualizations have been used to highlight discriminating words– simple ranked lists of words, word clouds, word bubbles, and word-based scatter plots. These techniques have a number of limitations. For example, the difficulty in comparing the relative frequencies of two terms in a word cloud, or in legibly displaying term labels in scatterplots.

Scattertext[1] is an interactive, scalable tool which overcomes many of these limitations. It is built around a scatterplot which displays a high number of words and phrases used in a corpus. Points representing terms are positioned to allow a high number of unobstructed labels and to indicate category association. The coordinates of a point indicate how frequently the word is used in each category.

Figure 1 shows an example of a Scattertext plot comparing Republican and Democratic political speeches. The higher up a point is on the y-axis, the more it was used by Democrats, and similarly, the further right on the x-axis a point appears, the more its corresponding word was used by Republicans. Highly associated terms fall closer to the upper left and lower right-hand corners of the chart, while stop words fall in the far upper right-hand corner. Words occurring infrequently in both classes fall closer to the lower left-hand corner. When used interactively, mousing-over a point shows statistics about a term's relative use in the two contrasting categories, and clicking on a term shows excerpts from convention speeches used.

The point placement, intelligent word-labeling, and auxiliary term-lists ensure a low-whitespace, legible plot. These are issues which have plagued other scatterplot visualizations showing discriminative language.

§2 discusses different views of term-category association that make up the basis of visualizations. In §3, the objectives, strengths, and weaknesses of existing visualization techniques. §4 presents the technical details behind Scattertext.

---

[1] github.com/JasonKessler/scattertext

Proceedings of the 55th Annual Meeting of the Association for Computational Linguistics-System Demonstrations, pages 85–90
Vancouver, Canada, July 30 - August 4, 2017. ©2017 Association for Computational Linguistics
https://doi.org/10.18653/v1/P17-4015

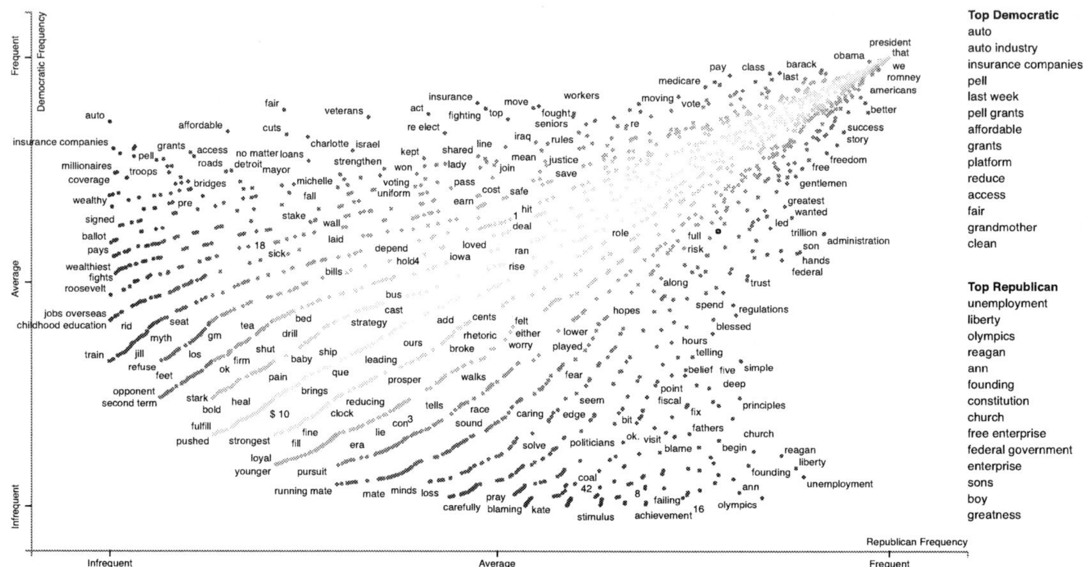

Figure 1: Scattertext visualization of words and phrases used in the 2012 Political Conventions. 2,202 points are colored red or blue based on the association of their corresponding terms with Democrats or Republicans, 215 of which were labeled. The corpus consists of 123 speeches by Democrats (76,864 words) and 66 by Republicans (58,138 words). The most associated terms are listed under "Top Democrat" and "Top Republican" headings. Interactive version: https://jasonkessler.github.io/st-main.html

§5 discusses how Scattertext can be used to identify category-discriminating terms that are semantically similar to a query.

2 On text visualization

The simplest visualization, a list of words ranked by their scores, is easy to produce, interpret and is thus very common in the literature. There are numerous ways of producing word scores for ranking which are thoroughly covered in previous work. The reader is directed to Monroe et al. (2008) (subsequently referred to as MCQ) for an overview of model-based term scoring algorithms. Also of interest, Bitvai and Cohn (2015) present a method for finding sparse words and phrase scores from a trained ANN (with bag-of-words features) and its training data.

Regardless of how complex the calculation, word scores capture a number of different measures of word-association, which can be interesting when viewed independently instead of as part of a unitary score. These loosely defined measures include:

Precision A word's discriminative power regardless of its frequency. A term that appears once in the categorized corpus will have perfect precision. This (and subsequent metrics) presuppose a balanced class distribution. Words close to the x and y-axis in Scattertext have high precision.

Recall The frequency a word appears in a particular class, or $P(\text{word}|\text{class})$. The variance of precision tends to decrease as recall increases. Extremely high recall words tend to be stop-words. High recall words occur close to the top and right sides of Scattertext plots.

Non-redundancy The level of a word's discriminative power given other words that co-occur with it. If a word w_a always co-occurs with w_b and word w_b has a higher precision and recall, w_a would have a high level of redundancy. Measuring redundancy is non-trivial, and has traditionally been approached through penalized logistic regression (Joshi et al., 2010), as well as through other feature selection techniques. In configurations of Scattertext such as the one discussed at the end of §4, terms can be colored based on their regression coefficients that indicate non-redundancy.

Characteristicness How much more does a word occur in than the categories examined than in background in-domain text? For example, if comparing positive and negative reviews of a single movie, a logical background corpus may be reviews of other movies. Highly associated terms tend to be characteristic because they frequently appear in one category and not the other. Some visualizations explicitly highlight these, ex. (Coppersmith and Kelly, 2014).

3 Past work and design motivation

Text visualizations manipulate the position and appearance of words or points representing them to indicate their relative scores in these measures. For example, in Schwartz et al. (2013), two word clouds are given, one per each category of text being compared. Words (and selected n-grams) are sized by their linear regression coefficients (a composite metric of precision, recall, and redundancy) and colored by frequency. Only words occurring in $\geq 1\%$ of documents and having Bonferroni-corrected coefficient p-values of <0.001 were shown. Given that these words are highly correlated to their class of interest, the frequency of use is likely a good proxy for recall.

Coppersmith and Kelly (2014) also describe a word-cloud based visualization for discriminating terms, but intend it for categories which are both small subsets of a much larger corpus. They include a third, middle cloud for terms that appear characteristic.

Word clouds can be difficult to interpret. It is difficult to compare the sizes of two non-horizontally adjacent words, as well as the relative color intensities of any two words. Longer words unintentionally appear more important since they naturally occupy more space in the cloud. Sizing of words can be a source of confusion when used to represent precision, since a larger word may naturally be seen as more frequent.

Bostock et al. (2012)[2] features an interactive word-bubble visualization for exploring different word usage among Republicans and Democrats in the 2012 US presidential nominating conventions. Each term displayed is represented by a bubble, sized proportionate to their frequency. Each bubble is colored blue and red, s.t. the blue partition's size corresponds to the term's relative use by Democrats. Terms were manually chosen, and arranged along the x-axis based on their discriminative power. When clicked, sentences from speeches containing the word used are listed below the visualization.

The dataset used in Bostock et al. (2012) is used to demonstrate the capabilities of Scattertext

---

[2]nytimes.com/interactive/2012/09/06/us/politics/convention-word-counts.html

in each of these figures. The dataset is available via the Scattertext Github page.

3.1 Scatterplot visualizations

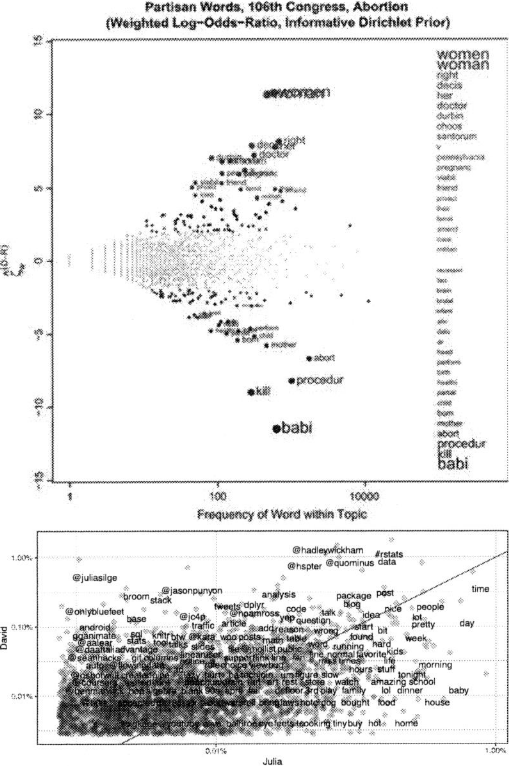

Figure 2: A sample of existing scatterplot visualizations. MCQ's is at the top. Tidytext is below.

MCQ present a visualization to illustrate the use of their proposed word score, log-odds-ratio with an informative Dirichlet prior (top of Figure 2). This visualization plots word-representing points along two axes. The axes are $\log_{10}$ recall vs. the difference in word scores z-scores. Points with a z-score difference <1.96 are grayed-out, while the top and bottom 20 are labeled, both by each point and on the right-hand side. The side-labeling is necessary because labels are permitted to overlap, hindering their on-plot readability. The sizes of points and labels are increased proportionally to the word score. This word score encompasses precision, recall, and characteristicness since it penalizes scores of terms used more frequently in the background corpus. MCQ used this type of plot to illustrate the different effects of various scoring techniques introduced in the paper. However, the small number of points which are possible to label limit its utility for in-depth corpus analysis.

Schofield and Mehr (2016) use essentially the

same visualization, but plot over 100 corresponding n-grams next to an unlabeled frequency/z-score plot. While this is appropriate for publication, displaying associated terms and the shape of the score distribution, it is impossible to align all but the highest scoring points to their labels.

The tidytext R-package (Silge and Robinson, 2016) documentation includes a non-interactive ggplot2-based scatter plot that is very similar to Scattertext. The x and y-axes both, like in Scattertext, correspond to word frequencies in the two contrasting categories, with jitter added.[3] In the example in Figure 2 (bottom), the contrasting categories are tweets from two different accounts. The red diagonal line separates words based on their odds-ratio. Importantly, compared to MCQ, less of this chart's area is occupied by whitespace.

While tidytext's labels do not overlap each other (in contrast to MCQ) they do overlap points. The points' semi-transparency makes labels in less-dense areas legible, the dense interior of the chart is nearly illegible, with both points and labels obscured. Figure 3 shows an excerpt of the same

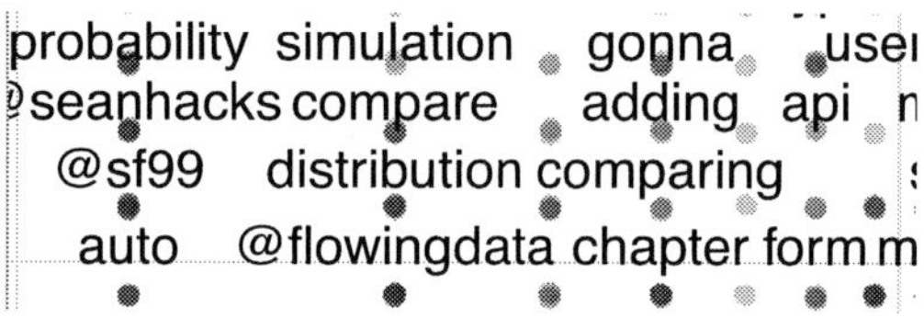

Figure 3: A small cropping from an un-jittered version at the bottom of Figure 2. The dark, opaque points indicate stacks of points.

plot, but with no jitter. Words appearing with the same frequency in both categories all become stacked atop each other, however, this provides more interior space for labeling.

As a side note, many text visualizations plot words in a 2D space according to their similarity in a high dimensional space. For example, Cho et al. 2014 uses the Barnes-Hut-SNE to plot words in a 2D space s.t. those with similar representations are grouped close together. Class-association does not play a role in this line of research, and global position is essentially irrelevant.

The next section presents Scattertext and how its approach to word ordering solves the problems discussed above.

---

[3]This type of visualization may have first been introduced in Rudder (2014).

4 Scattertext

Scattertext builds on tinytext and Rudder (2014). It plots a set of unigrams and bigrams (referred to in this paper as "terms") found in a corpus of documents assigned to one of two categories on a two-dimensional scatterplot.

In the following notation, user-supplied parameters are in bold typeface.

Consider a corpus of documents C with disjoint subsets A and B s.t. $A \cup B \equiv C$. Let $\phi^T(t, C)$ be the number of times term t occurs in C, $\phi^T(t, A)$ be the the number of times t occurs in A. Let $\phi^D(t, A)$ refer to the number of documents in A containing t. Let t_{ij} be the jth word in term t_i. In practice, $j \in \{1, 2\}$. The parameter ϕ may be ϕ^T or ϕ^D.[4] Other feature representations (ex., tf.idf) may be used for ϕ.

$$Pr[t_i] = \frac{\phi(t_i, C)}{\sum_{t \in C \wedge |t| \equiv |t_i|} \phi(t, C)}. \tag{1}$$

The construction of the set of terms included in the visualization V is a two-step process. Terms must occur $geqm$ times, and if bigrams, appear to be phrases. In order to keep the approach language neutral, I follow Schartz et al. (2013), and use a pointwise mutual information score to filter out bigrams that do not occur far more frequently than would be expected. Let

$$PMI(t_i) = \log \frac{Pr[t_i]}{\prod_{t_{ij} \in t_i} Pr[T_{ij}]}. \tag{2}$$

The minimum PMI accepted is p. Now, V can be defined as

$$\{t \mid \phi(t, C) \geq m \wedge (|t| \equiv 1 \vee PMI(t) > p)\} \tag{3}$$

Let a term t's coordinates on the scatterplot be (x_t^A, x_t^B), where A and B are the two document categories. Although x_t^K is proportional to $\phi(t, K)$, many terms will have identical $\phi(t, K)$ values. To break ties the word that appears last alphabetically will have a larger x_t^K.

Let us define r_t^K s.t. $t \in V$ and $K \in \{A, B\}$ as the ranks of $\phi(t, K)$, sorted in ascending order, where ties are broken by terms' alphabetical order. This allows us to define

$$x_t^K = \frac{r_t^K}{\mathrm{argmax}\, r^K} \tag{4}$$

---

[4]ϕ^D is useful when documents contain unique, characteristic, highly frequent terms. For example, names of movies can have high ϕ^T when finding differences in positive and negative film reviews. The may lead to them receiving higher scores than sentiment terms.

This limits x values to $[0,1]$, ensuring both axes are scaled identically. This keeps the chart from becoming lopsided toward the corpus that had a larger number of terms.[5]

The charts in Figures 1, 4, and 5, were made with parameters $m{=}5$, $p{=}8$, and $\phi{=}\phi^T$.

Breaking ties alphabetically is a simple but important alternative to jitter. While jitter (i.e., randomly perturbing x_t^A and x_t^B) breaks up the stacked points shown in Figure 3, it eliminates empty space to legibly label points. Jitter can make it seem like identically frequent points are closer to an upper left or lower right corner. Alphabetic tie-breaking makes identical adjustments to both axes, leading to the horizontal (lower-left to upper-right) alignments of identically frequent points. This angle does not cause one point to be substantially closer to either of the category associated corners (the upper-left and lower-right).

These alignments provide two advantages. First, they open up point-free tracts in the center of the chart which allow for unobstructed interior labels. Second, they arrange points in a way that it is easy to hover a mouse over all of them, to indicate what term they correspond to, and be clicked to see excerpts of that term.

In the running example, 154 points were labeled when a jitter of 10% of each axis and no tie-breaking was applied. 210 points (a 36% lift) were labeled when no jitter was applied. 140 were labeled if no tie breaking was used.

Rudder (2014) observed terms closer to the lower-right corner were used frequently in A and infrequently in B, indicating they have both high recall and precision wrt category A. Symmetrically, the same relationship exists for B and the upper-right corner. I can formalize this score between a point's coordinates and it's respective corner. This intuition is represented by a score function $s_K(t)$ ($K \in \{A, B\}$ and $t \in V$) where

$$s_K(t) = \begin{cases} \|\langle 1 - x_t^A, x_t^B \rangle\| & \text{if } K = A, \\ \|\langle x_t^A, 1 - x_t^B \rangle\| & \text{if } K = B \end{cases}. \quad (5)$$

Other term scoring methods (e.g., regression weights or a weighted log-odd-ratio with a prior) may be used in place of Formula 5.

Maximal non-overlapping labeling of scatterplots is NP-hard (Been et al., 2007). Scattertext's heuristic is labeling points if space is available in one of many places around a point. This is performed iteratively, beginning with points having the highest score (regardless of category) and proceeding downward in score. An optimized data structure automatically constructed using Cozy (Loncaric et al., 2016) holds the locations of drawn points and labels.

The top scoring terms in classes B and A (Democrats and Republicans in Figure 1) are listed to the right of the chart. Hovering over points and terms highlights the point and displays frequency statistics.

Point colors are determined by their scores on s. Those corresponding to terms with a high s_B colored in progressively darker shades of blue, while those with a higher s_A are colored in progressively darker shades of red. When both scores are about equal, the point colors become more yellow, which creates a visual divide between the two classes. The colors are provided by D3's "RdYlBu" diverging color scheme from Colorbrewer[6] via d3[7].

Other point colors (and scorings) can be used. For example, Figure 4 shows coefficients of an $\ell 1$ penalized log. reg. classifier on V features. Scattertext, in this example, is set to color 0-scoring coefficients light gray. Terms' univariate predictive power are still evident by their chart position. See below[8] for an interactive version.

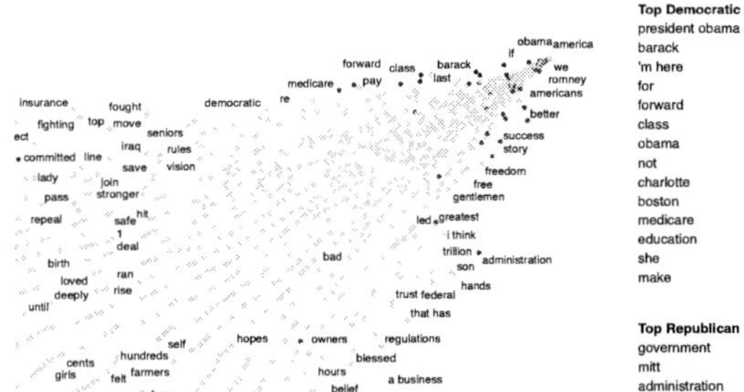

Figure 4: A cropped view of points being colored using $\ell 1$-logreg coefficients. Interactive version: jasonkessler.github.io/st-sparse.html

5 Topical category discriminators

In 2012, how did Republicans and Democrats use language relating to "jobs", "healthcare", or "military" differently? Figure 5 shows, in the running example, words similar to "jobs" that were characteristic of the political parties.

---

[5]While both are available, ordinal ranks are preferable to log frequency since uninteresting stop-words often occupy disproportionate axis space.

[6]colorbrewer2.org
[7]github.com/d3/d3-scale-chromatic
[8]jasonkessler.github.io/sparseviz.html

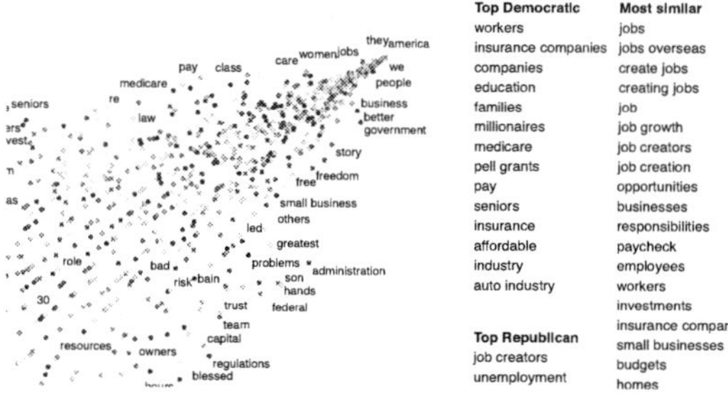

Figure 5: Words and phrases that are semantically similar to the word "jobs" are colored darker on a gray-to-purple scale, and general and category-specific related terms are listed to the right. Note that this is a cropping of the upper left-hand corner of the plot. Interactive version: jasonkessler.github.io/st-sim.html.

In this configuration of Scattertext, words are colored by their cosine similarity to a query phrase. This is done using spaCy[9]-provided GloVe (Pennington et al., 2014) word vectors (trained on the Common Crawl corpus). Mean vectors are used for phrases.

The calculation of the most similar terms associated with each category is a simple heuristic. First, sets of terms closely associated with a category are found. Second, these terms are ranked based on their similarity to the query, and the top rank terms are displayed to the right of the scatterplot (Figure 5).

A term is considered associated if its p-value is <0.05. P-values are determined using MCQ's difference in the weighted log-odds-ratio with an uninformative Dirichlet prior. This is the only model-based method discussed in Monroe et al. that does not rely on a large in-domain background corpus. Since I am scoring bigrams in addition to the unigrams scored by MCQ, the size of the corpus would have to be larger to have high enough bigram counts for proper penalization.

This function relies the Dirichlet distribution's parameter $\alpha \in \mathbf{R}_{+}^{|V|}$. Following MCQ, $\alpha_t = 0.01$. Formulas 16, 18 and 22 are used to compute z-scores, which are then converted to p-values using the Normal CDF of $\hat{\zeta}_w^{A-B}$, letting $y_t^{(K)} = \phi(t, K)$ st $K \in \{A, B\}$ and $t \in V$.

As seen in Figure 5, the top Republican word related to "jobs" is "job creators", while "workers" is the top Democratic term.

---

[9]spacy.io

6 Conclusion and future work

Scattertext, a tool to make legible, comprehensive visualizations of class-associated term frequencies, was introduced. Future work will involve rigorous human evaluation of the usefulness of the visualization strategies discussed.

Acknowledgments

Jay Powell, Kyle Lo, Ray Little-Herrick, Will Headden, Chuck Little, Nancy Kessler and Kam Woods helped proofread this work.

References

Ken Been, Eli Daiches, and Chee Yap. 2007. Dynamic map labeling. *IEEE-VCG* .

Zsolt Bitvai and Trevor Cohn. 2015. Non-linear text regression with a deep convolutional neural network. In *ACL*.

Mike Bostock, Shan Carter, and Matthew Ericson. 2012. At the national conventions, the words they used. In *The New York Times*.

Kyunghyun Cho, Bart van Merrienboer, Çaglar Gülçehre, Fethi Bougares, Holger Schwenk, and Yoshua Bengio. 2014. Learning phrase representations using RNN encoder-decoder for statistical machine translation. *CoRR* .

Glen Coppersmith and Erin Kelly. 2014. Dynamic wordclouds and vennclouds for exploratory data analysis. In *ACL-ILLVI*.

Justin Ryan Grimmer. 2010. *Representational Style: The Central Role of Communication in Representation*. Ph.D. thesis, Harvard University.

Mahesh Joshi, Dipanjan Das, Kevin Gimpel, and Noah A. Smith. 2010. Movie reviews and revenues: An experiment in text regression. In *HLT-NAACL*.

Dan Jurafsky, Victor Chahuneau, Bryan Routledge, and Noah Smith. 2014. Narrative framing of consumer sentiment in online restaurant reviews. *First Monday* .

Calvin Loncaric, Emina Torlak, and Michael D. Ernst. 2016. Fast synthesis of fast collections. In *PLDI*.

Burt L. Monroe, Michael P. Colaresi, and Kevin M. Quinn. 2008. Fightin' words: Lexical feature selection and evaluation for identifying the content of political conflict. *Political Analysis* .

Jeffrey Pennington, Richard Socher, and Christopher D. Manning. 2014. Glove: Global vectors for word representation. In *EMNLP*.

Christian Rudder. 2014. *Dataclysm: Who We Are (When We Think No One's Looking)*. Crown Publishing Group.

Alexandra Schofield and Leo Mehr. 2016. Gender-distinguishing features in film dialogue. *NAACL-CLfL* .

H. Andrew Schwartz, Johannes C. Eichstaedt, and Margaret L. et al. Kern. 2013. Personality, gender, and age in the language of social media: The open-vocabulary approach. *PLOS ONE* .

Julia Silge and David Robinson. 2016. tidytext: Text mining and analysis using tidy data principles in r. *JOSS* .

SEMEDICO:
A Comprehensive Semantic Search Engine for the Life Sciences

Erik Faessler
Jena University Language & Information
Engineering (JULIE) Lab
Friedrich-Schiller-Universität Jena
Jena, Germany
`erik.faessler@uni-jena.de`

Udo Hahn
Jena University Language & Information
Engineering (JULIE) Lab
Friedrich-Schiller-Universität Jena
Jena, Germany
`udo.hahn@uni-jena.de`

Abstract

SEMEDICO is a semantic search engine designed to support literature search in the life sciences by integrating the semantics of the domain at all stages of the search process—from query formulation via query processing up to the presentation of results. SEMEDICO excels with an ad-hoc search approach which directly reflects relevance in terms of information density of entities and relations among them (events) and, a truly unique feature, ranks interaction events by certainty information reflecting the degree of factuality of the encountered event.

1 Introduction

The exponential growth of scientific publications in the life science domain (Lu, 2011) has inspired a wide range of information retrieval services over the last decade (for a brief survey, see Section 2). Simple term-based retrieval techniques, including frequency-based approaches based on TF-IDF scores, rapidly hit their limits given the enormous complexity of the sublanguage in the life sciences, not only due to the sheer vocabulary size (amounting to millions of specialized terms) but also due to factors such as excessive ambiguity, non-canonicity of complex phrases, extensive terminological paraphrasing, etc.

Overly long hit lists returned for standard queries in PUBMED (Lu, 2011), the most prominent literature hub for life scientists, make focused search strategies a major desideratum. Current search mechanisms are unable to distinguish between semantically tightly bound informational units, like semantic relations (events) between entities (e.g., protein-protein interactions), and much looser relations between entities, like co-occurrence of search terms within the same paragraph or entire document.

Hence, in order to improve literature search, a retrieval system should take into account the domain knowledge of the domain under scrutiny, connect it with the contents of the publications in the document collection in a meaningful way, decide which information pieces to present with high priority and display them to the user in an easily digestable way. However, existing search engines only partially match these requirements.

As an alternative, we here present the semantic search engine SEMEDICO. It features a frontend with interactive disambiguation for query concepts that share a common name with other concepts, including abbreviations which have been automatically extracted from documents. Due to the incorporation of several life science ontologies (see Section 3) all subordinates of search terms are included in a search. This semantic enrichment not only plays a major role in retrieving relevant documents (implicitly, all subordinates are OR-ed) but also supports searchers in the formulation of adequate queries since it makes conceptual neighborhoods lucid, thus easing query formulation.

At the back end side, gene interactions are scored relative to the degree of factuality explicitly expressed in the document (*"we have evidence for the interaction of X and Y"* is a stronger claim than *"X might potentially interact with Y"* and will thus be ranked higher than the second statement; see Section 5). For ranking, we also take into account the proximity of occurrences of search terms within well-defined document portions. We deem shorter text passages populated by several query terms to be more informative to the researcher than wider dispersed term occurrences. The most informative units, from this perspective, are tightly connected semantic relations where constituent entities are syntactically

91

Proceedings of the 55th Annual Meeting of the Association for Computational Linguistics-System Demonstrations, pages 91–96
Vancouver, Canada, July 30 - August 4, 2017. ©2017 Association for Computational Linguistics
https://doi.org/10.18653/v1/P17-4016

related as well. This means that SEMEDICO prefers shorter passage matches over larger ones and scores document hits accordingly. In the final hit list, matching entities and relations are highlighted in order to orient the reader immediately to the relevant text parts (as defined by the query).

2 Related Semantic Search Engines

Several search engines for the life sciences have been developed to address the needs of researchers (for a survey, cf. Lu (2011)). A common characeristic of these systems is the incorporation of the semantics of the underlying domain, by design, in terms of domain-specific terminologies, thesauri and ontologies. GOPUBMED (Doms and Schroeder, 2005) integrates the Medical Subject Headings (MESH),[1] GENE ONTOLOGY (GO)[2] and UNIPROT.[3] It allows to browse PUBMED citations taxonomically structured by the MESH and GO. Search results also include hits for taxonomic descendants of search concepts, as does SEMEDICO. However, GOPUBMED does not integrate any relational information (such as protein-protein interactions) or factuality detection and operates on PUBMED abstracts only.

FACTA+ (Tsuruoka et al., 2011) recognizes a range of biomedical entity types (genes/proteins, diseases, symptoms, drugs, enzymes and compounds) in MEDLINE abstracts and analyzes documents for biomedical event triggers (Kim et al., 2008). FACTA+ offers multiple search modes. The *Find Associated Concepts* mode finds indirect associations between entities in the spirit of Swanson's notion of undiscovered public knowledge (Swanson, 1986) and thus is not the focus of this comparison. The *View Documents* mode is the information retrieval part of the system and lists highlighted MEDLINE titles and abstracts. This mode retrieves keyword-based results without making use of conceptual knowledge. FACTA+ detects event triggers and also gene mentions, but it does not include the gene arguments in its event model. Thus, one cannot search specifically, for example, a regulation of the gene *BRCA1*. SEMEDICO, on the other hand, exploits its ontological resources for concept synonyms, recognizes event trigger-argument structures and stores them as searchable items in the index.

QUETZAL (Coppernoll-Blach, 2011) stores hundreds of millions (250 million as of 2011) subject-verb-object relations that are matched against query terms to produce focused sentence-level retrieval results. In this regard, QUETZAL shares the basic idea of SEMEDICO that semantic relations between query terms are more relevant than longer text passages mentioning the query terms only in a loosely connected way. QUETZAL includes arbitrary relations of all kinds rather than domain-specific types of relations like SEMEDICO. The advantage of this approach is a higher domain coverage. On the downside, QUETZAL's restriction fails to account for a large number of interactions which are expressed using nouns, e.g., *"the regulation of mTOR"*. QUETZAL does not incorporate factuality information to the best of our knowledge.

FERRET's (Srinivasan et al., 2015) focus lies on the exploration of sentence-level gene-centric relationships in MEDLINE citations. The system performs gene name disambiguation and allows for query expansion via gene homologues. Retrieved sentences contain findings for gene-gene or gene-keyword pairs. SEMEDICO, in contradistinction, flexibly searches genes in a larger variety of text segment block sizes, including sentences.

POLYSEARCH2 (Liu et al., 2015) finds associations between an extensive range of entity types. Given a query with a specified entity class, the user may ask for relationships to another entity class. POLYSEARCH2 searches associations in a wide range of resources, including PUBMED, PUBMED CENTRAL, Wikipedia and life-science related databases. It does not support ad hoc free-text queries and does not employ dedicated recognition tools for entities or relations and always operates on the sentence level, much in contrast to SEMEDICO.

GENEVIEW (Thomas et al., 2012) employs an large variety of named entity recognition tools to automatically annotate different entity classes in MEDLINE and PUBMED CENTRAL, including SNPs, species, chemicals, histone modifications, genes, protein-protein interactions (PPIs) and more. Document scoring includes field length normalization, such that term matches in titles achieve higher scores than comparable matches across a whole section. In this way, GENEVIEW implements the idea that shorter text portions with entity matches are more relevant than longer stretches

---

[1] https://www.nlm.nih.gov/mesh/
[2] http://www.geneontology.org/
[3] http://www.uniprot.org/

of texts in a similar way as SEMEDICO does, but is restricted to formal title, abstract and full text sections. Unlike SEMEDICO, which automatically searches gene name query terms within molecular events, GENEVIEW requires the exact database identifier (e.g., NCBI GENE ID to search for a gene or an input of the form PPI:GENEID to search for PPIs including the given gene ID). There is no possibility to rank PPIs according to the degree of factuality.

HYPOTHESISFINDER (Malhotra et al., 2013) is one of the few life science search engines besides SEMEDICO that employs factuality statements. Accordingly, it provides the user with speculative sentences from MEDLINE matching a keyword query. Its goal is to explicitly provide speculative statements in order to find scientific hypotheses, yet there is no ranking for factuality in the sense of SEMEDICO, nor makes it use of sophisticated entity or event extraction methods.

3 Resources Used in SEMEDICO

Literature input for SEMEDICO comes from two sources, *viz.* more than 27 million life science abstracts from MEDLINE/PUBMED[45] and approximately 1,5 million life science full texts from the open access subset of PUBMED CENTRAL. They are stored in a POSTGRESQL database.[6]

Domain knowledge for the life sciences is gathered from several terminological and ontological resources. Each document from MEDLINE is indexed with entries from the Medical Subject Headings (MESH), a hierarchically organized thesaurus with rather general entries at the top (e.g., "Anatomy") and quite specific entries at the hierarchy's leaves (e.g., "Ankle"). SEMEDICO makes use of the MESH headings as encoded in the original XML files, while it also recognizes mentions of MESH entry terms within the document text by its named entity recognizers.

Another extensively used resource is the NCBI GENE database.[7] Our gene recognition and normalization engine (see Section 4) maps gene mentions in document text to unique NCBI GENE database entries to handle gene name synonymy and ambiguity. Additionally, SEMEDICO integrates the GENE ONTOLOGY and the GENE REG-

ULATION ONTOLOGY (GRO)[8] for the semantic description of different types of gene events.

All resources are stored in a NEO4J[9] graph database for direct access to their hierarchical structure. All terminologies, ontologies and databases are converted into a common JSON format. This format is then imported into NEO4J using a custom NEO4J server plugin.

4 Text Analytics

The complete document set of all MEDLINE/PUBMED abstracts and PMC full texts (roughly, 28,5m documents) is represented in SEMEDICO's index. Before indexing, each document undergoes an extensive text analytics as depicted in Figure 1. The goal is to identify textual units referring to gene/protein mentions, MESH headings, ontology concepts, gene interaction events and associated factuality markers.

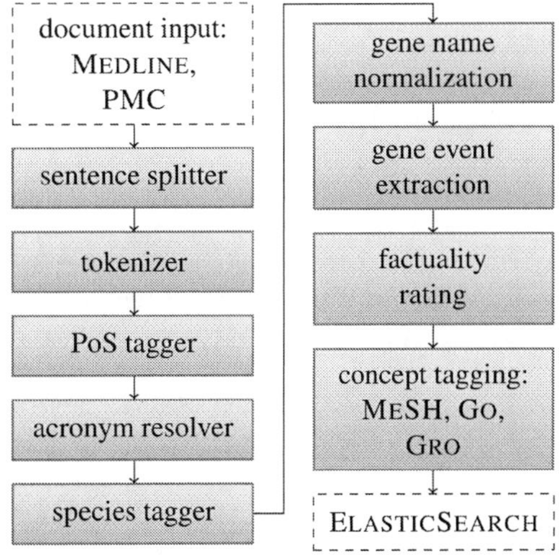

Figure 1: SEMEDICO's text analytics pipeline.

The morpho-syntactic analysis includes the resolution of acronyms (Schwartz and Hearst, 2003). This step is crucial for the interactive disambiguation feature of SEMEDICO. For most of these tasks, we employ JCORE (Hahn et al., 2016), our UIMA (Unstructured Information Management Architecture)[10] component repository.

Semantic analysis includes species tagging by the LINNAEUS tagger (Gerner et al., 2010), gene mention tagging and normalization using GENO

[4]https://www.ncbi.nlm.nih.gov/pubmed
[5]https://www.nlm.nih.gov/databases/download/pubmed_medline.html
[6]https://www.postgresql.org/
[7]https://www.ncbi.nlm.nih.gov/gene
[8]https://bioportal.bioontology.org/ontologies/GRO
[9]https://neo4j.com/
[10]https://uima.apache.org/

(Wermter et al., 2009), gene / protein event recognition with BIOSEM (Bui et al., 2013) and identification of event confidence ratings using the factuality rating determined by Hahn and Engelmann (2014). For BIOSEM, we use a model trained on the BIONLP SHARED TASK 2011 (Kim et al., 2011) training data that includes abstracts as well as full texts. MESH, GO and GRO concepts are tagged by a dictionary component. We then store the annotation results together with the original, raw documents in the document database.

In a last step, the analysis results are sent to an ELASTICSEARCH cluster for indexing. We use a custom ELASTICSEARCH plugin to have ELASTICSEARCH accept a term format that allows to exactly specify index terms within the ELASTICSEARCH index. This way, the exact linguistic analysis results are channeled into the index.

5 Document Indexing and Scoring

All concepts, i.e., entities like species, MESH headings, GO or GRO concepts, are indexed including their taxonomical ascendants such that a search for *Dementia* also includes text mentions of *Alzheimer's Disease* or *Huntington's Disease*.

As the basic document scoring algorithm, ELASTICSEARCH's *TF-IDF* scoring function is used. Additionally to this concept-centric scoring strategy, SEMEDICO splits MEDLINE citations and PMC full texts into their titles, sentences, abstract sections, paragraphs, full text sections, table and figure captions and the complete document text, if applicable. In a technically similar manner, relations between genes/proteins are extracted directly from the documents and stored as searchable items in the ELASTICSEARCH index as nested documents, still being connected to the original document. Relations are stored with information about the event types playing a role in the gene/protein interaction (e.g., Binding, Phosphorylation, Positive/Negative Regulation, etc.) and the actual gene/protein arguments involved.

Additionally, each relation item in the index is assigned an ordinal value representing the factuality status of the relation as expressed by the authors through explicit linguistic signals using epistemic modalities (such as *'could'*, *'probably'*, *'we believe'*, etc.). Based on experiments described in Hahn and Engelmann (2014), each lexical indicator for the expression of factuality is assigned an empirically determined "likelihood"

value which is subsequently transferred to each relation that carries such an epistemic labeling. The lowest likelihood value is issued when a negation is encountered because the authors express the firm belief that such a statement is false. If no epistemic modalities are detected in a sentence, we assign the highest likelihood.

SEMEDICO uses such factuality information to rank gene interaction relations according to their certainty, by default prioritizing statements with a higher factuality rating over lower ones. The final document score for the result list ranking is derived from the individual text portion and relation scores the document has, weighted by ELASTICSEARCH field length normalization on the basis of the spatial proximity of the text portions in which search terms co-occur. This way, SEMEDICO prefers query matches on shorter text passages over those in larger ones.

6 Web Application

SEMEDICO is realized as an APACHE TAPESTRY 5 web application.[11] Its start page presents itself with an input field for query input. It expects the user to enter query terms and prompts suggestions derived from the items in the NEO4J concept database (see Section 3) as soon as the user types into the input field (see Figure 2).

Enzymes × apc		
APC (Antigen-presenting cells)		Blood Cells
APC1 (PC1)		Genes and Proteins
APC2 (morula)		Genes and Proteins
APC5		Genes and Proteins
APC7		Genes and Proteins
APC9		Genes and Proteins
ApCp (adenylyl(3'-5')cytidine-3'-phosphate)		Chemicals and Drugs
ApCy (adenylyl cytidine)		Chemicals and Drugs
apc1 (slc25a24-b)		Genes and Proteins
APC11 (lmgA)		Genes and Proteins
apc		Keyword

Figure 2: SEMEDICO finds suggestions in the concept database.

We use an adapted version of the JQUERY TOKEN PLUGIN[12] to segment the query into "tokens" to clarify what is searched for. A token

[11]http://tapestry.apache.org/
[12]http://loopj.com/jquery-tokeninput/

94

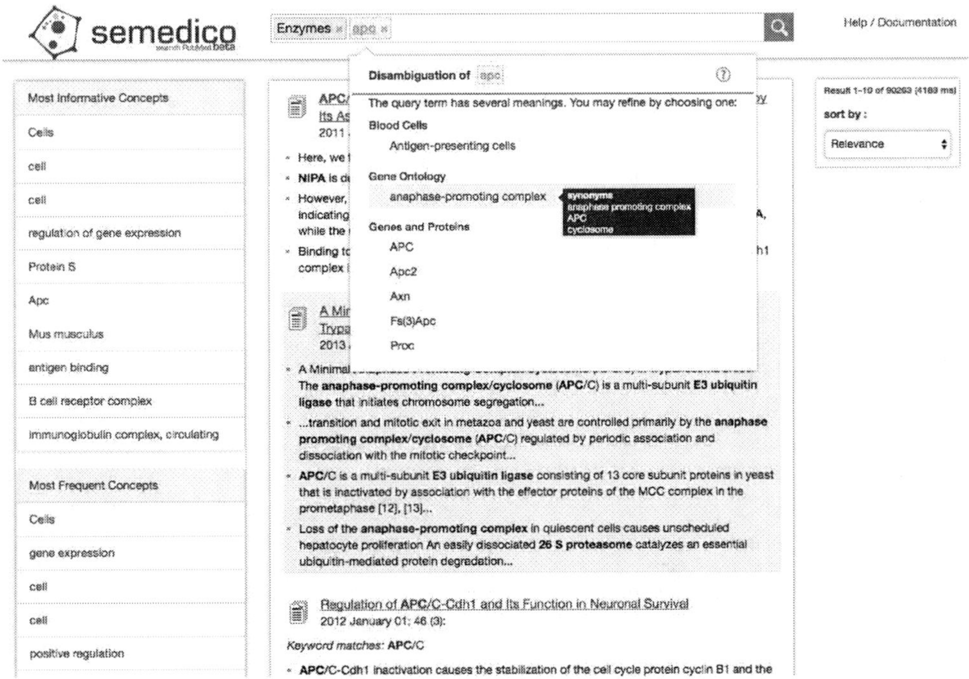

Figure 3: SEMEDICO highlights query concept matches in document snippets and allows explicit disambiguation of concept names.

may consist of multiple words and either represents a database concept or a keyword that cannot be (or, as decided by the user, should not be) resolved to a concept name.

If the user does not select any of these suggestions, SEMEDICO automatically recognizes concepts in the query. For query portions which can be mapped to multiple concepts, SEMEDICO assigns a specific graphical styling to the query tokens in question after the search process and displays disambiguation options when the cursor is hovered over the tokens (see Figure 3). All disambiguation options are concepts from the database and contain their synonyms as tooltips to help the user in the disambiguation process.

SEMEDICO makes extensive use of highlighting to clarify at first glance why a document match was deemed relevant. Since SEMEDICO does not only search for the exact query concepts but also for their taxonomic subordinates, subordinate matches are also highlighted. For example, Figure 3 shows that a search for *Enzymes* also leads to matches like *E3 ubiquitin ligase*, which is a taxonomic descendant of the *Enzymes* heading in the MESH. Again, matches in shorter text snippets

are expected to be more valuable to the user than those in larger text portions, and are thus displayed to the user with higher preference. On the left side, SEMEDICO shows concepts occurring in the document result list, sorted either by frequency or by using the ELASTICSEARCH "Significant Terms Aggregation".[13] These concepts may be added to the current query for refinement.

Clicking on an article title opens a new page showing the abstract with highlighted search concept matches and, for PMC hits, a list of highlighted full text matches, showing the highest ranking query matches without the need for further search within a – possibly very long – document. Links to PUBMED, PMC and publisher full text sources allow easy access to the original publication.

7   Conclusion

We presented SEMEDICO, a semantic search engine for PUBMED and PUBMED CENTRAL that assists users with query formulation by con-

---

[13]`https://www.elastic.co/guide/en/elasticsearch/guide/2.x/significant-terms.html`

cept suggestion, recognition and interactive disambiguation. SEMEDICO covers multiple levels of semantics, from simple abbreviation resolution over entity recognition to relation extraction for gene interaction events. Sentences are tagged for varying degrees of factuality and relations are ranked by scoring these degrees. The semantic units are further scored by varying levels of textual proximity—first, looking for explicitly expressed gene relations, co-occurrences of query concepts within sentences, paragraphs or even larger text blocks. All sources of evidence are translated into a measure of semantic tightness between query concepts. Furthermore, the ranking reflects a preference for grouping query terms together in a closer textual context, while textually more dispersed co-occurrences are sorted on lower ranks.

Acknowledgments.

This work is part of the Collaborative Research Center AQUADIVA (SFB 1076: AQUADIVA) established at Friedrich-Schiller-Universität Jena and funded by *Deutsche Forschungsgemeinschaft* (DFG). Initial funding of SEMEDICOwas due to the *German Ministry of Education and Research* (BMBF) for the *Jena Centre of Systems Biology of Ageing* (JENAGE) (grant no. 0315581D).

References

Quoc-Chinh Bui, David Campos, Erik M. van Mulligen, and Jan A. Kors. 2013. A fast rule-based approach for biomedical event extraction. In *BioNLP 2013 — Proceedings of the BioNLP Shared Task 2013 Workshop @ ACL 2013. Sofia, Bulgaria, August 9, 2013*. pages 104–108.

Penny Coppernoll-Blach. 2011. Quertle: The conceptual relationships alternative search engine for PubMed. *Journal of the Medical Library Association* 99(2):176–177.

Andreas Doms and Michael Schroeder. 2005. GoPubMed: exploring PubMed with the Gene Ontology. *Nucleic Acids Research* 33(Suppl 2):W783–W786.

Martin Gerner, Goran Nenadic, and Casey M. Bergman. 2010. Linnaeus: a species name identification system for biomedical literature. *BMC Bioinformatics* 11:#85.

Udo Hahn and Christine Engelmann. 2014. Grounding epistemic modality in speakers' judgments. In Duc-Nghia Pham and Seong-Bae Park, editors, *Trends in Artificial Intelligence. PRICAI 2014 — Proceedings of the 13th Pacific Rim International Conference on Artificial Intelligence. Gold Coast, Australia, 1-5 Dec, 2014*. Springer, number 8862 in Lecture Notes in Artificial Intelligence, pages 654–667.

Udo Hahn, Franz Matthies, Erik Faessler, and Johannes Hellrich. 2016. UIMA-based JCoRe 2.0 goes GitHub and Maven Central: state-of-the-art software resource engineering and distribution of NLP pipelines. In *LREC 2016 — Proceedings of the 10th International Conference on Language Resources and Evaluation. Portorož, Slovenia, 23-28 May 2016*. pages 2502–2509.

Jin-Dong Kim, Tomoko Ohta, and Jun'ichi Tsujii. 2008. Corpus annotation for mining biomedical events from literature. *BMC Bioinformatics* 9:10.

Jin-Dong Kim, Sampo Pyysalo, Tomoko Ohta, Robert Bossy, Ngan Nguyen, and Jun'ichi Tsujii. 2011. Overview of BioNLP Shared Task 2011. In *BioNLP 2011 — Proceedings of the BioNLP Shared Task 2011 Workshop @ ACL-HLT 2011. Portland, Oregon, USA, 24 June 2011*. pages 1–6.

Yifeng Liu, Yongjie Liang, and David S. Wishart. 2015. PolySearch2: a significantly improved text-mining system for discovering associations between human diseases, genes, drugs, metabolites, toxins and more. *Nucleic Acids Research* 43(W1):W535–W542.

Zhiyong Lu. 2011. Pubmed and beyond: a survey of web tools for searching biomedical literature. *Database: The Journal of Biological Databases and Curation* page #baq036.

Ashutosh Malhotra, Erfan Younesi, Harsha Gurulingappa, and Martin Hofmann-Apitius. 2013. 'HypothesisFinder:' a strategy for the detection of speculative statements in scientific text. *PLoS Computational Biology* 9(7):e1003117.

Ariel S. Schwartz and Marti A. Hearst. 2003. A simple algorithm for identifying abbreviation definitions in biomedical text. In *PSB 2003 – Proceedings of the Pacific Symposium on Biocomputing 2003. Kauai, Hawaii, USA, January 3-7, 2003*. pages 451–462.

Padmini Srinivasan, Xiao-Ning Zhang, Roxane Bouten, and Caren Chang. 2015. Ferret: a sentence-based literature scanning system. *BMC Bioinformatics* 16(1):#198.

Don R. Swanson. 1986. Fish oil, Raynaud's Syndrome, and undiscovered public knowledge. *Perspectives in Biology and Medicine* 30(1):7–18.

Philippe E. Thomas, Johannes Starlinger, Alexander Vowinkel, Sebastian Arzt, and Ulf Leser. 2012. GeneView: a comprehensive semantic search engine for PubMed. *Nucleic Acids Research* 40(W1):W585–W591.

Yoshimasa Tsuruoka, Makoto Miwa, Kaisei Hamamoto, Jun'ichi Tsujii, and Sophia Ananiadou. 2011. Discovering and visualizing indirect associations between biomedical concepts. *Bioinformatics* 27(13):i111–i119.

Joachim Wermter, Katrin Tomanek, and Udo Hahn. 2009. High-performance gene name normalization with GeNo. *Bioinformatics* 25(6):815–821.

SuperAgent: A Customer Service Chatbot for E-commerce Websites

Lei Cui,* **Shaohan Huang**,* **Furu Wei**, **Chuanqi Tan**, **Chaoqun Duan**, and **Ming Zhou**

Microsoft Research Asia

`{lecu,shaohanh,fuwei,v-chutan,v-chadu,mingzhou}@microsoft.com`

Abstract

Conventional customer service chatbots are usually based on human dialogue, yet significant issues in terms of data scale and privacy. In this paper, we present SuperAgent, a customer service chatbot that leverages large-scale and publicly available e-commerce data. Distinct from existing counterparts, SuperAgent takes advantage of data from in-page product descriptions as well as user-generated content from e-commerce websites, which is more practical and cost-effective when answering repetitive questions, freeing up human support staff to answer much higher value questions. We demonstrate SuperAgent as an add-on extension to mainstream web browsers and show its usefulness to user's online shopping experience.

1 Introduction

Customer service plays an important role in an organization's ability to generate income and revenue. It is often the most resource-intensive department within a company, consuming billions of dollars a year to change the entire perception customers hold. Support staff spend a lot of time answering questions via telephone or messaging applications to make sure are customers satisfied with their business. This traditional customer service has two problems: First, staff usually receive repetitive questions asked by a variety of customers, which can be cost-effectively answered by machines. Second, it is difficult to support 7×24 services, especially for most non-global businesses. Therefore, chatbots can be a great way to supplement customer service offerings since they are more economical and indefati-

gable, and free up support staff to answer much higher value queries.

Recently, virtual assistants for customer service have become more and more popular with customer oriented businesses. Most of them are built from human conversations in the past, which is straightforward but faced with problems of data scale and privacy. Most of the time, customers need to wait online to get a support staff person's answer, which is less effective and difficult to scale up. Meanwhile, customers may have privacy concerns about the conversations, hence conversations with customers cannot be easily leveraged to train a chatbot. It is essential to find large-scale and publicly available customer service data sources on which to build such assistants.

In this paper, we demonstrate SuperAgent, a powerful customer service chatbot leveraging large-scale and publicly available e-commerce data. Nowadays, large e-commerce websites contain a great deal of in-page product descriptions as well as user-generated content, such as Amazon.com, Ebay.com, and JD.com. Figure 1 shows a product page from Amazon.com, which contains detailed Product Information (PI), a set of existing customer Questions & Answers (QA), as well as sufficient Customer Reviews (CR). This crowdsourcing style of data provides appropriate information to feed into chat engines, accompanying human support staff to deliver better customer service experience when online shopping.

We define the problem as follows: given a specific product page and a customer question, SuperAgent selects the best answer from existing data sources within the page (PI+QA+CR). If it cannot find the answer, it indicates that no replies will be generated. Specifically, we decompose the chat engine into three sub-engines: 1) a fact question answering engine for PI; 2) an FAQ search engine for QA; 3) an opinion mining & text question an-

---

The first two authors contribute equally to this work.

Proceedings of the 55th Annual Meeting of the Association for Computational Linguistics-System Demonstrations, pages 97–102
Vancouver, Canada, July 30 - August 4, 2017. ©2017 Association for Computational Linguistics
https://doi.org/10.18653/v1/P17-4017

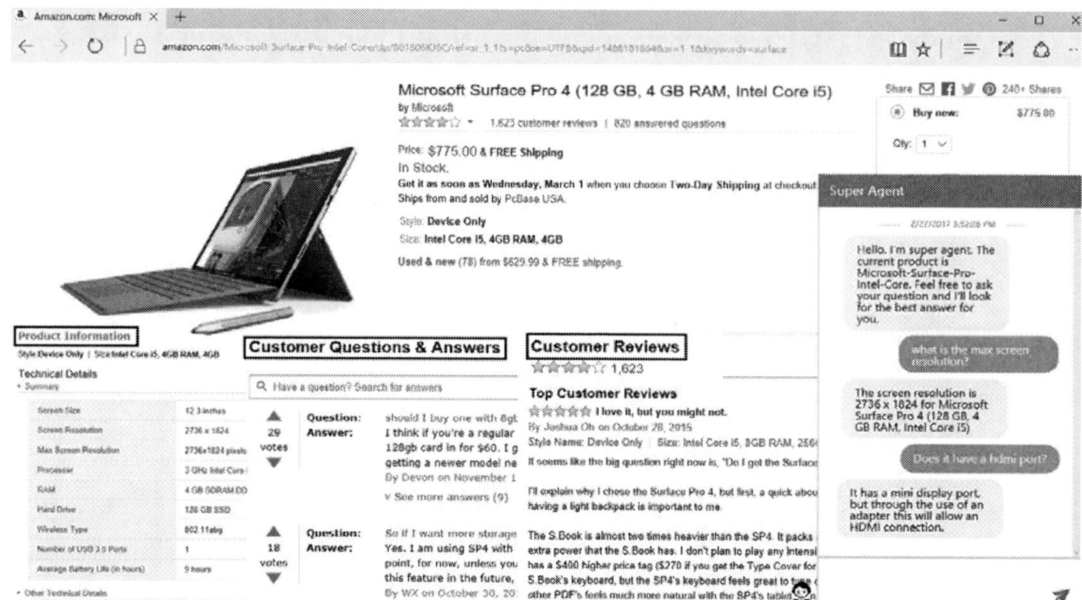

Figure 1: An example of a product page from Amazon.com, including product information, customer Q&A, and reviews. SuperAgent is an add-on extension located at the bottom right corner.

swering engine for CR. In addition, we also add a chit-chat engine as the back-fill to make conversations as smooth as possible. To improve the overall online shopping experience, we demonstrate SuperAgent as an add-on extension to mainstream web browsers such as Microsoft Edge and Google Chrome, where the conversation UI is shown at the bottom right corner, as shown in Figure 1.

Compared to conventional customer service chatbots, SuperAgent has several promising advantages:

1. SuperAgent can easily leverage crowd-sourcing styles, as well as large-scale and publicly available e-commerce data,

2. SuperAgent contains a set of state-of-the-art NLP and machine learning techniques, including fact QA, FAQ search, opinion mining, text QA, and chit-chat conversation.

3. SuperAgent is integrated into e-commerce websites as an add-on extension, which can directly improve customer's online shopping experience.

The rest of the paper is organized as follows: The system details are described in Section 2. The usability analysis is presented in Section 3. Section 4 introduces some related work. Section 5 concludes the paper and suggests future directions.

2 System Details

2.1 Overview

Figure 2 shows the system overview of SuperAgent. As the figure shows, when the product page is first visited, SuperAgent crawls the html information and scrape PI+QA+CR data from the webpage. The advantage of this design pattern is that we do not need to deploy web crawlers for the websites. Instead, when users visit the page, SuperAgent will be notified since the add-on extension is associated with each webpage. Therefore, SuperAgent brings very few additional web loads to the host websites. Besides, this architecture makes data updates very easy to implement, where frequently-visited pages get updated frequently and vice versa. After that, given an input query from a customer, different engines are processed in parallel. If one of the answers from the first three engines has high confidence, the chatbot returns with the answer as the response. Otherwise, the chit-chat engine will generate a reply from the predefined permitted response sets. Next, we introduce these engines in detail.

2.2 Fact QA for Product Information

The fact QA engine is designed for answering questions regarding the facts of the product. The product information is stored in the

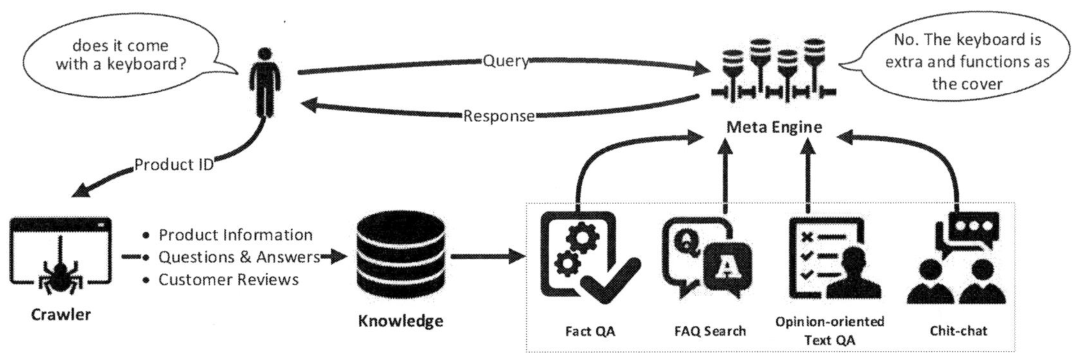

Figure 2: The system overview of SuperAgent

format of knowledge triples ⟨#, attribute_name, attribute_value⟩, where # represents the product name in our scenario. We focus on simple fact inquiry in this paper. As a result, the task is transformed to matching the question to the attribute names in the product information. This is achieved with a deep learning based matching framework. Specifically, the input question is matched with every attribute name using the DSSM model (Huang et al., 2013). We select the top-ranked attribute name which passes a predefined threshold as the result from attribute matching. The corresponding attribute value is further used to generate the response sentences with predefined templates. The engine's output is shown as follows:

Q: What's the CPU?

A: The processor is 3 GHz Intel Core i5 for Microsoft Surface Pro 4 (128 GB, 4 GB RAM, Intel Core i5)

Q: What is the pre-installed operating system?

A: The operating system is Windows 10 Pro for Microsoft Surface Pro 4 (128 GB, 4 GB RAM, Intel Core i5)

2.3 FAQ Search for Customer QA Pairs

The FAQ search engine is defined as follows: given a set of QA pairs $P = \{q_i, a_i\}_{i=1}^n$ and a customer's question q, we find the most similar q_j in P and return the corresponding a_j as the reply. For example, given two QA pairs:

Q: does it come with a keyboard

A: No. The keyboard is extra and functions as the cover

Q: does it come with the pen

A: yes it does

Then, if the user asks "does it have a keyboard", the question "does it come with a keyboard" will be matched and the answer should be "No. The keyboard is extra and functions as the cover". Therefore, the question ranking problem is essential for an FAQ search engine.

Formally, given two questions q and $q\prime$, the question ranker will learn a mapping function f where $f(q, q\prime) \rightarrow [0, 1]$, so f is actually a semantic similarity metric between two questions, indicating whether they convey the same meaning. We train a regression forest model (Meinshausen, 2006) and use the following features: monolingual word aligner (Sultan et al., 2014), DSSM model (Huang et al., 2013), word embedding composition (max, sum, idf-sum) with GloVe (Pennington et al., 2014), n-gram overlap, subsequence matching, PairingWords (Han et al., 2013), word mover's distance (Kusner et al., 2015).

The model is evaluated on the dataset for SemEval-2016 Task 1. The mean accuracy (Pearson Correlation) of our model on five datasets (0.78455) significantly outperforms the 1st place team (0.77807)[1]. Specifically, the accuracy on the question-to-question dataset is 0.75773, surpassing the 1st place team (0.68705) by a large margin. This confirms the effectiveness of our model on the FAQ search task.

2.4 Opinion-Oriented Text QA for Reviews

Customer reviews provide rich information for different aspects of the product from users' per-

---

[1] http://alt.qcri.org/semeval2016/task1/index.php?id=results

spective. They are very important resources for answering opinion-oriented questions. To this end, we first split the review text into sentences and run opinion mining modules to extract the aspects and corresponding opinions. We then use the text question answering module to generate responses (i.e. review sentences).

For opinion mining, we use a hybrid approach (Qiu et al., 2011) to extract the aspects from review sentences. We also run the sentiment classifier (Tang et al., 2014) to determine the polarity (i.e. positive, negative, and neutral) of the sentence regarding the specific aspect mentioned. The aspects and polarity are indexed together with keywords using the Lucene toolkit[2].

For text QA, given an input query, it outputs the answer based on the following three steps:

- *Candidate retrieval*, which searches the query by Lucene to get candidate sentences.

- *Candidate ranking*, which ranks all candidate sentences with a regression based ranking framework.

- *Candidate triggering*, which decides whether it is confident enough to output the candidate.

Specifically, for candidate retrieval, we use the default ranker in Lucene to retrieve the top 20 candidate sentences. For candidate ranking, we build a regression based framework to rank all candidate sentences based on features designed at different levels of granularity. Our feature set consists of WordCnt, translation model, type matching, WordNet, and two neural network based methods BiCNN (Yu et al., 2014) and MatchLSTM (Wang and Jiang, 2016). We conduct experiments on the WikiQA (Yang et al., 2015) dataset. The results show that we achieve state-of-the-art results with 0.7164 in terms of MAP and 0.7332 in terms of MRR. For candidate triggering, as the ranking model outputs a regression score for each candidate sentence, we only output the candidate sentence whose score is higher than the threshold selected on the development set. The engine's output examples are shown as follows:

> Q: what do you think of the battery life of surface pro 4?
>
> R: I've been getting ˜7-9 hours of battery life on the SP4 which is more than enough to get me through a school day.

^{2}`http://lucene.apache.org`

Q: Is the screen size of surface pro 4 appropriate for reading?

R: The screen is not too small like the iPad, neither is it bulky like a laptop.

2.5 Chit-chat Conversation Modeling

The chit-chat engine is mainly designed to reply to greeting queries such as "hello" and "thank you", as well as queries that cannot be answered by the previous three engines, such as "you are so cute". However, general chit-chat engines tend to be topic-deviated so that the replies may be irrelevant. To avoid such deviations, we follow the smart reply approach for email reply suggestions (Kannan et al., 2016) to predefine a permitted response set. Formally, the chit-chat model is an attention-based LSTM seq2seq model (Bahdanau et al., 2014) trained on twitter conversation data (˜43 million query-reply pairs). We select the 5 million most frequent non-duplicate short replies (less than 15 words) as the permitted response set, most of which are greetings and common replies. The end-to-end perplexity of the seq2seq model is 16.9, which is similar to Kannan et al.'s result. The engine's output is very topic-coherent, which is shown as follows:

> Q: hello
>
> R: hey how are you?
>
> Q: thank you
>
> R: you're very welcome sir
>
> Q: you are so cute
>
> R: u r more

2.6 Meta Engine

For each query, SuperAgent will call the above-mentioned sub-engines in parallel. The meta engine is then used to merge and prioritize the results from the different engines. We use a simple strategy to implement the meta engine, which prefers results from the engines in order of fact QA, FAQ search, text QA and chit-chat engine according to tunable threshold.

3 Usability Analysis

In this section, we discuss the reason why SuperAgent is necessary and how customers use it. When customers visit e-commerce websites, they often need to know what other people feel after the purchase. In addition, customers are also interested in the answers to similar questions that other people have. We randomly select 670 product pages from Amazon.com and get a total of 29,471 customer QA pairs, almost 44 pairs per product on average. We also get 72,402 customer reviews, about 108 reviews per product on average. The number is much higher for a popular product, making it difficult for users to read all of them. For example, in Figure 1, there are more than 800 QA pairs existing within the page, which is impossible to go through by customers. Besides, there are also more than 1,200 high quality customer reviews in the page of Figure 1, which is overwhelming for users to read. Therefore, it is crucial to integrate these data into a unified knowledge base and provide easy access to all customers.

Figure 3 shows a typical scenario when a customer asks SuperAgent for help. When the customer opens up the chat window within web browsers, SuperAgent first detects which product is being visited. SuperAgent then makes a self-introduction and confirms that the customer is visiting the product. Subsequently, customers may greet SuperAgent or ask specific questions. As Figure 3 shows, SuperAgent is able to answer fact questions using in-page product information, conduct an FAQ search from customer QA pairs, get text QA answers from customer reviews, and finally greet customers using the chit-chat engine. The dialogs are coordinated by the meta engine so that different queries go to corresponding engines respectively. Since e-commerce websites get updated frequently and fresh user-generated content emerges continuously, SuperAgent also updates the data and models periodically according to the frequency of customers' visits.

4   Related Work

Customer service chatbots can be roughly categorized into two types: first-party and third-party. First-party chatbots refer to conversation engines developed by large enterprises for their own business to improve customer service quality and reduce overall customer service budget. This often happens in consumer-driven industries such as banking, telecoms, and e-commerce. One example is the recently launched chatbot Erica from Bank of America, which helps customers with banking-related problems. Another example is the

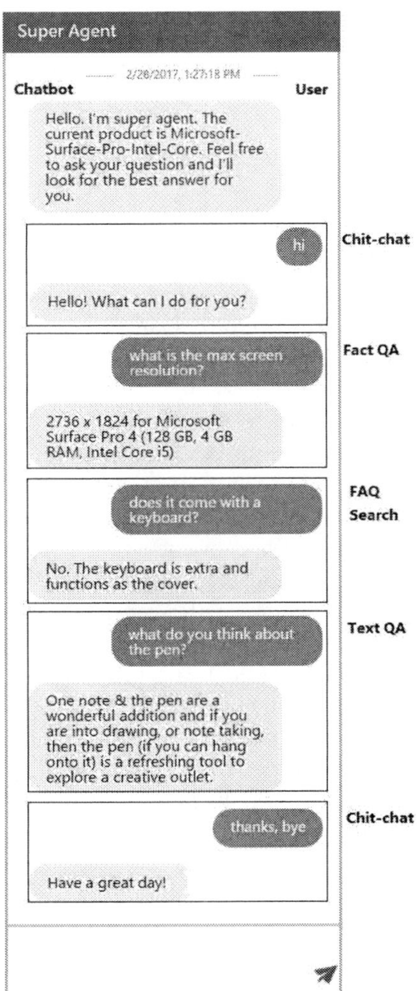

Figure 3: A case study of SuperAgent

AT&T support chatbot that helps people answer FAQs related to different business questions.

Third-party chatbots refer to open source building blocks that help developers to build their conversation engines, such as Microsoft Bot Framework[3], Facebook Messenger[4], Google Assistant[5], and Amazon Lex[6]. These chatbot makers build and connect intelligent conversation engines to interact with customers naturally wherever they are. In addition, they are highly customizable in terms of real scenarios with third-party data.

It is worth mentioning that we position SuperAgent as a third-party chatbot because it utilizes

---

[3]https://dev.botframework.com/
[4]https://messengerplatform.fb.com/
[5]https://assistant.google.com/
[6]https://aws.amazon.com/lex/

publicly available third-party data. Moreover, it improves the overall online shopping experience for various products in an e-commerce website.

5 Conclusion and Future Work

We have developed SuperAgent, a customer service chatbot for e-commerce websites. Compared to conventional customer service chatbots, SuperAgent takes advantage of large-scale, publicly available, and crowd-sourced customer data. In addition, SuperAgent leverages state-of-the-art NLP and machine learning techniques, including fact QA, FAQ search, opinion-oriented text QA, as well as chit-chat conversation modeling. Usability analysis shows that SuperAgent has improved the end-to-end user experience in terms of online shopping. It is more convenient for customer's information acquisition especially when a product page contains too much user-generated content.

In the future, we will focus on two main problems. First, we need to integrate a customer's query intent detection module, so that we can better leverage individual engines. Second, we will have a deeper delve on multi-turn queries, where context modeling will be further investigated.

References

Dzmitry Bahdanau, Kyunghyun Cho, and Yoshua Bengio. 2014. Neural machine translation by jointly learning to align and translate. *CoRR* abs/1409.0473. http://arxiv.org/abs/1409.0473.

Lushan Han, Abhay L. Kashyap, Tim Finin, James Mayfield, and Jonathan Weese. 2013. Umbc_ebiquity-core: Semantic textual similarity systems. In *Second Joint Conference on Lexical and Computational Semantics (*SEM), Volume 1: Proceedings of the Main Conference and the Shared Task: Semantic Textual Similarity*. Association for Computational Linguistics, Atlanta, Georgia, USA, pages 44–52. http://www.aclweb.org/anthology/S13-1005.

Po-Sen Huang, Xiaodong He, Jianfeng Gao, Li Deng, Alex Acero, and Larry Heck. 2013. Learning deep structured semantic models for web search using clickthrough data. In *Proceedings of the 22Nd ACM International Conference on Information & Knowledge Management*. ACM, New York, NY, USA, CIKM '13, pages 2333–2338. https://doi.org/10.1145/2505515.2505665.

Anjuli Kannan, Karol Kurach, Sujith Ravi, Tobias Kaufman, Balint Miklos, Greg Corrado, Andrew Tomkins, Laszlo Lukacs, Marina Ganea, Peter Young, and Vivek Ramavajjala. 2016. Smart reply: Automated response suggestion for email. In *Proceedings of the ACM SIGKDD Conference on Knowledge Discovery and Data Mining (KDD) (2016)..* http://www.kdd.org/kdd2016/papers/files/Paper_1069.pdf.

Matt J. Kusner, Yu Sun, Nicholas I. Kolkin, and Kilian Q. Weinberger. 2015. From word embeddings to document distances. In *Proceedings of the 32Nd International Conference on International Conference on Machine Learning - Volume 37*. JMLR.org, ICML'15, pages 957–966. http://dl.acm.org/citation.cfm?id=3045118.3045221.

Nicolai Meinshausen. 2006. Quantile regression forests. *J. Mach. Learn. Res.* 7:983–999. http://dl.acm.org/citation.cfm?id=1248547.1248582.

Jeffrey Pennington, Richard Socher, and Christopher D. Manning. 2014. Glove: Global vectors for word representation. In *Empirical Methods in Natural Language Processing (EMNLP)*. pages 1532–1543. http://www.aclweb.org/anthology/D14-1162.

Guang Qiu, Bing Liu, Jiajun Bu, and Chun Chen. 2011. Opinion word expansion and target extraction through double propagation. *Comput. Linguist.* 37(1):9–27. https://doi.org/10.1162/coli_a_00034.

Md Sultan, Steven Bethard, and Tamara Sumner. 2014. Back to basics for monolingual alignment: Exploiting word similarity and contextual evidence. *Transactions of the Association for Computational Linguistics* 2:219–230. https://transacl.org/ojs/index.php/tacl/article/view/292.

Duyu Tang, Furu Wei, Nan Yang, Ming Zhou, Ting Liu, and Bing Qin. 2014. Learning sentiment-specific word embedding for twitter sentiment classification. In *Proceedings of the 52nd Annual Meeting of the Association for Computational Linguistics (Volume 1: Long Papers)*. Association for Computational Linguistics, Baltimore, Maryland, pages 1555–1565. http://www.aclweb.org/anthology/P14-1146.

Shuohang Wang and Jing Jiang. 2016. Learning natural language inference with LSTM. In *NAACL HLT 2016, The 2016 Conference of the North American Chapter of the Association for Computational Linguistics: Human Language Technologies, San Diego California, USA, June 12-17, 2016*.

Yi Yang, Wen-tau Yih, and Christopher Meek. 2015. Wikiqa: A challenge dataset for open-domain question answering. In *Proceedings of the 2015 Conference on Empirical Methods in Natural Language Processing*. Association for Computational Linguistics, pages 2013–2018. https://doi.org/10.18653/v1/D15-1237.

Lei Yu, Karl Moritz Hermann, Phil Blunsom, and Stephen Pulman. 2014. Deep learning for answer sentence selection. *Proceedings of the Deep Learning and Representation Learning Workshop: NIPS* .

Swanson linking revisited: Accelerating literature-based discovery across domains using a conceptual influence graph

Gus Hahn-Powell   **Marco Valenzuela-Escárcega**   **Mihai Surdeanu**
University of Arizona, Tucson, AZ, USA
{hahnpowell, marcov, msurdeanu}@email.arizona.edu

Abstract

We introduce a modular approach for literature-based discovery consisting of a machine reading and knowledge assembly component that together produce a graph of influence relations (e.g., "A promotes B") from a collection of publications. A search engine is used to explore direct and indirect influence chains. Query results are substantiated with textual evidence, ranked according to their relevance, and presented in both a table-based view, as well as a network graph visualization. Our approach operates in both domain-specific settings, where there are knowledge bases and ontologies available to guide reading, and in multi-domain settings where such resources are absent. We demonstrate that this deep reading and search system reduces the effort needed to uncover "undiscovered public knowledge", and that with the aid of this tool a domain expert was able to drastically reduce her model building time from months to two days.

1   Introduction

Since at least 1990, there has been exponential growth in the number of academic papers published annually in the biomedical domain (Pautasso, 2012). For example, the number of English language biomedical publications indexed by PubMed[1] alone since 1900 has now surpassed 25 million[2]. Over 17 million of these were published between 1990 and 2015.

Although a number of information extraction (IE) systems have been developed to mine individual facts (e.g., biochemical interactions) from these publications, there is limited work on assembling and interpreting these fragments. This limitation may result in solutions to critical problems being overlooked, as many tasks today cross several disciplines that interact only minimally. Swanson (1986) described this problem as "undiscovered public knowledge".

In this work, we propose a machine reading and assembly approach that facilitates connections between different research efforts and research communities across several fields. Following past efforts in literature-based discovery (Smalheiser and Swanson, 1998; Bekhuis, 2006), we introduce a modular system that performs (a) information extraction and assembly from publications, and (b) hypothesis exploration using a custom search engine that queries the knowledge graph of direct and indirect links uncovered by the machine.

We elected to focus on links that highlight influence relations between two concepts (e.g., "CTCF activates FOXA1") in the biomedical domain. Importantly, our approach reads statements about influence relations from publications, and does not attempt to verify these findings directly through separate modeling.[3] We apply our system to build influence graphs for two scenarios: (a) biomolecular explanations of cell signaling pathways with applications to cancer research (this is a single domain rich with knowledge base (KB) resources to guide information extraction), and (b) factors influencing children's health (this task crosses multiple domains, and has limited supported from KBs).

---

[1] http://www.ncbi.nlm.nih.gov/pubmed
[2] https://www.ncbi.nlm.nih.gov/pubmed/?term=%221900%22%5BPDAT%5D%20%3A%20%222017%22%5BPDAT%5D&cmd=DetailsSearch

[3] In other words, we trust that the authors' statements are correct. Although these statements often contain causal language (e.g., "A causes B"), we avoid referring to these relations as causal, since our approach does not attempt to verify quantitative findings directly.

Proceedings of the 55th Annual Meeting of the Association for Computational Linguistics-System Demonstrations, pages 103–108
Vancouver, Canada, July 30 - August 4, 2017. ©2017 Association for Computational Linguistics
https://doi.org/10.18653/v1/P17-4018

2 Previous Work

There is a substantial body of work addressing open-domain machine reading (Banko et al., 2007; Carlson et al., 2010; Zhang, 2015), as well as systems that target specific domains (Björne et al., 2009; Nédellec et al., 2013; Peters et al., 2014). All of these systems read individual facts, which makes Swanson's observation even more valid today. Attempts have been made in the biomedical domain to assemble relations extracted by machine reading into coherent models (Hahn-Powell et al., 2016). This domain is known for the complexity of its models (Lander, 2010), which has spurred research on improved visualizations for actionable insights (Dang et al., 2015).

Our work builds on these previous efforts by assembling complex influence graphs from the extractions of a machine reading system, and through a novel search engine that efficiently searches this graph and visualizes the results in a simple and intuitive interface.

3 Approach

Our approach consists of two stages: (a) machine reading and assembly (MRA), which produces a graph of influence relations from a collection of publications, and (b) a search engine that explores both direct and indirect connections in this graph. In this section, we describe our machine reading and assembly approach. In Section 4 we describe the search engine over this influence graph.

We introduce methods for machine reading and assembly in two scenarios: (a) a domain-specific machine reading system for molecular biology, and (2) an open-domain system for discovering factors influencing children's health. Both systems are rule-based, which has the desirable property of producing an interpretable extraction model that allows for incremental, isolated improvements by an end user that understands the task at hand but is not a natural language processing (NLP), or a machine learning (ML) expert (the likely maintainer of such a system). Although the IE models we discuss in the next section are rule-based, the modular design of the system means that the graph explorer interface is agnostic of and independent to the IE component.

3.1 Domain-specific Reading and Assembly

Our MRA system for the biomedical literature is called REACH (from REading and Assembling

Contextual and Holistic mechanisms from text)[4]. This system extracts entities (e.g., proteins, other chemicals, biological processes) and events (e.g., biochemical interactions) from biomolecular literature. REACH is built on top of the Odin IE framework (Valenzuela-Escarcega et al., 2016) and captures 17 kinds of events, including *nested* events (i.e., events involving other events). The event grammars are applied in cascades composed of rules that describe patterns over both syntactic dependencies and token sequences, using constraints over a token's attributes (part-of-speech tag, lemma, etc.). The system architecture is summarized in Figure 1, and described below.

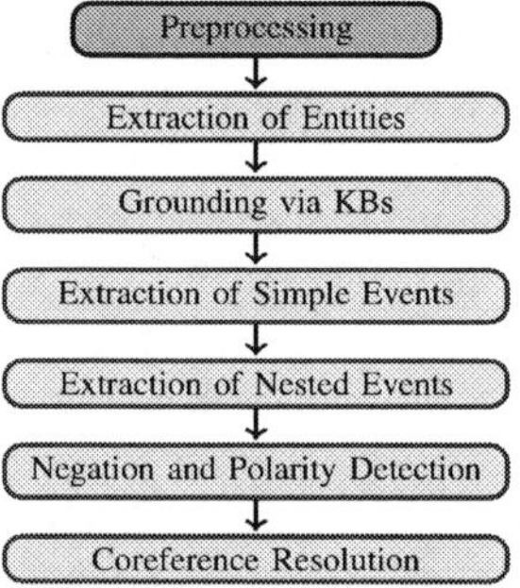

Figure 1: The REACH pipeline, which includes detection of hedging and negation. In addition to the components shown, REACH detects the scope of biological contexts such as cell line, tissue type, and species (not covered here).

Entity Extraction and Resolution

Because of its focus on a single domain (molecular biology), REACH leverages domain-specific resources such as curated knowledge bases (e.g., Uniprot[5] for protein names, and PubChem[6] for other chemicals) to perform entity recognition and resolution.

REACH's named entity recognizer (NER) is a hybrid model that combines a rule-based component with a statistical one.[7] The output of the NER system is then matched against the set of knowledge bases in order to "ground" these textual mentions to real-world entities through ID assignment. This grounding component enables the deduplication of entity nodes during graph construction (the assembly phase). That is, all synonyms of the

---

[4]`https://github.com/clulab/reach`
[5]`http://www.uniprot.org`
[6]`https://pubchem.ncbi.nlm.nih.gov`
[7]The details of this hybrid NER architecture are omited for brevity.

same protein are mapped to the same node in the influence graph.

Event Extraction

REACH uses a two-stage bottom-up strategy for event extraction, following biochemical semantics inspired by BioPAX (Demir et al., 2010). First, we identify biochemical reactions that operate directly on entities, initially ignoring their catalysts and other controllers, e.g., phosphorylation of a protein. We call these events "simple". REACH uses a domain-specific taxonomy for specifying the selectional restrictions on event arguments. Next, nested events are captured. For example, during this stage, catalysts that control simple events such as phosphorylations are extracted. During graph construction, these nested events are "flattened" into binary influence links. For example, the nested interaction `PositiveRegulation(Controller:A, Controlled:Phosphorylation(B))` is reduced to A → B, where the arrow indicates a left-to-right influence relation. Additionally, these links preserve the type (e.g., phosphorylation) and polarity of the biochemical interaction, e.g., a positive regulation is equivalent to a "promotes" link, whereas a negative regulation reduces to "inhibits".[8]

Coreference Resolution and Negation

The coreference resolution component in REACH adapts the algorithm of Lee et al. (2013) to the biomedical domain, where it operates both over entity mentions (e.g., by resolving pronominal and nominal mentions such as "it" or "this protein" to the corresponding entity) and event mentions (e.g., "this interaction" is resolved to an actual event) (Bell et al., 2016).

The negation detection module identifies explicit statements that a reaction does not occur (e.g., "ZAP70 does not induce TRIM phosphorylation") in a particular experimental context. REACH also handles more subtle linguistic phenomena such as reversing the polarity of events. For example, the naive interpretation of the text "decreased PTPN13 expression enhances EphrinB1 phosphorylation" yields a positive regulation (due to "enhances"). The polarity correction module changes this to a negative regulation due to the presence of the "decreased" modifier.

---

[8]Polarity detection is more complicated in practice, because some simple events have polarity information as well, which needs to be taken into account when flattening events. We ignore this situation here for brevity.

3.2 Multi-domain Reading and Assembly

Our second use case for MRA models children's health, which involves complex influence chains that span multiple levels of abstraction, linking low-level biomolecular processes with nutritional and socio-economic issues.

In such a setting, comprehensive resources are unavailable. Unlike in REACH, we cannot rely on a taxonomy to guide our extractions. While incomplete resources are available for a subset of the covered domains, we treat this use case as an opportunity to explore what can be extracted and assembled when no knowledge base is available for entity recognition or resolution.

Entity Extraction

Following Banko et al. (2007), we instead consider expanded noun phrases as a coarse approximation of the concepts we wish to link. Starting at each noun, we traverse `amod`, `advmod`, `ccmod`, `dobj`, `nn`, `vmod`, and `prep_*` Stanford collapsed dependency relations and promote only the longest span to our pool of candidate concepts. For example, starting at *infections* in "viral infections among infants are [...]", the expansion procedure produces *viral infections among infants* as a candidate entity.

Event Extraction and Resolution

For event extraction, we adapted the REACH grammars that capture influence statements (e.g., positive and negative regulations) to the current task by removing selectional restrictions on the arguments of each event predicate. That is, we extract any lexicalized variation of "A causes B" where A and B are entities identified in the previous step. Matches to these rules produce a directed influence relation that maintains polarity (i.e., increase or decrease). Any mention that is detected as being negated (e.g., "X was not found to increase Y") is discarded from further consideration.

Surviving edges are consolidated through a conservative deduplication procedure where two edges are considered identical if and only if the set of lemmatized content terms[9] for corresponding source-destination concepts between two edges is identical (e.g., "children's stunting" = "stunted children"). When merging duplicates, textual provenance of the extractions is aggregated.

---

[9]Function words are ignored.

4 Influence Graph Search Engine

Conventional visualization of any sufficiently complex network suffers from the "hairball" (Lander, 2010) problem. To mitigate this obfuscation, we introduce a search user interface (UI)[10] that allows for structured queries where a user can explore the influence neighborhood around a CAUSE and/or EFFECT to a configurable distance in terms of "hops" in the graph. Alternatively, the user may choose to explore direct and indirect chains of influence linking a possible CAUSE and EFFECT pair (see Figure 2 for a detailed description of the UI).

As the pool of analyzed documents grows, possible connections may become so numerous that the results of a query could overwhelm a user. For this reason, we rank query results using a relevance score designed to bring surprising findings to the attention of the user. The scoring procedure is discussed in Section 4.1.

4.1 Estimating Event Relevance

In order to rank the results of extraction by an estimate of their relative novelty, each deduplicated edge is scored according to a relevance metric based on the inverse document frequency (IDF) of the lemmatized terms in its concept nodes. We provide several scores for each edge, which differ by (a) whether or not the score incorporates all of the terms in the source and destination concepts or only their head lemmas, and (b) whether the score is an average or maximum. IDF scores were calculated for the lemma of each term in the vocabulary using the entire open access subset of PubMed. To simplify ranking, the scores were normalized using the maximum IDF possible for the dataset.

4.2 Influence Graphs

In Figure 3, we show an example of output for our domain-specific IE system (see §3.1). The output demonstrates the system's ability to capture chains of biomolecular interactions. Output for our open domain IE system (see §3.2) is shown in Figure 4, which showcases the system's ability to uncover indirect links between concepts across domains.

5 Evaluation

An early version of this system was evaluated by a biologist who used the tool to augment her model

building process for the topic of children's health. The biologist provided the system a set of terms as input. The terms were used to formulate a information retrieval query against the open access subset of PubMed to identify papers relevant to her use case. We then extracted influence relations from the retrieved documents and presented the ranked results to the biologist.

Through her exploration, the biologist refined her search terms of interest and the process was repeated for three cycles over two days. The result was a model containing 35 core concepts such as "EBF", "improved water access", and "government subsidy", and 48 directed influence relations holding between these concepts (e.g., *rapid urbanization* PROMOTES (availability of) *cheap processed food*). Importantly, all influence relations incorporated in her model were substantiated by evidence from the literature.

According to the biologist, the system reduced the model building process from months to two days, remarking that "finding one of these links manually may well take 1–3 days – sometimes one is lucky and comes across a review paper where someone has already drawn a fairly mature mental model – but filling in the details and making sure they are not biased can take much longer." We consider this success as a first step toward bridging research islands through Swanson linking.

6 Conclusion

We introduced a search engine that operates over influence graphs that were automatically mined from scientific literature. Our approach consists of two high-level components. The first component is a machine reading and assembly system that extracts entities of interest and influence relations that hold between them (e.g., "promotes" or "inhibits"). The reading system can operate in both domain-specific settings, where there are knowledge bases that can support reading (e.g., lists of protein names), and in multi-domain settings where such resources are not available. The second component of our approach is a search engine interface that allows the user to explore not by keywords, but by direct and indirect influence patterns. The results are displayed in a network graph format depicting the subgraph matching the query, and in a table-based view that lists the matching influence relations in descending order of relevance. Through a user study we demonstrated

---

[10]More information on this system can be found at `http://clulab.cs.arizona.edu/demos/influence-search`

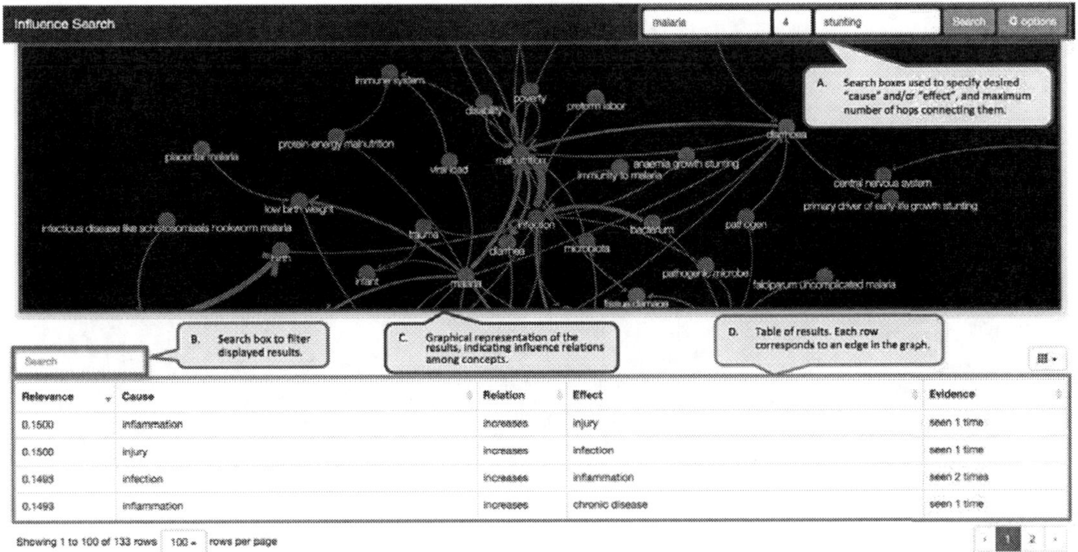

Relevance	Cause	Relation	Effect	Evidence
0.1500	inflammation	increases	injury	seen 1 time
0.1500	injury	increases	infection	seen 1 time
0.1493	infection	increases	inflammation	seen 2 times
0.1493	inflammation	increases	chronic disease	seen 1 time

Figure 2: The search engine UI for the conceptual influence graph. **A**: search boxes used to specify the purported CAUSE and/or EFFECT, and the maximum number of intervening edges that connect these concepts. **B**: search box used to further filter query results. **C**: network representation of the query results, displaying how the concepts influence each other. Green edges indicate promotion; red ones indicate inhibition. The width of a link is proportional to the amount of evidence supporting it. **D**: results as a table in which each row corresponds to an edge in the graph shown in **C**. The provenance (textual mentions) of an edge can be viewed by clicking on the "seen X times" entry corresponding to that row.

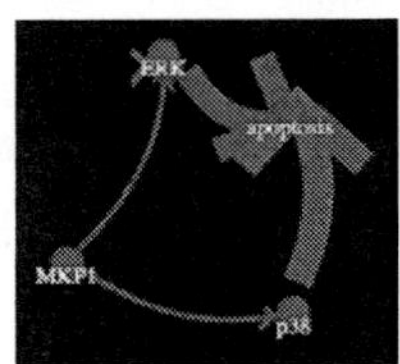

Figure 3: One result of *MKP1*'s role in *apoptosis*, which demonstrates multiple pathways with competing downstream effects. The query for this result was constrained to a maximum distance of three intervening nodes.

that this deep reading and search approach reduces the effort needed to uncover "undiscovered public knowledge" (Swanson, 1986). With the aid of this tool, a domain expert reduced her model building time from months to two days.

In future work, we will strengthen our assembly approach by improving node and edge deduplication. This remains a challenging problem in the multi-domain setting where comprehensive knowledge bases are not available. For example, minimal pairs differing in a single modifier such as *"acute* diarrhea" vs. *"chronic* diarrhea" have clinical definitions with clear distinctions. Care must be taken in determining which syntactic constituents (e.g., prepositional phrases) can be safely ignored during comparisons. Additionally, we plan to add a context filter to the search fields, which will allow the user to focus results by context, e.g., "show results just for *pancreatic cancer*", or "show impact factors to children's health in *Sudan*."

Acknowledgments

This work was funded by the DARPA Big Mechanism program under ARO contract W911NF-14-1-0395 and by the Bill and Melinda Gates Foundation HBGDki Initiative. The authors declare a financial interest in lum.ai, which licenses the intellectual property involved in this research. This interest has been properly disclosed to the University of Arizona Institutional Review Committee and is managed in accordance with its conflict of interest policies.

References

Michele Banko, Michael J Cafarella, Stephen Soderland, Matthew Broadhead, and Oren Etzioni. 2007.

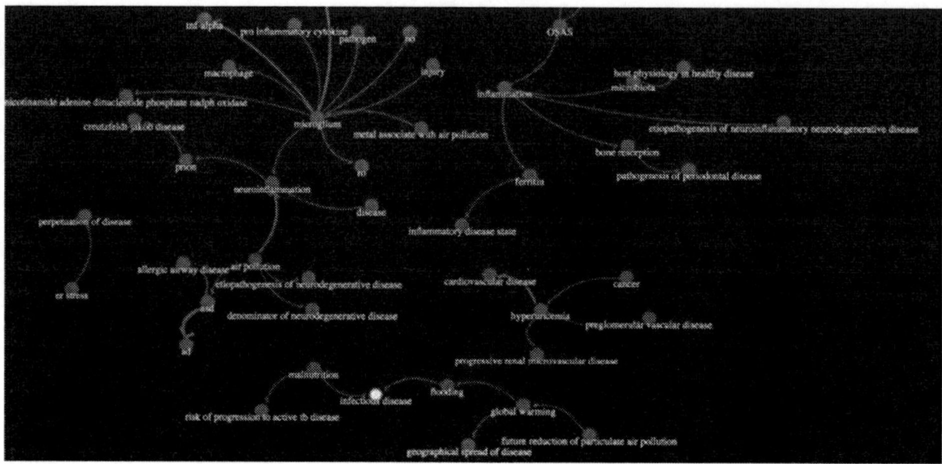

Figure 4: A sample of the top 50 indirect connections between *pollution* and *disease*. In this example, the connection is constrained to at most three intervening nodes between these two concepts.

Open information extraction from the web. In *IJ-CAI*. volume 7, pages 2670–2676.

Tanja B Bekhuis. 2006. Conceptual biology, hypothesis discovery, and text mining: Swanson's legacy. *Biomedical Digital Library* 3(2).

Dane Bell, Gus Hahn-Powell, Marco A Valenzuela-Escárcega, and Mihai Surdeanu. 2016. Sieve-based coreference resolution in the biomedical domain. In *LREC*.

Jari Björne, Juho Heimonen, Filip Ginter, Antti Airola, Tapio Pahikkala, and Tapio Salakoski. 2009. Extracting complex biological events with rich graph-based feature sets. In *Proceedings of the Workshop on BioNLP: Shared Task*. ACL, pages 10–18.

Andrew Carlson, Justin Betteridge, Bryan Kisiel, Burr Settles, Estevam R Hruschka Jr, and Tom M Mitchell. 2010. Toward an architecture for never-ending language learning. In *AAAI*. volume 5, page 3.

Tuan Nhon Dang, Paul Murray, and Angus Graeme Forbes. 2015. Pathwaymatrix: Visualizing binary relationships between proteins in biological pathways. In *BMC Proceedings*. BioMed Central Ltd, volume 9, page S3.

Emek Demir, Michael P Cary, Suzanne Paley, Ken Fukuda, Christian Lemer, Imre Vastrik, Guanming Wu, Peter D'eustachio, Carl Schaefer, Joanne Luciano, et al. 2010. The biopax community standard for pathway data sharing. *Nature biotechnology* 28(9):935–942.

Gus Hahn-Powell, Dane Bell, Marco A Valenzuela-Escárcega, and Mihai Surdeanu. 2016. This before that: Causal precedence in the biomedical domain. In *Proceedings of the 15th Workshop on Biomedical Natural Language Processing*.

Arthur D Lander. 2010. The edges of understanding. *BMC biology* 8(1):40.

Heeyoung Lee, Angel Chang, Yves Peirsman, Nathanael Chambers, Mihai Surdeanu, and Dan Jurafsky. 2013. Deterministic coreference resolution based on entity-centric, precision-ranked rules. *Computational Linguistics* 39(4).

Claire Nédellec, Robert Bossy, Jin-Dong Kim, Jung-Jae Kim, Tomoko Ohta, Sampo Pyysalo, and Pierre Zweigenbaum. 2013. *Proceedings of the BioNLP Shared Task 2013 Workshop*, Association for Computational Linguistics, chapter Overview of BioNLP Shared Task 2013, pages 1–7. http://aclweb.org/anthology/W13-2001.

Marco Pautasso. 2012. Publication growth in biological sub-fields: patterns, predictability and sustainability. *Sustainability* 4(12):3234–3247.

Shanan E. Peters, Ce Zhang, Miron Livny, and Christopher Ré. 2014. A machine reading system for assembling synthetic paleontological databases. *PLOS ONE* 9(12):1–22. https://doi.org/10.1371/journal.pone.0113523.

Neil R Smalheiser and Don R Swanson. 1998. Using arrowsmith: a computer-assisted approach to formulating and assessing scientific hypotheses. *Computer methods and programs in biomedicine* 57(3):149–153.

Don R Swanson. 1986. Undiscovered public knowledge. *The Library Quarterly* 56(2):103–118.

Marco A Valenzuela-Escarcega, Gustave Hahn-Powell, and Mihai Surdeanu. 2016. Odin's runes: A rule language for information extraction. In *LREC*.

Ce Zhang. 2015. *DeepDive: a data management system for automatic knowledge base construction*. Ph.D. thesis, Citeseer.

UCCAApp: Web-application for Syntactic and Semantic Phrase-based Annotation

Omri Abend, Shai Yerushlami, Ari Rappoport

Department of Computer Science, The Hebrew University of Jerusalem
`{oabend|shaiy|arir}@cs.huji.ac.il`

Abstract

We present UCCAApp, an open-source, flexible web-application for syntactic and semantic phrase-based annotation in general, and for UCCA annotation in particular. UCCAApp supports a variety of formal properties that have proven useful for syntactic and semantic representation, such as discontiguous phrases, multiple parents and empty elements, making it useful to a variety of other annotation schemes with similar formal properties. UCCAApp's user interface is intuitive and user friendly, so as to support annotation by users with no background in linguistics or formal representation. Indeed, a pilot version of the application has been successfully used in the compilation of the UCCA Wikipedia treebank by annotators with no previous linguistic training. The application and all accompanying resources are released as open source under the GNU public license, and are available online along with a live demo.[1]

1 Introduction

We present UCCAApp, a web-application for semantic and general phrase strucutre annotation, which has been developed for annotation using the UCCA scheme (Abend and Rappoport, 2013), but can support the annotation of most phrase-structure annotation schemes, including support for discontiguous units, multiple categories for a phrase, and reentrancy (multiple parents for a phrase, resulting in DAG structures). Despite the recent interest in web-based annotation applications, very few open source applications support phrase-structure annotation (see Section 5), a gap we address in this work.

UCCA (Universal Conceptual Cognitive Annotation) is a cross-linguistically applicable semantic representation scheme, building on the Basic Linguistic Theory typological framework (Dixon, 2010a,b, 2012), and Cognitive Linguistics literature (Croft and Cruse, 2004). It has demonstrated applicability to multiple languages, including English, French, German and Czech, support for rapid annotation, accessibility to non-expert annotators and stability under translation (Sulem et al., 2015). The scheme has recently proven useful for machine translation evaluation (Birch et al., 2016).

UCCA emphasizes accessibility and intuitive distinctions in the definition of its categories. UCCAApp complements this effort by offering an intuitive user interface (see Figure 1 and Section 4), which does not require background in formal representation and linguistics, as attested by the steep learning curve of annotators with no background in these fields that used UCCAApp in the annotation of the UCCA Wikipedia corpus (Abend and Rappoport, 2013).[2]

Aside from the annotation interface, the application includes modules for defining annotation schemes (layers), and for project management. Importantly, the system supports a multi-layered architecture, where the same text passage may be annotated by multiple layers. See Section 3.

In order to facilitate the adoption of UCCAApp by other research groups, we built UCCAApp using recent, standard web technology. The server is based on Django, accompanied with a Post-

---

[1] `https://github.com/omriabnd/UCCA-App`

[2] UCCA's resources are freely available through `http://www.cs.huji.ac.il/~oabend/ucca.html`.

Proceedings of the 55th Annual Meeting of the Association for Computational Linguistics-System Demonstrations, pages 109–114
Vancouver, Canada, July 30 - August 4, 2017. ©2017 Association for Computational Linguistics
https://doi.org/10.18653/v1/P17-4019

greSQL database. The API follows the *apigee* style guide,[3] and the client is based on AngularJS.

2 The UCCA Framework

UCCA graphs are edge-labeled, directed acyclic graphs (DAGs), whose leaves correspond to the tokens of the text. A node (or *unit*) corresponds to a terminal or to several sub-units (not necessarily contiguous) viewed as a single entity according to semantic or cognitive considerations.

Edges bear a category, indicating the role of the sub-unit in the parent relation. Figure 2 presents a few examples. One incoming edge for each non-root node is marked as *primary*, and the rest (mostly used for implicit relations and arguments) as *remote* edges, a distinction made by the annotator (see Section 4). The primary edges thus form a tree structure, whereas the remote edges enable reentrancy, forming a DAG. The primary tree structure can be equivalently viewed as a node-labeled tree, where each node is labeled with the category of the edge leading to its primary parent. We adopt this view in our user interface.

UCCA is a multi-layered framework, where each layer corresponds to a "module" of semantic distinctions. UCCA's *foundational layer*, with which existing UCCA corpora are annotated, covers predicate-argument relations for predicates of all grammatical categories (verbal, nominal, adjectival and others), their inter-relations, and other major linguistic phenomena such as coordination and multi-word expressions. The layer's basic notion is the *scene*, describing a movement, action or state. Each scene contains one main relation (marked as either a Process or a State), as well as one or more Participants. For example, the sentence "After graduation, John moved to Paris" (Figure 2a) contains two scenes, whose main relations are "graduation" and "moved". "John" is a Participant in both scenes, while "Paris" only in the latter. Further categories account for inter-scene relations and the internal structure of complex arguments and relations .

3 System Architecture

The system is built as two completely separate modules: a RESTful web API for monitoring and manipulating the system's resources, and a client which interfaces with the system's resources through http requests to the API. This modular architecture allows to create, read, update and delete

the system's resources without using the client, which is useful for the integration of external resources, such as parsers and analysis tools.

The system's resources can largely be categorized into resources that define annotation schemes (layers and categories), and resources for managing the annotation projects and tasks.

Defining Annotation Schemes. The atomic units of annotation schemes are the *categories*. A *layer* is a set of categories, paired with a set of restrictions over the joint occurrence of these categories (see Section 4). The grouping of categories into layers and the definition of restrictions are fully configurable either through chart-based admin interface or through the web API.

UCCAApp supports a multi-layered architecture, which is implemented using three types of inter-layer relations. The first is REFINEMENT, where one layer defines sub-categories for the parent layer (e.g., a Participant category may be refined to Agent and Patient categories). The second is COARSENING, where one layer defines super-categories for sub-sets of categories in the other layer (i.e., the inverse of REFINEMENT). The third is EXTENSION, where two disjoint sets of categories, that may inform the annotation of one another, are annotated one on top of the other (e.g., information structural categories and phrase structure annotation).

Passages and Users. UCCAApp includes standard management tools for text passages and users. There are four types of roles in the system. ADMIN users are super-users who administrate the system, and have complete access to its resources. PROJECT MANAGERS oversee one or more projects, and may create new layers and categories, invite new users and assign annotators with tasks. ANNOTATORS carry out tasks assigned to them, while GUESTS can view all the layers and categories defined in the system, as well as try out the annotation interface, in order to get an impression of the system's capabilities.

Passages are the source texts that the annotation procedure targets. The system allows inserting passages either through a web interface, or by uploading a delimited text file.

Projects. An annotation project is managed by a project manager, and consists of a layer (possibly shared across projects), and a set of tasks. Tasks come in several types, where each is defined according to the type of input it receives and what it

---

[3] https://apigee.com/

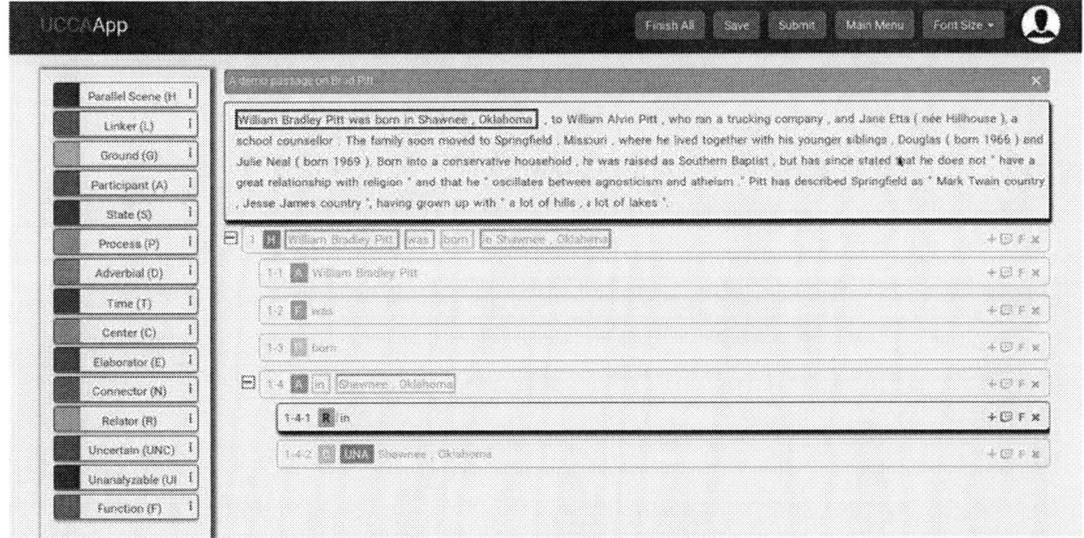

Figure 1: The layout of UCCAApp's annotation interface. See Section 4.

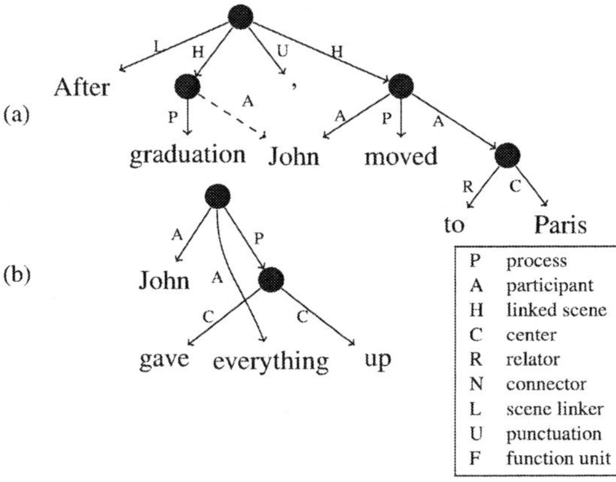

P	process
A	participant
H	linked scene
C	center
R	relator
N	connector
L	scene linker
U	punctuation
F	function unit

Figure 2: UCCA structures demonstrating two structural properties exhibited by the scheme. (a) includes a remote edge (dashed), resulting in "John" having two parents. (b) includes a discontinuous unit ("gave ... up"). Pre-terminal nodes are omitted for brevity. Right: legend of edge labels.

allows annotators to do.

- **Tokenization tasks**, whose input is a passage of text and whose output is a sequence of tokens. Tokenization tasks are carried out by hand-correcting the output of an automatic tokenizer.

- **Annotation task**, whose input is a set of tokens, and whose output is a DAG structure, whose leaves are the tokens. The task proceeds by iteratively grouping tokens into units.

- **Review task**, which is similar to an annotation task, but whose input is a full annotation of a given passage, and not only its set of tokens.

Annotation tasks in a project that uses a derived layer (i.e., a layer which is either a REFINEMENT, an EXTENSION or a COARSENING of a parent layer), start where a full annotation of a passage using the parent layer is in place. Such tasks are thus created by selecting a completed task that uses the parent layer as a parent task.

A complete documentation of the API is included in the project's repository. Figure 3 presents a screenshot of the admin screens used for managing the different resources. The admin interface is designed to scale to tens of thousands of tasks and passages, and supports advanced pagination, search and filtering capabilities.

4 Annotation Interface

The system's core is its annotation interface. Annotation is carried out over passages, rather than individual sentences. The application thus supports the annotation of inter-sentence relations, which feature in many annotation schemes, including the Penn Discourse Treebank (Miltsakaki et al., 2004), the Groningen Meaning Bank (Basile et al., 2012), and UCCA. UCCAApp fully supports both mouse functionality, for novice annotators, and keyboard functionality, which we have found to be faster, and more suitable for experienced annotators.

Layout. The layout of the web-interface is presented in Figure 1. Its main components are (1) a navigation bar with general functionality such as saving, submitting and returning to the main

111

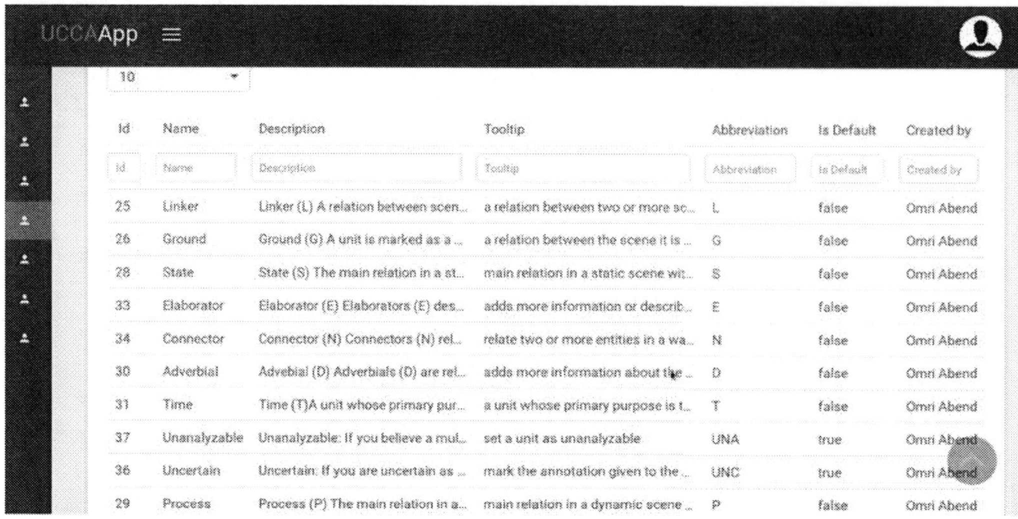

Id	Name	Description	Tooltip	Abbreviation	Is Default	Created by
25	Linker	Linker (L) A relation between scen…	a relation between two or more sc…	L	false	Omri Abend
26	Ground	Ground (G) A unit is marked as a …	a relation between the scene it is …	G	false	Omri Abend
28	State	State (S) The main relation in a st…	main relation in a static scene wit…	S	false	Omri Abend
33	Elaborator	Elaborator (E) Elaborators (E) des…	adds more information or describ…	E	false	Omri Abend
34	Connector	Connector (N) Connectors (N) rel…	relate two or more entities in a wa…	N	false	Omri Abend
30	Adverbial	Adverbial (D) Adverbials (D) are rel…	adds more information about the …	D	false	Omri Abend
31	Time	Time (T)A unit whose primary pur…	a unit whose primary purpose is t…	T	false	Omri Abend
37	Unanalyzable	Unanalyzable: If you believe a mul…	set a unit as unanalyzable	UNA	true	Omri Abend
36	Uncertain	Uncertain: If you are uncertain as …	mark the annotation given to the …	UNC	true	Omri Abend
29	Process	Process (P) The main relation in a…	main relation in a dynamic scene …	P	false	Omri Abend

Figure 3: An example admin screen, for accessing and manipulating the system's resources.

menu; (2) a left sidebar that includes buttons for creating new categories, and assigning and removing categories from existing units, and (3) the annotation panel on which the annotation is carried out, and which takes up most of the screen.

Within the annotation panel, the passage box is presented at the top of the annotation panel, and corresponds to the root of the DAG. Upon the creation of a unit, a unit box is created, indented below its parent. Each unit thus appears twice in the annotation panel: as a nested unit box, and as a bordered span in the unit box of its parent. The cursor is always found within one of the unit boxes, which is highlighted (henceforth, the *focus unit*).

Creating and Deleting Units. Annotation is carried out by iteratively grouping tokens and units into larger units. Units are created by marking spans of text (not necessarily contiguous), declaring them as units, and assigning them any number of categories.

Preliminary user studies conducted with a pilot version of the application have shown that most annotators find it most intuitive and efficient to perform the annotation top-down, starting off by creating larger units (e.g., sentences), and iteratively analyzing their sub-parts, until the resulting unit cannot be further decomposed.

We consequently designed the interface to optimally support top-down annotation flow. Once an annotation unit has been created, the focus immediately shifts to the newly formed unit, allowing the user to internally analyze it. Once the annotation of a unit has been completed, the user may mark it as "finished". The system then validates the annotation of the unit and its sub-tree (according to the layer's restrictions), collapses its sub-unit tree and shifts the focus to the parent unit. Such a procedure minimizes the number of keystrokes required for a user who is annotating bottom-up. Still, the user is free to override this action order, and annotate the passage in any order she pleases.

Remote Sub-Units. In order to support the annotation of remote sub-units, we note that most schemes that allow DAG structures, including UCCA, use multiple parents to express shared argumenthood, namely a single argument participating in multiple relations (see Figure 2a). However, supporting such structures does not require general DAG annotation functionality, but only support for drawing additional edges between units that otherwise form a tree. For instance, UCCA annotation does not require a functionality for forming partially overlapping sub-units, such as having both w_1, w_2 and w_2, w_3 be sub-units of a unit whose span is w_1, w_2, w_3.

Remote edges are annotated by allowing the user to set any previously annotated unit (except for its descendant and ancestor units) as a remote sub-unit. For instance, in the sentence "After graduation, John moved to Paris", "John" is an argument of both "graduation" and "moved". UCCAApp can capture this shared argumenthood by annotating "John" as a sub-unit of "John moved to Paris" and a remote sub-unit of "graduation".[4]

Remote sub-units may not have any children and are displayed in a different color in the unit hierarchy. For example:

Implicit Sub-Units. Many annotation schemes encode units that do not correspond to any span of text. Examples include traces, such as in the Penn Treebank (Marcus et al., 1993), and implicit arguments (Gerber and Chai, 2010). UCCAApp supports this functionality by allowing units to have remote sub-units that do not correspond to any span of text. Implicit sub-units may receive categories just like any other unit.

Restrictions Module. UCCAApp supports the introduction of restrictions over the joint occurrence of different categories within a layer. Restrictions may either forbid a category from having any children, require that two categories appear together as siblings or children of one another, or forbid them from doing so. Restrictions are validated when a unit is declared finished, or when the passage is submitted. If the validation fails, an error message pops up, indicating what the user should fix.

Multi-layered Annotation. In order to keep the user interface user friendly, annotation tasks that use derived layers, i.e., layers that were derived from another layer through extension, refinement or coarsening, are built upon a complete annotation according to the parent layer. The annotation task in a derived layer thus only includes adding units and categories to an existing annotation, which in itself is not editable.

For instance, assume L is a refinement layer of L_{parent}. Then an annotation task t by L begins with the submitted annotation of a parent task t_{parent}, annotated with L_{parent}. Completing t requires traversing the units created in t_{parent}, and for each of the units that is annotated with a category $c \in L_{parent}$, selecting which of the refined categories in L applies to it.

---

[4]There is some arbitrariness in selecting which unit "John" is a remote sub-unit of. Both assigning "John" to be a remote sub-unit of "graduation" and of "moved to Paris" are valid options, although annotators tend to prefer selecting contiguous units wherever possible.

5 Previous Work

While there are a number of open-source web-applications for corpus annotation, very few of them support phrase-based annotation in general, and the formal properties required by UCCA in particular. Annotald[5] is a web application for phrase structure annotation, originally developed for Icelandic. It is however difficult to use in a web-based setting, as it requires all annotators to be logged in to the same system, which often leads to security issues. Folia FLAT[6] is an open-source web-application with support for distributed collaborative annotation in a variety of annotation formats, including phrase-structure annotation. However, as it is mostly geared towards flat annotations, phrase structure annotation with FLAT is somewhat difficult. SynTree[7] also supports phrase-structure annotation, focusing on Chinese. Its applicability, however, has so far been limited due to its documentation being formulated only in Chinese. To the best of our knowledge, none of these applications support DAG annotation, or full keyboard functionality.

The AMR editor[8] (Banarescu et al., 2013) supports annotation through an interface based on the linearization of the AMR DAGs using the PENMAN notation. The application has a number of dedicated functionalities both for facilitating the annotation process (e.g., nodes and edges can be added either by directly inputting their textual representations, or through more elaborate modals), and for validating that the resulting annotation is indeed well-formed. The editor is also well integrated with the AMR category set, facilitating the navigation through its rich ontology. UCCAApp supports many of the properties required for AMR annotation, including reentrancy, and offers a graphical user interface that does not require annotators to be versed in formal notation. While not all functionalities required for AMR annotation are currently supported in UCCAApp (importantly, the application does not support representations that are not anchored in the words and phrases of the text), future work will address the adaptation of UCCAApp to AMR annotation.

A number of recent annotation web applications support dependency annotation, and provide ef-

---

[5]https://annotald.github.io/
[6]https://github.com/proycon/flat
[7]http://syntree.github.io/
[8]http://www.isi.edu/~ulf/amr/AMR-editor.html

fective tools for collaborative annotation by geographically dispersed parties. The brat application (Stenetorp et al., 2012) is a popular web-based annotation tool that supports a wide variety of annotation types, including dependency analysis, chunking and named entity recognition. However, annotation in brat is carried out through dialogue boxes, which slows down the annotation process. WebAnno (Eckart de Castilho et al., 2016) is a generic and flexible annotation tool for collaborative annotation, which supports the joint annotation of semantic and syntactic dependencies. One of its major design principles is multi-layered analysis and the effective browsing of rich category sets, which it supports using a suggestion engine, and both manually-configurable and automatically-induced constraints on the joint appearance of categories. It also improves upon brat's (and earlier versions of WebAnno) user interface, allowing improved keyboard functionalities and visualization. Arborator (Gerdes, 2013) is a lightweight, web-based annotation application which focuses on dependency structures. The tool is easily configurable, and has a mouse-based interface for creating annotations. None of these recently proposed tools support phrase-structure grammar annotation.

6 Conclusion

We presented UCCAApp, an open-source web application for phrase-based and UCCA annotation, with an intuitive and accessible design. An earlier version of UCCAApp was developed as part of the compilation of the English UCCA corpus, and was successfully employed by annotators with no background in linguistics or formal representation.

UCCAApp supports annotation with a variety of formal properties, including discontiguous units, inter-sentence annotation, reentrancy and multi-layered annotation, making it suitable for other syntactic and semantic annotation schemes that use these properties. Future extensions of UCCAApp will include further analysis capabilities, such as inter-annotator agreement tools, as well as support for AMR annotation.

Given the scarcity of freely available annotation web applications for phrase structures, UCCAApp's modular and extensible design, and its intuitive user interface, we believe UCCAApp will make a substantial contribution to the field of linguistic annotation.

References

Omri Abend and Ari Rappoport. 2013. Universal Conceptual Cognitive Annotation (UCCA). In *Proc. of ACL*. pages 228–238.

Laura Banarescu, Claire Bonial, Shu Cai, Madalina Georgescu, Kira Griffitt, Ulf Hermjakob, Kevin Knight, Philipp Koehn, Martha Palmer, and Nathan Schneider. 2013. Abstract meaning representation for sembanking. In *Proc. of LAW*. pages 178–186.

Valerio Basile, Johan Bos, Kilian Evang, and Noortje Venhuizen. 2012. Developing a large semantically annotated corpus. In *Proc. of LREC*. pages 3196–3200.

Alexandra Birch, Omri Abend, Ondřej Bojar, and Barry Haddow. 2016. HUME: Human UCCA-based evaluation of machine translation. In *Proc. of EMNLP*. pages 1264–1274.

William Croft and Alan Cruse. 2004. *Cognitive linguistics*. Cambridge University Press.

R.M.W. Dixon. 2010a. *Basic Linguistic Theory: Grammatical Topics, Vol. 2*. Oxford University Press.

R.M.W. Dixon. 2010b. *Basic Linguistic Theory: Methodology, Vol. 1*. Oxford University Press.

R.M.W. Dixon. 2012. *Basic Linguistic Theory: Further Grammatical Topics, Vol. 3*. Oxford University Press.

Richard Eckart de Castilho, Eva Mujdricza-Maydt, Seid Muhie Yimam, Hartmann Silvana, Iryna Gurevych, Annette Frank, and Chris Biemann. 2016. A web-based tool for the integrated annotation of semantic and syntactic structures. In *Proc. of the LT4DH workshop*. pages 76–84.

Matthew Gerber and Joyce Chai. 2010. Beyond NomBank: A study of implicit arguments for nominal predicates. In *Proc. of ACL*. pages 1583–1592.

Kim Gerdes. 2013. Collaborative dependency annotation. In *Proc. of DepLing*. pages 88–97.

Mitch Marcus, Beatrice Santorini, and Mary Ann Marcinkiewicz. 1993. Building a large annotated corpus of English: The Penn Treebank. *Computational Linguistics* 19:313–330.

Eleni Miltsakaki, Rashmi Prasad, Aravind Joshi, and Bonnie Webber. 2004. The penn discourse treebank. In *LREC*. pages 2237–2240.

Pontus Stenetorp, Sampo Pyysalo, Goran Topić, Tomoko Ohta, Sophia Ananiadou, and Jun'ichi Tsujii. 2012. Brat: a web-based tool for nlp-assisted text annotation. In *Proc. of EACL*. pages 102–107.

Elior Sulem, Omri Abend, and Ari Rappoport. 2015. Conceptual annotations preserve structure across translations: A French-English case study. In *Proc. of Semantics-Driven Statistical Machine Translation (S2MT) Workshop*. pages 11–22.

WebChild 2.0:
Fine-Grained Commonsense Knowledge Distillation

Niket Tandon
Allen Institute for Artificial Intelligence
Seattle, WA, USA
nikett@allenai.org

Gerard de Melo
Rutgers University
Piscataway, NJ, USA
gdm@demelo.org

Gerhard Weikum
Max Planck Institute for Informatics
Saarbrücken, Germany
weikum@mpi-inf.mpg.de

Abstract

Despite important progress in the area of intelligent systems, most such systems still lack commonsense knowledge that appears crucial for enabling smarter, more human-like decisions. In this paper, we present a system based on a series of algorithms to distill fine-grained disambiguated commonsense knowledge from massive amounts of text. Our WebChild 2.0 knowledge base is one of the largest commonsense knowledge bases available, describing over 2 million disambiguated concepts and activities, connected by over 18 million assertions.

1 Introduction

With the continued advances in natural language processing and artificial intelligence, the general public is increasingly coming to expect that systems exhibit what may be considered *intelligent* behavior. While machine learning allows us to learn models exploiting increasingly subtle patterns in data, our systems still lack more abstract, generic forms of *commonsense knowledge*. Examples of such knowledge include the fact that fire causes heat, the property of ice being cold, as well as relationships such as that a bicycle is generally slower than a car. Previous work in this area has mostly relied on handcrafted or crowdsourced data, consisting of ambiguous assertions, and lacking multimodal data. The seminal work on ConceptNet (Havasi et al., 2007), for instance, relied on crowdsourcing to obtain an important collection of commonsense data. However, it conflates different senses of ambiguous words (e.g., *"hot"* in the sense of temperature vs. *"hot"* in the sense of being trendy). It also lacks fine-grained details such as specific kinds of properties, comparisons

between objects, and detailed knowledge of activities. We attempt to fill these significant gaps.

This paper presents automated methods targeting the acquisition of large-scale, semantically organized commonsense knowledge. This goal poses challenges because commonsense knowledge is: (i) *implicit and sparse*, as humans tend not to explicitly express the obvious, (ii) *multimodal*, as it is spread across textual and visual sources, (iii) *affected by reporting bias*, as uncommon facts are reported disproportionally, and (iv) *context dependent*, which implies, among other things, that at an abstract level it is perhaps best described as merely holding with a certain confidence. Prior state-of-the-art methods to acquire commonsense are either not automated or based on shallow representations. Thus, they cannot automatically produce large-scale, semantically organized commonsense knowledge.

To achieve this challenging goal, we divide the problem space into three research directions.

- Properties of objects: acquisition of properties like `hasSize`, `hasShape`, etc. We develop a transductive approach to compile semantically organized properties.

- Relationships between objects: acquisition of relations like `largerThan`, `partOf`, `memberOf`, etc. We develop a linear-programming based method to compile comparative relations, and, we further develop a method based on statistical and logical inference to compile part-whole relations.

- Their interactions: acquisition of knowledge about activities such as *drive a car*, *park a car*, etc., with expressive frame based representation including temporal and spatial attributes. For this, our Knowlywood approach is based on semantic parsing and probabilistic graphical models to compile activity knowledge.

115

Proceedings of the 55th Annual Meeting of the Association for Computational Linguistics-System Demonstrations, pages 115–120
Vancouver, Canada, July 30 - August 4, 2017. ©2017 Association for Computational Linguistics
https://doi.org/10.18653/v1/P17-4020

Together, these methods result in the construction of a large, clean and semantically organized Commonsense Knowledge Base that we call the WebChild 2.0 knowledge base.

2 Web-Scale Fact Extraction

Our framework consists of two parts. First, we rely on massive amounts of text to extract substantial amounts of raw extractions. Subsequently, in Section 3, we will present a series of algorithms to distill fine-grained disambiguated knowledge from raw extractions of this sort. For details on the input dataset leading to raw extractions, refer to the original publications, cited through each subsection in Section 3.

Pattern-Based Information Extraction. For knowledge acquisition, it is well-known that one can attempt to induce patterns based on matches of seed facts, and then use pattern matches to mine new knowledge. Unfortunately, this bootstrapping approach suffers from significant noise a) when using a very large number of seeds, and b) when applied to large Web-scale data (Tandon et al., 2011), which appears necessary to mine adequate amounts of training data. Specifically, for many of our extractions, Google's large Web N-Gram dataset, which provides Web-scale data. Additionally, many of our experiments use a large subset of ConceptNet as seed facts, resulting in a seed set that is many orders of magnitude larger than the typical set of perhaps 10 seeds used in most other bootstrapped information extraction systems. This problem is exacerbated by the fact that we are aiming at commonsense knowledge, which is not typically expressed using explicit relational phrases. We thus devise a custom bootstrapping approach designed to minimize noise when applied to Web-scale data.

We assume that we have a set of relations $\mathcal{R}$, a set of seed facts $S(r)$ for a given $r \in \mathcal{R}$, as well as a $\mathrm{domain}(r)$ and $\mathrm{range}(r)$, specified manually to provide the domain and range of a given r as its type signature. For pattern induction, we look for co-occurrences of words in the seed facts within the n-grams data (for $n = 3,4,5$). Any match is converted into a pattern based on the words between the two occurrences, e.g. "*that apple is red*" would become "$<x>$ *is* $<y>$".

Pattern Scoring. The acquired patterns are still rather noisy and moreover very numerous, due to our large set of seeds. To score the reliability of patterns, we invoke a ranking function that rewards patterns with high distinct seed support but also discounts patterns that occur across multiple dissimilar relations (Tandon et al., 2011). The intuition is that a good pattern should match many of the seed facts (reward function), but must be discounted at matching too many relations (discount function). As, e.g., the pattern "$<x>$ *and* $<y>$" is unreliable because it matches seeds from too many relations.

This discount must be softened when the pattern matches related relations. To allow for this, we first define a relatedness score between relations. We can either provide these scores manually, or consider Jaccard overlap statistics computed directly from the seed assertion data. Let p be a candidate pattern and $r \in \mathcal{R}$ be the relation under consideration. We define $|S(r, p)|$ as the number of distinct seeds $s \in S(r)$ under the relation r that p matches. We then define the discount score of the pattern p for relation r as:

$$\phi(r,p) = \sum_{r' \in \mathcal{R}, r' \neq r} \frac{|S(r,p)|}{|S(r)|} - (1 - \mathrm{sim}(r,r')) \frac{|S(r',p)|}{|S(r')|}$$

where $\mathrm{sim}(r, r')$ is the similarity between relations r and r'. The final score is a combination of the discount score $\phi(r, p)$ and the judiciously calculated reward score. At the end, we choose the top-k ranked patterns as the relevant patterns for the extraction phase.

Assertion Extraction. We apply the chosen patterns to find new occurrences in our (Google Web N-grams) data. For instance, "$<x>$ *is* $<y>$" could match "*the sun is bright*", yielding ("*sun*", "*bright*") as an assertion for the `hasProperty` relation. To filter out noise from these candidate assertions, we check if the extracted words match the required domain and range specification for the relation, using WordNet's hypernym taxonomy. Finally, we rank the candidate assertions analogously to the candidate patterns, but treating the patterns as seeds.

3 Distilling Fine-Grained Knowledge

The techniques described above provide a sizable set of extractions that serve as the the basis for WebChild 2.0. Next, we consider a family of algorithms that take raw extractions of this form and exploit them to distill detailed fine-grained knowledge.

3.1 Fine-Grained Properties

The first algorithm we consider (Tandon et al., 2014a) aims at compiling a large and clean set of fine-grained commonsense properties, connecting noun senses with adjective senses by a variety of relations. In contrast to prior work that only dealt with a generic `hasProperty` relation, we use 19 different (sub-)relations such as `hasShape`, `hasSize`, `hasTaste`, `hasAbility`, `evokesEmotion`, etc. This list is systematically derived from WordNet based on its `attribute` information.

Moreover, our goal is to distinguish the specific senses (e.g. $green_a^2$, or `green#a#2` refers to the second sense of WordNet adjective `green`) of the arguments of these relations as well. For example, for ⟨*plant* `hasProperty` *green*⟩, there are two competing interpretations with very different meanings: ⟨*industrial-plant* `hasQuality` *green-environmental*⟩ vs. ⟨*botanical-plant* `hasColor` *green-color*⟩.

We start out by constructing the range and domain of the property relations with a small set of seed examples. Such seeds would normally be gathered manually, but in our work, we observed that an ensemble of two very different, automated, and noisy sources can also produce high-quality seeds. We construct a graph where the nodes are words and word senses and the edge weights are computed based on taxonomic and distributional similarities (these edge weights are depicted in Figure 1). We then use a judiciously designed form of label propagation (Talukdar and Crammer, 2009) to learn the domain set, the range set, and the extension of such relations, at large scale and in terms of specific word senses. An example of a range graph is given in Figure 1. The highlighted seed nodes mark specific senses of words as pertaining to a specific relation (e.g., `hasTemperature`). Via label propagation, we can infer such information for additional nodes, such as the "pleasantly cold" sense of "*crisp*" (for the range of the relation), but not other irrelevant senses of "*crisp*". The same label propagation technique can then also be applied to infer entire relation tuples.

Our graph-based semi-supervised approach is generic enough to extract any type of fine-grained sub-property or attribute, for which we need only a few seeds to begin.

3.2 Comparative Knowledge

The second algorithm (Tandon et al., 2014b) aims at extracting and organizing large-scale comparative commonsense knowledge. Prior to our work, semantically organized comparative commonsense knowledge had not been studied or compiled before.

We first gather a set of new raw extractions using patterns targeting comparisons. These include the word "*to be*" followed by comparative forms of adjectives (e.g. "*smaller than*", "*more educated than*"). While we again follow a Web-scale extraction strategy as in Section 2, note that these patterns are generic in the sense that they cover all words identified as adjectives. Thus, this constitutes a form of open information extraction for comparative knowledge.

The next step is to refine and extend these extractions. The constituents of a comparative assertion are strongly related (e.g., *car*, *fast*, and *bike* in ⟨*car* `faster than` *bike*⟩); our method builds upon this observation to jointly disambiguate and connect these assertions, while inferring additional ones. Disambiguation is important because relationships such as "*richer than*" could refer to financial assets or to calories. The joint algorithm is also necessary to exploit dependencies and transitivity between extractions (e.g., "*is smaller than*", "*is larger than*", "*is not bigger than*"), with the goal of validating input extractions as well as inferring new relationships. This is achieved via a custom Integer Linear Program with constraints accounting for the coherence and logical consistency of the interpretation .

3.3 Detailed Part-Whole Relationships

The third algorithm (Tandon et al., 2016) focuses on extracting and organizing large-scale part-whole commonsense knowledge. In contrast to prior work, our algorithm distinguishes `physicalPartOf` (e.g., ⟨`wheel physicalPartOf bike`⟩), `memberOf` (e.g., ⟨`cyclist memberOf team`⟩), and `substanceOf` (e.g., ⟨`rubber substanceOf wheel`⟩), and the arguments are disambiguated. We also estimate *cardinality*, describing the typical number of parts in a whole, and *visibility* information, i.e., whether the part can be perceived visually.

We again rely on raw assertions extracted from text, but distill these via statistical scoring combined with logical inference to account for tran-

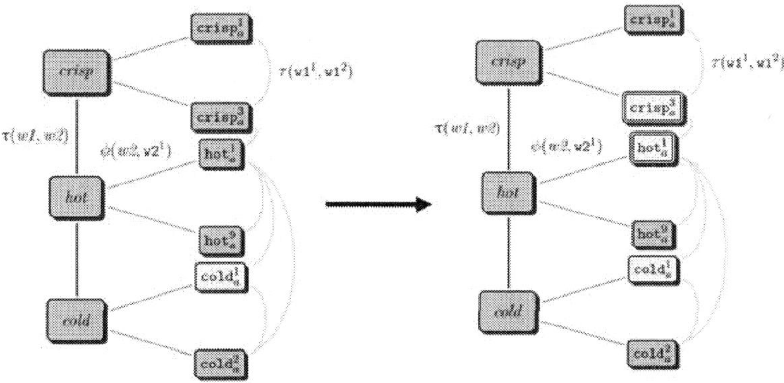

Figure 1: Inferring range of `hasTemperature`. Violet nodes indicate noisy candidate range. Starting with seeds (yellow single outlined), the algorithm enforces that similar nodes have similar labels, and infers range (yellow double outlined). For details on edge weights, see (Tandon et al., 2014a).

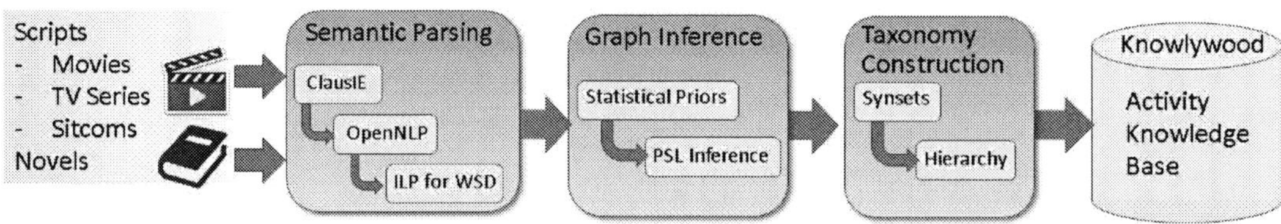

Figure 2: Knowlywood pipeline to extract activity frames.

sitivity and inheritance of assertions (via WordNet's hypernym hierarchy). To estimate visibility, we verify the assertions in images (we call this quasi-visual verification). Quasi-visual verification leverages the best of text-only verification (which is inaccurate due to reporting bias), and visual-only verification (which is inaccurate due to the object detectors' inaccuracies).

Our method generalizes to any relation with finer-grained sub-relations. This specific multimodal approach generalizes to any commonsense relation that has multiple sub-relations and is verifiable in images, e.g., `hasLocation` relation (with sub-relations `hasLocationAbove/Below`, etc.).

3.4 Activity Knowledge

The fourth algorithm (Tandon et al., 2015) is a novel method for a new task to extract and organize semantic frames of human activities, together with their visual content. The Knowlywood pipeline, illustrated in Figure 2, distills such knowledge from raw text, rather than starting with the extractions from Section 2. In particular, we acquire knowledge about human activities from narrative text, focusing in particular on movie scripts, which are structured in terms of scenes, and provide descriptions of scene settings/locations, speakers, etc. Moreover, when scripts come with representative images or time points in the movie, it is possible to align a scene description with the actual visual contents of the movie. The main difficulty, however, is that all this rich contents in movie scripts is merely in textual form – still far from structured KB representation.

Table 1: Semantic Parse Example

Input	WordNet Mapping	VerbNet Mapping	Expected Frame
the man	man#1	Agent . animate	Agent: man#1
begin to shoot	shoot#4	shoot#vn#3	Action: shoot#4
a video	video#1	Patient . solid	Patient:video#1
in	in	PP . in	
the moving bus	bus#1	NP . Location . solid	Location: moving bus#1

Our method considers joint semantic role labeling and word sense disambiguation for parsing these scripts to generate candidate items for the activity frames. In particular, we rely on

118

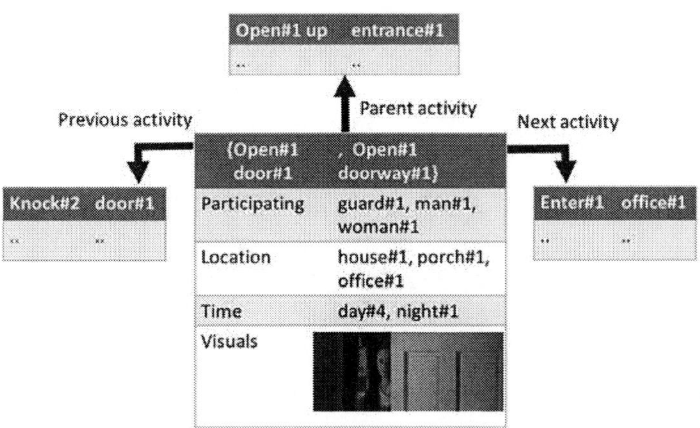

Figure 3: Example of an activity frame

Table 2: Knowlywood Coverage and Precision: manual assessments over a sample of 100 activity frames

Source	#Scenes	#Unique Activities	Parent	Parti.	Prev	Next	Loc.	Time	Avg.
Movie scripts	148,296	244,789	0.87	0.86	0.78	0.85	0.79	0.79	0.84
TV series	886,724	565,394	0.89	0.85	0.81	0.84	0.82	0.84	0.86
Sitcoms	286,266	200,550	0.88	0.85	0.81	0.87	0.81	0.83	0.87
Novels	383,795	137,365	0.84	0.84	0.78	0.88	0.85	0.72	0.84
Crowdsrc.	3,701	9,575	0.82	0.91	0.91	0.87	0.74	0.40	0.86
Knowlywood	1,708,782	964,758	0.87	0.86	0.84	0.85	0.78	0.84	**0.85±0.01**
ConceptNet 5	-	4,757	0.15	0.81	0.92	0.91	0.33	N/A	**0.46±0.02**

a semantic parsing like approach that fills the slot values of such frames (activity type, location, participants, etc.), while also jointly disambiguating the verb and the slot fillers with respect to WordNet. This is achieved by computing strong priors that are fed into an integer linear program. In the example in Table 1, we see how this process also jointly relies on information from VerbNet. For the WordNet verb sense number 2: `shoot#2` (killing), VerbNet provides a role restriction `Agent.animate V Patient.animate PP Instrument.solid`, where `animate` refers to living beings, as opposed to inanimate objects. This allows us to infer that this `shoot#2` sense is not compatible with the argument "the video", which is not `animate`. This way, we can disqualify the incorrect interpretation of "shoot".

We then perform inference using probabilistic graphical models that can encode joint dependencies among different candidate activity frames. Unlike the previous contribution, this method goes beyond disambiguation of the arguments of an assertion; and, additionally assign roles to these arguments. A final taxonomy construction step groups together similar activity frames and forms a hierarchy of activities. For movie scripts with aligned movie data, we associate the correspond video key frames with our activities. Figure 3 provides an example of the resulting activity frames.

4   Results and Demonstration

Together, these methods have been used to create the WebChild 2.0 KB, which is one of the largest commonsense knowledge bases available, describing over 2 million disambiguated concepts and activities, connected by over 18 million assertions.

Among this data, we highlight the Knowlywood pipeline that produced 964,758 unique activity instances, grouped into 505,788 activity synsets. In addition to the edges mentioned above, we also obtain 581,438 `location`, 71,346 `time`, and 5,196,156 `participant` attribute entries over all activities. This is much larger than other commonsense KBs such as ConceptNet, refer Table 2.

The WebChild 2.0 KB is bigger and richer than any other automatically constructed commonsense KB. It can also be viewed as an extended WordNet (comprising not just words, but also activi-

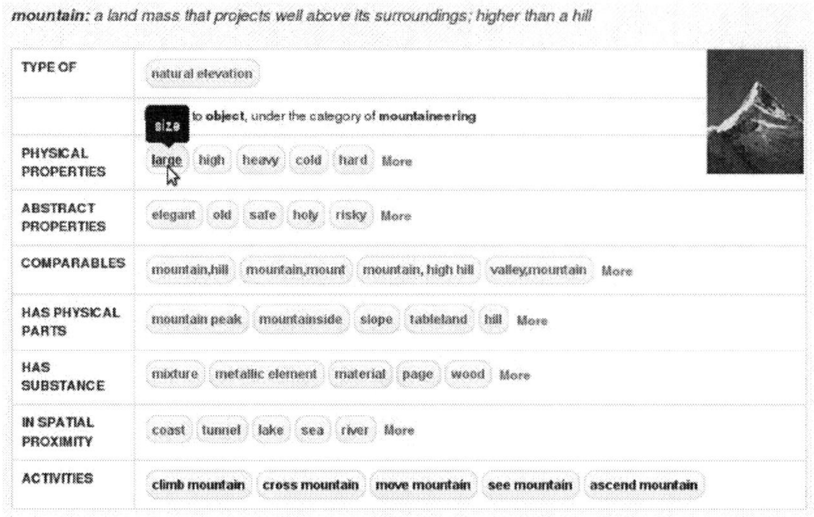

Figure 4: WebChild 2.0 browser results for `mountain`. It presents semantic knowledge for concepts, comparisons, and activities. For more examples, visit `gate.d5.mpi-inf.mpg.de/webchild`

ties and other concepts expressed via multi-word expressions), with an orders of magnitude denser relationship graph (connecting the concepts with novel relations such as comparatives), and with additional multimodal content.

The WebChild 2.0 browser provides a user interface to semantically browse the current commonsense database, combining the knowledge from all of the above algorithms, refer to Figure 4.

5 Conclusion

From a resource perspective, people looking for commonsense knowledge bases had few options available before our construction of the WebChild 2.0 knowledge base. The available alternatives do not offer the same level of size, richness and semantic rigor over multiple modalities. In ongoing work, we are developing improved algorithms to prune noisy extractions, and computing the weights for the inference steps to distill cleaner knowledge.

WebChild 2.0 has already been effective in providing background knowledge to applications such as visual question answering (Wang et al., 2016) and neural relation prediction (Chen et al., 2016). The WebChild 2.0 data is freely downloadable at `http://www.mpi-inf.mpg.de/yago-naga/webchild/`, and browsable at `https://gate.d5.mpi-inf.mpg.de/webchild/`.

References

Jiaqiang Chen, Niket Tandon, Charles Darwis Hariman, and Gerard de Melo. 2016. Webbrain: Joint neural learning of large-scale commonsense knowledge. In *Proceedings of ISWC 2016*.

Catherine Havasi, Robert Speer, and Jason Alonso. 2007. Conceptnet 3: a flexible, multilingual semantic network for common sense knowledge. In *Proceedings of RANLP*.

Partha P. Talukdar and Koby Crammer. 2009. New regularized algorithms for transductive learning. In *Proceedings of ECML/PKDD*.

Niket Tandon, Gerard de Melo, Abir De, and Gerhard Weikum. 2015. Knowlywood: Mining activity knowledge from hollywood narratives. In *Proceedings of CIKM*.

Niket Tandon, Gerard de Melo, Fabian Suchanek, and Gerhard Weikum. 2014a. Webchild: Harvesting and organizing commonsense knowledge from the web. In *Proceedings of WSDM*.

Niket Tandon, Gerard de Melo, and Gerhard Weikum. 2011. Deriving a web-scale commonsense fact database. In *Proceedings of AAAI*.

Niket Tandon, Gerard De Melo, and Gerhard Weikum. 2014b. Acquiring comparative commonsense knowledge from the web. In *Proceedings of AAAI*.

Niket Tandon, Charles Hariman, Jacopo Urbani, Anna Rohrbach, Marcus Rohrbach, and Gerhard Weikum. 2016. Commonsense in parts: Mining part-whole relations from the web and image tags. In *Proceedings of AAAI*.

Peng Wang, Qi Wu, Chunhua Shen, Anton van den Hengel, and Anthony R. Dick. 2016. FVQA: fact-based visual question answering. *CoRR* abs/1606.05433. http://arxiv.org/abs/1606.05433.

Zara Returns: Improved Personality Induction and Adaptation by an Empathetic Virtual Agent

Farhad Bin Siddique[†], Onno Kampman[†], Yang Yang[†], Anik Dey[†*], Pascale Fung[†*]
[†]Human Language Technology Center
Department of Electronic and Computer Engineering
Hong Kong University of Science and Technology, Hong Kong
*EMOS Technologies Inc.
pascale@ece.ust.hk,
[fsiddique, opkampman, yyangag, adey]@connect.ust.hk

Abstract

Virtual agents need to adapt their personality to the user in order to become more empathetic. To this end, we developed Zara the Supergirl, an interactive empathetic agent, using a modular approach. In this paper, we describe the enhanced personality module with improved recognition from speech and text using deep learning frameworks. From raw audio, an average F-score of 69.6 was obtained from real-time personality assessment using a Convolutional Neural Network (CNN) model. From text, we improved personality recognition results with a CNN model on top of pre-trained word embeddings and obtained an average F-score of 71.0. Results from our Human-Agent Interaction study confirmed our assumption that people have different agent personality preferences. We use insights from this study to adapt our agent to user personality.

1 Introduction

According to Miner et. al's research (Miner et al., 2016), various world renowned virtual assistants respond inconsistently and impersonally to affect-sensitive topics such as mental health, domestic violence, and emergencies. This situation calls for a need in empathy and adaptive personality in the virtual agents (VA). In human-human interactions (HHI), personality compatibility is important for relationship satisfaction and interpersonal closeness (Long and Martin, 2000; Berry et al., 2000). With the rising number of interactive products in the market these days, it is important to emphasize machine adaptability to different users of varying needs. Here we propose an adaptive personality module that can be embedded in interactive dia-

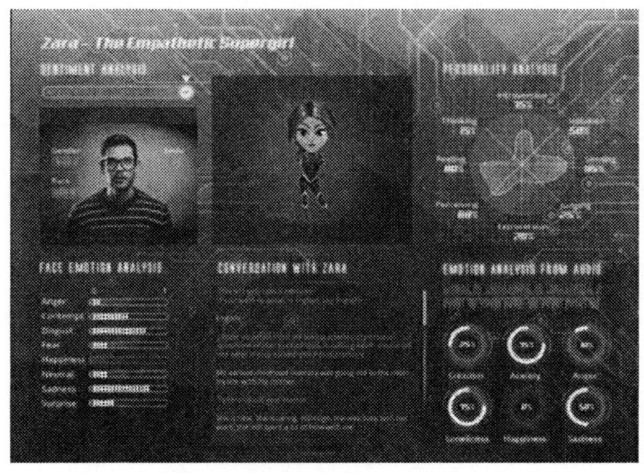

Figure 1: System UI design

log systems. In our new version of Zara, we start with recognizing user personality through speech and text based on the Big Five traits of personality (Gosling et al., 2003; Barrick and Mount, 1991). Our module includes two separate Convolutional Neural Network (CNN) models, one with real-time raw audio analysis and the other trained on text with pre-trained word embeddings. To justify our concept of adaptive personality, we did a user study after developing three virtual agents (two with distinct personalities and a robotic version as a control).

2 System Description

We are building our current work on top of our previous interactive system of Zara the Supergirl (Fung et al., 2015), with an updated user interface (see Figure 1). Zara assesses user personality based on the answers users provide at each turn. The entire conversation lasts around five minutes. The dialog is system-initiated when the user's face is detected. Zara asks a series of personal questions with increasing intimacy, including topics like childhood memory, travel, work-life, and affiliation towards human-agent interactions. At every

Proceedings of the 55th Annual Meeting of the Association for Computational Linguistics-System Demonstrations, pages 121–126
Vancouver, Canada, July 30 - August 4, 2017. ©2017 Association for Computational Linguistics
https://doi.org/10.18653/v1/P17-4021

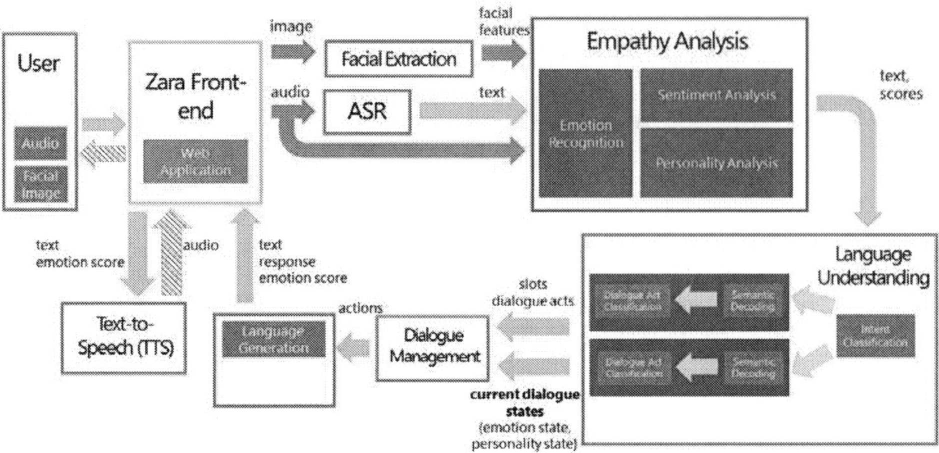

Figure 2: System architecture

utterance, the system gives an empathetic response based on the user's sentiment and emotion scores (Bertero et al., 2016; Fung et al., 2016). A separate module handles user-initiated queries, which chats with the user until the user desires to go back and finish the test. Abusive language - such as swearing, explicit sexist, or racist remarks - are also handled by a separate module. A simplified system architecture diagram is given in Figure 2. Zara is a web application, run on a server, and can be rendered on a browser.

3 Big Five Personality Induction

Personality is the complex pattern of individual differences, behavior, and thinking style. It is predominantly described with the Big Five model of personality (Goldberg, 1993), which defines five personality traits and rates a person along them. The traits are (abbreviations used in this paper are bolded): **Extr**aversion vs. introversion, **Agree**ableness vs. detachment, **Cons**cientiousness vs. carelessness, **Neur**oticism vs. emotional stability, and **Open**ness to Experience vs. cautiousness. Big Five personalities can be determined by self-reported assessments, such as the NEO-PI-R (Costa and McCrae, 2008). An automatic system of personality recognition is useful for situations where this is not practical.

Early work on automatic personality recognition was mostly concerned with text and audio-visual features. Argamon et al. focused on text-based personality recognition (Argamon et al., 2005), and used four sets of lexical features to determine a document's author's Extraversion and Neuroticism levels. In 2007, Mairesse et al. extracted lexical features from text, and prosodic features from speech clips (Mairesse et al., 2007). These were then mapped to the Big Five traits using different algorithms. Researchers using prosodic features commonly extract them using a pre-existing toolkit such as openSMILE (Eyben et al., 2010), after which they use classifiers such as SVMs to classify personality traits. More recently, in the ChaLearn Looking at People workshop of 2016, Gucluturk et al. experimented with a CNN approach on video snapshots and raw audio to train their model (Güçlütürk et al., 2016).

3.1 Personality perception from raw audio

We propose a method for automatically detecting someone's personality without the need for complex feature extraction upfront, as in (Mohammadi and Vinciarelli, 2012). This speeds up the computation, which is essential for dialog systems. Raw audio is inserted straight into a CNN. These architectures have been applied very successfully in speech recognition tasks recently (Palaz et al., 2015).

Our CNN architecture is shown in Figure 3. The audio input has sampling rate 8 kHz. The first convolutional layer is applied directly on a raw audio sample $\mathbf{x}$:

$$\mathbf{x}_i^C = \text{ReLU}(\mathbf{W}_C \mathbf{x}_{[i,i+v]} + \mathbf{b}_C) \qquad (1)$$

where v is the convolution window size. We apply a window size of 25ms and move the convolution window with a step of 2.5ms. The layer

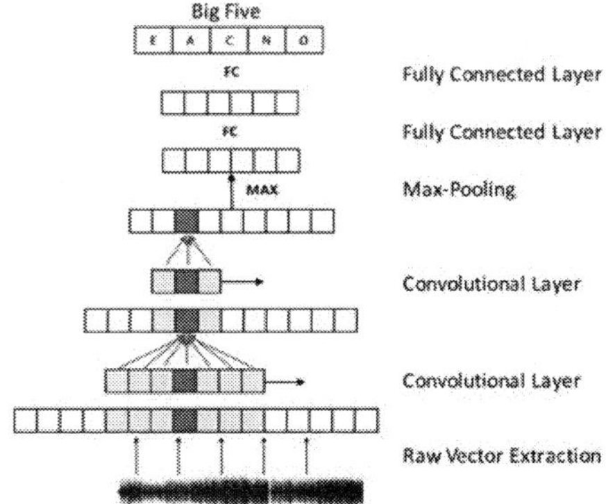

Figure 3: CNN to extract personality features from raw audio, mapped to Big Five personality traits

uses 15 filters. It essentially makes a feature selection among neighbouring frames. The second convolutional layer (identical to the first, but with a window size of 12.5ms) captures the differences between neighbouring frames again, and a global max-pooling layer selects the most salient features among the entire input speech sample and combines them into a fixed-size vector. Two fully connected rectified-linear layers and a final sigmoid layer output the predicted scores of each of the five personality traits.

The dataset trained on is the ChaLearn First Impressions dataset (Ponce-López et al., 2016). The dataset consists of 10,000 clips (15 seconds each) of YouTube bloggers talking about diverse topics. Each clip is annotated with the Big Five personality traits by Amazon Mechanical Turk workers. The dataset used a pre-defined split of a Training set of 6,000 videos, a Validation set of 2,000 videos, and a Test set of 2,000 videos. In our experiment we use the Training set for training (using cross-validation), and the Validation set for testing performance.

We implement our model using Tensorflow on a GPU setting. The model is iteratively trained to minimize the Mean Squared Error (MSE) between trait predictions and corresponding training set ground truths, using Adam (Kingma and Ba, 2014) as optimizer and Dropout (Srivastava et al., 2014) in between the two fully connected layers to prevent model overfitting.

3.2 Personality induction from text

CNNs have also gained popularity recently in efficiently carrying out the task of text classification (Kalchbrenner et al., 2014; Kim, 2014). In particular, using pre-trained word embeddings like word2vec (Mikolov et al., 2013) to represent the text has proved to be useful in classifying text from different domains. We have trained a model that takes as input text represented with the pre-trained word embeddings, followed by a single CNN layer, and then a max pooling, and a fully connected layer with softmax at the end to map the features to the binary classification task.

The convolution window sizes of 3, 4 and 5 were used in order to represent the n-gram features, and a total of 128 filters were trained in parallel. For regularization, the L2 regularization with lambda 0.01, and Dropout of 0.5 was used. We used rectified linear (ReLu) to add non-linearity, and the Adam optimizer was used for the training update at each step.

The datasets used for the training are taken from the Workshop on Computational Personality Recognition (WCPR) (Kosinski and Stillwell, 2012; Celli et al., 2014). The Facebook and Youtube personality datasets were combined and used for training. The Facebook dataset consists of status updates taken from 250 users with their personality labeled via a form the users filled up, and the Youtube dataset has 404 different transcriptions of vloggers which are labeled via perceived personality with the help of mechanical turk. A median split of the scores is done to divide each of the big five personality groups into two classes, and so the task was five different binary classifications, one for each trait.

We trained a SVM classifier using LIWC (Pennebaker et al., 2001) lexical features to treat as baseline (Verhoeven et al., 2013) in order to compare with our own model.

3.3 Results

For personality perception from audio, our model outputs a continuous score between 0 and 1 for each of the five traits for any given sample. We evaluate its performance by turning the continuous labels and outputs into binary classes using median splits. Our classification performance is good when comparing, for instance, to the winner of the 2012 INTERSPEECH Speaker Trait sub-Challenge on Personality (Ivanov and Chen, 2012; Schuller et al., 2012). Table 1 shows the model performance on the ChaLearn Validation set for this 2-class problem. The average of the mean ab-

%	Average	Extr	Agre	Cons	Neur	Open
Accuracy	62.3	63.2	61.5	60.1	64.2	62.5
Precision	60.6	60.5	60.6	58.4	62.7	60.8
Recall	81.8	83.7	83.2	86.3	78.3	77.6
F − Score	69.6	70.2	70.1	69.6	69.7	68.2

Table 1: Classification performance on ChaLearn Validation dataset using CNN on raw audio

	Average	Extr	Agre	Cons	Neur	Open
CNN model	**71.0**	**70.8**	**72.7**	**70.8**	**72.9**	**67.9**
Baseline SVM	59.4	59.6	57.7	60.1	63.4	56.0

Table 2: F-Score results of CNN model on text compared to the baseline SVM with LIWC features

solute error over the traits is 0.1075.

For personality induction from text, the CNN model for text beats the F-score performance of the SVM baseline by a large margin (see Table 2). Our immediate future work will focus on combining the two models described in this paper and adding facial expression data to the input.

4 Adaptive Virtual Agent

Past research has shown the importance of VAs adapting to users in terms of culture (Al-Saleh and Romano, 2015), learning style (Liew and Tan, 2016), and social constructs (Youssef et al., 2015). These scenarios show improvement in user satisfaction and also better collaboration between the user and the VA (Hu et al., 2015; Liew and Tan, 2016). In addition, users prefer adaptive agents to non-adaptive VAs when completing a task (Hu et al., 2015). However, whether and how users would prefer adaptive personality in virtual agents has not yet been explored. To this end, we conducted a counter-balanced, three-by-three factorial within-subject study with 36 participants recruited from a local university.

Each participant filled in a big-five questionnaire and was shown three different virtual agents in random order. A Robotic VA was developed as control; it replies to affect-sensitive comments with impersonal responses like "I don't understand" and "No answer detected." The two personality-driven VAs were based on Clifford Nass' work on computers with personalities (Nass et al., 1995). The Tough VA (TVA) and the Gentle VA (GVA) embody the traits of dominance and submissiveness dimension of interpersonal behavior (Kiesler, 1983) respectively. Below, adjectives

that signify each dimension are listed:

- Dominance: able to give orders, assumes responsibilities, controlling, self-assertive

- Submissive: easily led, lets others make decisions, and avoids responsibilities

After interacting with each VA, the participants filled out a survey to indicate and explain their VA preference and user satisfaction. We looked at the correlations between users' Big Five scores and their VA personality preference. Especially the Openness trait correlates with Submissive preference, where higher scores indicate an increased preference for submissiveness in an agent (see Figure 4). Our results also show that 77.78% of the participants found GVA more desirable to converse with, 16.67% with TVA, and only 5% preferred the Robotic version. This is in line with human interactions, where empathy in physicians directly improves patient satisfaction and recovery (Derksen et al., 2013). Therefore, our preliminary results broadly showed that users prefer personality adaptation in VAs.

5 Future Work

Our future work would involve improving Zara's adaptation to user personality. To increase VA's personality flexibility, we can do a modelling of different personalities from movie and TV series characters using machine learning techniques. An adaptive personality module may also require some form of personality compatibility matching between users and the VA. To improve, we can seek works in psychology on friendship and relationship compatibility based on personality (Huston and Houts, 1998) to extract and match features

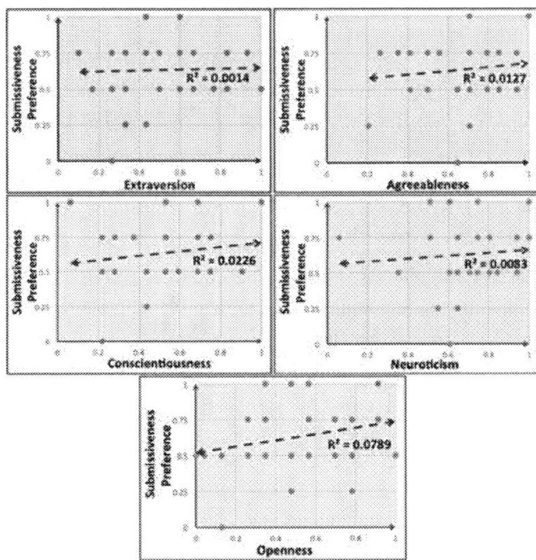

Figure 4: Correlation between user Big Five personality dimensions and VA personality

between the user and the VA. We are also designing more user experiments with more subjects and additional VA preference scales (apart from the Dominant-Submissive axis).

Furthermore, we have collected larger datasets to train our text model. One dataset contains 22 million status updates from 154,000 Facebook users, labeled with Big Five scores (Kosinski and Stillwell, 2012). Another way to improve the personality identification results is to train a separate ensemble model, which would take as input text, speech audio and facial features, and return the Big Five classifications as output.

6 Conclusion

We have described Zara the Supergirl, a multimodal interactive system that shows empathy to users and tries to assess their personality in the form of the Big Five traits, and have explained the personality modules used in detail. Training the classifier from raw audio directly without feature extraction enables real-time processing and hence makes it more suitable for applications like dialogue systems. We have also shown that our CNN classifier from text gives a much better performance when compared to the conventional SVM approach with lexical features. Our user study shows some interesting insights about the significance of personality adaptation in human-agent interactions. As we continue to build conversational systems that can detect and adapt to user personal-

ity, the interaction between user and machine can be more personal and human-like. This will in turn make it easier for people to consider virtual agents as their friends and counselors.

References

Mashael Al-Saleh and Daniela Romano. 2015. Culturally appropriate behavior in virtual agents: A review.

Shlomo Argamon, Sushant Dhawle, Moshe Koppel, and James W Pennebaker. 2005. Lexical predictors of personality type. In *Proceedings of the 2005 Joint Annual Meeting of the Interface and the Classification Society of North America.*

Murray R Barrick and Michael K Mount. 1991. The big five personality dimensions and job performance: a meta-analysis. *Personnel psychology* 44(1):1–26.

Diane S Berry, Julie K Willingham, and Christine A Thayer. 2000. Affect and personality as predictors of conflict and closeness in young adults' friendships. *Journal of Research in Personality* 34(1):84–107.

Dario Bertero, Farhad Bin Siddique, Chien-Sheng Wu, Yan Wan, Ricky Ho Yin Chan, and Pascale Fung. 2016. Real-time speech emotion and sentiment recognition for interactive dialogue systems .

Fabio Celli, Bruno Lepri, Joan-Isaac Biel, Daniel Gatica-Perez, Giuseppe Riccardi, and Fabio Pianesi. 2014. The workshop on computational personality recognition 2014. In *22nd ACM international conference on multimedia.* ACM, pages 1245–1246.

Paul T Costa and Robert R McCrae. 2008. The revised neo personality inventory (neo-pi-r). *The SAGE handbook of personality theory and assessment* 2:179–198.

Frans Derksen, Jozien Bensing, and Antoine Lagro-Janssen. 2013. Effectiveness of empathy in general practice: a systematic review. *Br J Gen Pract* 63(606):e76–e84.

Florian Eyben, Martin Wöllmer, and Björn Schuller. 2010. opensmile - the munich versatile and fast open-source audio feature extraction. In *18th ACM international conference on multimedia.* ACM, pages 1459–1462.

Pascale Fung, Dario Bertero, Yan Wan, Anik Dey, Ricky Ho Yin Chan, Farhad Bin Siddique, Yang Yang, Chien-Sheng Wu, and Ruixi Lin. 2016. Towards empathetic human-robot interactions. *arXiv preprint arXiv:1605.04072* .

Pascale Fung, Anik Dey, Farhad Bin Siddique, Ruixi Lin, Yang Yang, Wan Yan, and Ricky Chan Ho Yin. 2015. Zara the supergirl: An empathetic personality recognition system .

Lewis R Goldberg. 1993. The structure of phenotypic personality traits. *American psychologist* 48(1):26.

Samuel D Gosling, Peter J Rentfrow, and William B Swann. 2003. A very brief measure of the big-five personality domains. *Journal of Research in personality* 37(6):504–528.

Yağmur Güçlütürk, Umut Güçlü, Marcel AJ van Gerven, and Rob van Lier. 2016. Deep impression: audiovisual deep residual networks for multimodal apparent personality trait recognition. In *Computer Vision–ECCV 2016 Workshops*. Springer, pages 349–358.

Chao Hu, Marilyn A Walker, Michael Neff, and Jean E Fox Tree. 2015. Storytelling agents with personality and adaptivity. In *International Conference on Intelligent Virtual Agents*. Springer, pages 181–193.

Ted L Huston and Renate M Houts. 1998. The psychological infrastructure of courtship and marriage: The role of personality and compatibility in romantic relationships. *The developmental course of marital dysfunction* pages 114–151.

Alexei Ivanov and Xin Chen. 2012. Modulation spectrum analysis for speaker personality trait recognition. In *INTERSPEECH*. pages 278–281.

Nal Kalchbrenner, Edward Grefenstette, and Phil Blunsom. 2014. A convolutional neural network for modelling sentences. *arXiv preprint arXiv:1404.2188*.

Donald J Kiesler. 1983. The 1982 interpersonal circle: A taxonomy for complementarity in human transactions. *Psychological review* 90(3):185.

Yoon Kim. 2014. Convolutional neural networks for sentence classification. *arXiv preprint arXiv:1408.5882*.

Diederik Kingma and Jimmy Ba. 2014. Adam: A method for stochastic optimization. *arXiv preprint arXiv:1412.6980*.

Michal Kosinski and David Stillwell. 2012. mypersonality research wiki.

Tze Wei Liew and Su-Mae Tan. 2016. Virtual agents with personality: Adaptation of learner-agent personality in a virtual learning environment. In *Digital Information Management (ICDIM), 2016 Eleventh International Conference on*. IEEE, pages 157–162.

M Valora Long and Peter Martin. 2000. Personality, relationship closeness, and loneliness of oldest old adults and their children. *The Journals of Gerontology Series B: Psychological Sciences and Social Sciences* 55(5):P311–P319.

François Mairesse, Marilyn A Walker, Matthias R Mehl, and Roger K Moore. 2007. Using linguistic cues for the automatic recognition of personality in conversation and text. *Journal of artificial intelligence research* 30:457–500.

Tomas Mikolov, Ilya Sutskever, Kai Chen, Greg S Corrado, and Jeff Dean. 2013. Distributed representations of words and phrases and their compositionality. In *Advances in neural information processing systems*. pages 3111–3119.

Adam S Miner, Arnold Milstein, Stephen Schueller, Roshini Hegde, Christina Mangurian, and Eleni Linos. 2016. Smartphone-based conversational agents and responses to questions about mental health, interpersonal violence, and physical health. *JAMA internal medicine* 176(5):619–625.

Gelareh Mohammadi and Alessandro Vinciarelli. 2012. Automatic personality perception: Prediction of trait attribution based on prosodic features. *IEEE Transactions on Affective Computing* 3(3):273–284.

Clifford Nass, Youngme Moon, BJ Fogg, Byron Reeves, and Chris Dryer. 1995. Can computer personalities be human personalities? In *Conference companion on Human factors in computing systems*. ACM, pages 228–229.

Dimitri Palaz, Ronan Collobert, et al. 2015. Analysis of cnn-based speech recognition system using raw speech as input. Technical report, Idiap.

James W Pennebaker, Martha E Francis, and Roger J Booth. 2001. Linguistic inquiry and word count: Liwc 2001. *Mahway: Lawrence Erlbaum Associates* 71(2001):2001.

Víctor Ponce-López, Baiyu Chen, Marc Oliu, Ciprian Corneanu, Albert Clapés, Isabelle Guyon, Xavier Baró, Hugo Jair Escalante, and Sergio Escalera. 2016. Chalearn lap 2016: First round challenge on first impressions-dataset and results. In *Computer Vision–ECCV 2016 Workshops*. Springer, pages 400–418.

Björn Schuller, Stefan Steidl, Anton Batliner, Elmar Nöth, Alessandro Vinciarelli, Felix Burkhardt, Rob van Son, Felix Weninger, Florian Eyben, Tobias Bocklet, Gelareh Mohammadi, and Benjamin Weiss. 2012. The interspeech 2012 speaker trait challenge. In *INTERSPEECH*. pages 254–257.

Nitish Srivastava, Geoffrey E Hinton, Alex Krizhevsky, Ilya Sutskever, and Ruslan Salakhutdinov. 2014. Dropout: a simple way to prevent neural networks from overfitting. *Journal of Machine Learning Research* 15(1):1929–1958.

Ben Verhoeven, Walter Daelemans, and Tom De Smedt. 2013. Ensemble methods for personality recognition. In *Proceedings of the Workshop on Computational Personality Recognition*. pages 35–38.

Atef Ben Youssef, Mathieu Chollet, Hazaël Jones, Nicolas Sabouret, Catherine Pelachaud, and Magalie Ochs. 2015. Towards a socially adaptive virtual agent. In *International Conference on Intelligent Virtual Agents*. Springer, pages 3–16.

Author Index

Association for Computational Linguistics
209 N. Eighth Street
Stroudsburg, Pennsylvania 18360

ISBN 978-1-5108-4570-1